The Spoils of War

The Spoils of War

Greed, Power, and the Conflicts That Made Our Greatest Presidents

Bruce Bueno de Mesquita
and Alastair Smith

PUBLICAFFAIRS

New York

Published in the United States by PublicAffairs™, an imprint of Perseus Books, a division of PBG Publishing, LLC, a subsidiary of Hachette Book Group, Inc.

PublicAffairs books are available at special discounts for bulk purchases in the US by corporations, institutions, and other organizations. For more information, please contact the Special Markets Department at the Perseus Books Group, 2300 Chestnut Street, Suite 200, Philadelphia, PA 19103, call (800) 810-4145, ext. 5000, or e-mail special.markets@perseusbooks.com.

Book design by Amy Quinn

A CIP record is available from the Library of Congress.
ISBN 978-1-61039-662-2 (hardcover)
ISBN 978-1-61039-664-6 (ebook)

First Edition

10 9 8 7 6 5 4 3 2 1

With fond remembrance and gratitude for our colleague and friend, George W. Downs. And with love and appreciation for Arlene and Susan.

Contents

Preface

James Madison, an inordinately wise observer of politics and politicians, suggested that the "truth is that all men having power ought to be mistrusted." This book is about that truth. Hardly anyone these days would say that they trust their government completely; but do we mistrust them *enough*? In this book, we investigate a dangerous possibility: that even such great presidents as Washington, Lincoln, FDR, and Madison himself, as well as less revered leaders, such as JFK, LBJ, George W. Bush, and Barack Obama, allow their own interests to trump national best interests when it comes to making what is probably the most consequential decision of all—whether, and how, to go to war. We argue that war, even in a highly democratic society, sadly is not primarily about what is good for "We, the people." Of course, true as that is for democracies, there is even less chance that war is about the average citizen's welfare in other kinds of governments, such as dictatorships.

Mindful though we must be of Madison's warning, equally we must be careful not to too readily accept the modern-day translation of his wisdom into such bumper-sticker philosophy as "Question Authority." In democracies, leaders are chosen with the idea that they will faithfully represent what their subjects want, especially when it comes to making momentous choices between war and peace. Hence, we should be open to the possibility that they can be trusted but we should also recognize that their interests and ours do not necessarily coincide. We need to know how to ensure that our leaders represent our interests fairly, faithfully, and, when necessary, forcefully. This book is concerned with addressing who we should trust and what we should know before our nation or any nation commits itself to resolving crises by war, by negotiation, or by looking the other way.

From our cynical perspective, decisions about whether, when, and how to fight adversaries is primarily about what our chosen leaders think will do them the most good.

We illustrate this point by examining the self-interested actions of even our most revered presidents. Such extraordinary American presidents as George Washington, Abraham Lincoln, Franklin Roosevelt, and yes, James Madison, are taken to task. After introducing the central ideas in the Introduction, we connect history's dots in the subsequent chapters, exposing the mythology of the standard accounts of American presidents at war. We conclude each war chapter with a "What If?" section that shows realistically how the relevant politician's interests could have been advanced while avoiding or minimizing the heavy costs of their war, advancing instead an alternative approach that would have been better for the average American.

Chapter 1 looks at George Washington, the Declaration of Independence, and the motivation for the American Revolution. Washington, as an exemplar of the founding fathers, is seen to have been strongly driven to declare war against Britain not so much because of King George III's alleged tyranny and not even all that much because of taxation without representation, but because his vast personal wealth, like Jefferson's, Franklin's, and so many other founding fathers', was put at risk by Britain's policies. The average colonist, in contrast, was little affected by the policies pointed to by the founding fathers as the reasons for rebellion and, in fact, a substantial percentage of the colonists either opposed the war or were indifferent to it. America's wealthiest colonists, not "We, the people," were the immediate beneficiaries of a revolution whose issues could have been settled by peaceful means.

Chapter 2 investigates Madison's War of 1812, sometimes called the Second War for Independence. Here we see that ambitious presidents can go along with self-aggrandizing leaders in Congress just to curry their favor. This first declared American war has a powerful message for today's foreign policy debates. Many have bought into the folklore of a bipartisan foreign policy at least when it comes to the question of war. The War of 1812—like George W. Bush's Iraq War, taken up in Chapter 5—illustrates how partisan interests can overwhelm concern for national well-being. Madison, architect of the Constitution, abdicated his power as commander in chief, surrendering control over the nation's vital foreign policy to a pair of freshman members of Congress, Henry Clay and John C. Calhoun, with mostly bad results for the country but great results for them and for Madison. In the process of fighting what might be termed a farcical war, Madison ensured that he, and not some prowar alternative politician, was elected in 1812.

Chapter 3 suggests that Abraham Lincoln, a smoke-filled-room, dirty-tricks politician, was a changed man after the Supreme Court handed down the Dred Scott decision in March 1857. Before that, he did little to advance his own belief that slavery was immoral, since doing so would only have put his political ambitions (and his lucrative legal practice) in danger. After Dred Scott, he found a way to link his opposition to slavery to his burning ambition to be a person who mattered, with that desire to matter translated into his quest, starting in 1858, to become president. We demonstrate that to fulfill his ambition and his beliefs Lincoln needed a civil war.[1] Through a series of lawyerlike briefs (at which he was a master), Lincoln made himself a serious contender for the Republican presidential nomination by willfully provoking disunion even as he (and history's lore) declared that nothing was more important to him than preserving the Union. Tragically, his contemporaries, who viewed him as a big-hearted but broadly incompetent leader, were probably closer to the truth than we are today. As we demonstrate, he neither worked masterfully to preserve the Union nor did he conduct the war against the Confederacy skillfully. Reasonable estimates suggest the Civil War should have lasted only about five or six months, rather than four years. Lincoln failed to win it quickly or efficiently, contrary even to the expectations of such major Confederate figures as Jefferson Davis or John Breckinridge. But for the long, costly war he instigated, in all likelihood we would remember Lincoln no better than such one-term presidents as Franklin Pierce or Rutherford Hayes. War made Lincoln and Lincoln, with the help of short-sighted southern fire-eaters, made the costliest war in American history.

Chapter 4 jumps ahead in time, skipping some important wars, to focus on Franklin Roosevelt. We contend that there were two FDRs. One, a visionary leader, persuaded the American public to follow him, embracing his vision from 1933 through 1939. The other FDR, the one who chose to seek a third term in 1940, was strictly a follower. Despite believing in the importance of defending democracy and freedom from the dangers of Nazi Germany, he refused to join the war until American public opinion favored doing so following the Japanese attack on Pearl Harbor. By delaying the United States' entry into the war, it is likely that he allowed millions more people to die than otherwise would have. But FDR was not willing to lead public opinion to favor defending Europe if doing so added the slightest risk—and the evidence shows the risk would have been very small—that he would not win reelection in 1940. So fearful of electoral losses was he that he even refused to integrate the US armed forces, despite evidence that it would have made for a more efficient military and despite political pressure from his wife and from civil rights leaders—whose constituents had swung politically to the Democrats, thanks to the New Deal.

Chapter 5 provides a comparison between LBJ's Vietnam War and George W. Bush's Iraq War. We see that Johnson, a ruthless pursuer of office for much of his life, determined to use the presidency to advance his belief in equality even as it meant sacrificing electoral strongholds of the Democrats and, more critically for him, sacrificing his own prospects for reelection as his Selective Service reforms, aimed at making Vietnam a more equitable war effort, alienated many of his core liberal Democratic voters. In contrast, George W. Bush mirrored the partisanship of James Madison and his War Hawk Democrat-Republican colleagues. Bush shifted the tax burden onto Democrats while he reduced the cost of his war for fellow Republicans, much as Madison had made Federalists pay for the War of 1812 to benefit such Democrat-Republican frontier leaders as Henry Clay. LBJ, an exception to the cynical perspective we bring to American presidents at war, emerges as the tragic hero, a president who sacrificed his own political well-being for what he believed was best for the rest of us.

Chapter 6 contrasts the crisis foreign policies of John F. Kennedy and Barack Obama. In each case we see that partisan political concerns were at the forefront of their decision making, in Kennedy's case during the 1962 Cuban missile crisis and in Obama's during the pivotal confrontation with Syria over chemical weapons and the interrelated Russian expansion into Crimea and Eastern Ukraine in 2013–2014. These crises clearly illustrate the logic of when to make serious international threats and when not to. The evidence, as with the earlier chapters, helps us to see that short-term electoral and political considerations drive even the most major national security decisions today as they have done since before the nation was born and, in fact, as they do in all places and in all times in history.

In our conclusion, building on the insights of the connected dots from history and our "What If?" discussions, we propose procedural changes that could alter the profile of militarism in American foreign affairs and, indeed, in global foreign affairs. Being neither pacifists nor war advocates, we highlight when it is best to avoid the costs of war, instead pursuing peaceful dispute resolution, and when the pursuit of negotiated settlements is futile and the use of force or the decision just to wait things out is appropriate. We do so from the perspective of what is good for a broad swath of the nation's population while being mindful that improved policy must be compatible with the interests of the politicians who are asked to make it. In doing so, we recognize that rare is the politician who would make choices that harm their interests, however good those choices would be for the rest of us. Hence, we try to offer concrete proposals that our presidents and members of Congress should be able to live with and that "We, the people" will want as well. The big changes that are needed involve making sure that we citizens are in a position to make informed decisions, relying not on polemics and rhetoric but on logic and the evidence at hand.

We might as readily have selected other American wars to make our arguments, but chose to omit them in the interest of brevity. There is no powerful reason for discussing some wars and ignoring others— they all fit the account rather well. Perhaps someone else will reprise our argument and apply its logic to the Spanish-American War or World War I or the Korean War or the Indian Wars or the many other conflicts in which the United States has been involved. In any case, we hope that our message is laid out with the same clarity and evidence we should all demand from our leaders.

Acknowledgments

We have benefited from the guidance and feedback of colleagues and friends. Portions of the chapter on George Washington were inspired by earlier research and discussions with Professor Norman Schofield. Our analysis of Abraham Lincoln likewise benefited from long-ago discussions with Professors William Riker and Barry Weingast. They, of course, are not responsible for the directions we have taken in our analyses.

Professors Nathaniel Beck, Patrick Egan, Sanford Gordon, Alexander Rosenberg, Bruce Russett, Shanker Satyanath, Dustin Tingley, and Tyll Van Geel offered us a great deal of help in steering us toward important sources of information, in listening to our endless tales about American presidents, and in helping us to see how to provide a positive as well as a probing outlook on American presidents at war. Family members likewise listened to our endless storytelling and pushed us to defend, modify, or clarify our arguments. We especially benefited from suggestions made by Judy Berton, Steven Steiner, and Jason Wright after each read earlier versions of the manuscript.

Our agent, Eric Lupfer, from WME is a great delight to work with as he is smart, insightful, and routinely saves us from egregious errors. We thank him profusely! The publication team at PublicAffairs, especially Ben Adams, Sandra Beris, as well as copyeditor Iris Bass and proofreader Bill Warhop, saved us from errors and from lack of clarity. The NYU Department of Politics and the NYU Alexander Hamilton Center for Political Economy and its principle benefactor, Roger Hertog, made it possible for us to write this book in a most congenial environment. Additionally, we are grateful to Google Books, Amazon Books, Wikipedia, and the NYU Bobst Library, each of which helped us assemble information, data, and primary and secondary sources.

Any book project is a burden on those closest to the authors. That is certainly true in our case. Bruce's wife, Arlene, his three children and their spouses, Erin and Jason, Ethan and Rebecca, and Gwen and Adam, listened endlessly—if not tirelessly—to trial efforts at telling the story of American presidents at war, a burden even imposed on Bruce's grandchildren Nathan, Clara, Abraham, Hannah, Izzie, and Otis. Alastair likewise put his family through the miseries and excitement that comes with listening to a book unfold. He is particularly grateful to Susan Yun and his four wonderful children: Angus, Duncan, Molly, and Penelope.

In the end, of course, none of the above people are responsible for our errors or our point of view. As always, remaining errors and failings are the responsibility of the other author.

Introduction

E Pluribus Unum

MYTHOLOGY—THAT IS WHAT THE STANDARD ACCOUNTS OF America's most beloved presidents really are. Over the years, the imperfections and blemishes of our great leaders have been slowly erased, lovingly rubbed away by our reconstructions of history, or simply forgotten by our selective memories. We have turned Shakespeare's view of death and memory on its head. When eulogizing Julius Caesar, his Mark Antony observed, "The evil that men do lives after them; / The good is oft interred with their bones." Right for Caesar and exactly backward for America's most revered wartime presidents![1] The great good that Caesar did for the commoners of Rome is, indeed, interred with his bones.[2] But when we remember Abraham Lincoln, his unbridled ambition and its painful consequences are the memories that have been interred with *his* bones, all but forgotten beneath the historical reconstruction of his life and presidency. We know the mythological, larger-than-life Lincoln whose historical legacy, devoid of warts, was constructed by his personal secretaries and close advisers, John Hay and John Nicolay, and by a legion of subsequent historians. We do not much reflect on the Lincoln known to his contemporaries, such as the prominent African American abolitionist, H. Ford Douglas, who on

July 4, 1860, speaking to an audience of two thousand in Framingham, Massachusetts, said of Abraham Lincoln:

> I do not believe in the antislavery of Abraham Lincoln, because he is on the side of this slave power of which I am speaking, that has possession of the federal government. . . . Not only would I arraign Mr. Lincoln . . . for his proslavery character and principles, but when he was a member of the House of Representatives, in 1849, on the tenth day of January, he went through the District of Columbia and consulted the prominent proslavery men and slaveholders of the District, and then went into the House of Representatives and introduced, on his own responsibility, a fugitive-slave law for the District of Columbia.[3]

Mr. Douglas's Lincoln is not the man history would have us remember. The same can be said of a truer view of George Washington than the mythological perspective promulgated by Parson Mason Locke Weems but a year after the first president died. He invented the tale of honest George confessing that he chopped down his father's cherry tree. The story was harmless enough on its own, but in its retelling it became a source for the purification of mass memory, leaving us to believe Washington was nearly a saint, when the truth is much less flattering.[4]

We hope to correct the folklore behind America's wartime presidents, in the process acknowledging their many great acts while also exposing the reality of what drove them to action. We will assess what price "We, the people" pay for what James Madison described as the inevitable "ambition, avarice, and vanity" of the nation's future presidents. In doing so we also hope to highlight how "We, the people" can and should take responsibility for holding presidents to a more virtuous and less militaristic standard. That, indeed, is our ultimate goal. We do not relish challenging the folklore surrounding America's most distinguished leaders, but only in doing so can we establish the core principle guiding our political analysis: that when politicians are unconstrained, and thus left to their own devices, even the greatest among them forget what is good for the common people in their lust for personal aggrandizement and satisfaction.

The standard telling of the stories of America's greatest war presidents has certain common, misleading, threads. It is commonplace, for instance, and not altogether wrong, to think that Abraham Lincoln, Franklin Roosevelt, and George Washington were reluctant, victorious, and virtuous warriors. Lincoln, we might say, was prophetic in 1858 when he declared, "A house divided against itself cannot stand." Unable to achieve his greatest desire—to preserve the nation undivided and at peace—he reluctantly found himself at the helm of a nation at war against itself. In winning that war, he sought to reunite the country; he ended slavery; he promised "malice toward none" of the vanquished southern states and leaders; and he gave his life for the union he loved.

Perhaps even more reluctant a warrior, George Washington found himself the leader of a great struggle to establish a new form of government, one, as Lincoln would observe four score and seven years later, "of the people, by the people, for the people," although he personally fostered the belief that he wanted nothing more than to remain at home, tending to his lands and his beloved Mount Vernon. With the greatest humility and trepidation, he accepted the wishes of his countrymen, fighting a war to establish the dignified right of the people of the American colonies to representation as the price government must pay to engage in taxation.

As for Franklin Roosevelt, to borrow Woodrow Wilson's term for an earlier war, surely he fought to make the world safe for democracy. Hesitantly, seeking nothing more than to keep America at peace, he found himself confronted with a harsh choice. He could keep America aloof from the old world's troubles at the risk of living in a world that would succumb to the evils of tyrants or finally, reluctantly, he could commit the nation to a war intended to rescue the world from tyranny.

These iconic accounts of turning points in American history relate our essential mythological understanding of the greatest American presidents and the history they created. They are seen as the men who made the American way of life the envy of much of the world. Their story is our American story. These presidents are pushed forward as the exemplars whose tales forge the fundamental historical lessons learned by every American schoolchild, the glue that makes the United States into a melting pot of cultures and history, the foundation of a coherent unity of states. It is indeed the mythology of American history. It is the foundation of "e pluribus unum"—"one out of many."

Like so much folklore, the tales of America at war contain kernels of truth and yet in crucial ways are fundamentally false. We hope to help set the record of American presidents at war—and at peace—aright. We do so not through ideological critique, partisan bias, or some mistaken sense of malice, and with appreciation for the many extraordinary achievements accomplished by America's war presidents and with reverence for the idea of making one from many. Rather, we conduct a careful look at history that is stripped of preconceived, inherited ideas of our marble heroes. We assess these figures' motives and actions within the framework suggested by James Madison, one that applies to virtually all political leaders in all of time and in all places: a framework that focuses attention squarely on their quest for personal power and fame even if it comes at the expense of the average citizen.

This revision is essential if we are to advance beyond a love for the heroics of war to a love for the less heralded but greater heroics of the promotion of peace. The evidence will show, for instance, that Franklin Roosevelt was indeed a reluctant warrior but that his reluctance was not born so much out of a love for peace as it was out of a love for reelection. Likewise, history reveals that it is true that Washington wanted nothing more than to stay at home and tend to his lands; that is, his vast, far-reaching land holdings that made him one of the richest people in *all* of American history; land holdings whose value—estimated to have been in the billions of dollars by today's standards—was put at risk by the British government's policies, starting with King George III's Proclamation of 1763. The facts will demonstrate that Lincoln would surely have loved peace and unity on his terms, with those terms barely open to any notion of compromise. We will see that he was not hesitant to use rhetoric and to take actions with the knowledge that, through his words and deeds, he was stoking the engine of civil war as a price to be paid to advance his own ambition for high office.

Please do not misread our account as suggesting some special flaw in America's leaders or its government. Quite to the contrary, we believe the United States, because of the particulars of its national constitution, its federal structure, its separation of powers, and its history of mostly honest national elections,[5] is the toughest case in the world history of government for our thesis that politics is about using high office to improve, as James Madison put it, personal "ambition, avarice, vanity, the honourable or venial love of fame" and not about advancing national welfare.[6]

Making the rest of us well off certainly is not abhorrent to any leader, but taking actions to do so stands far back in line to a ruler's own personal advancement. Hence, we will carefully dissect how greed drove such founding fathers as Washington to revolution; how a burning personal ambition, coupled with a noble moral inclination, drove Lincoln to promote the division of the Union; and how the quest to stay in power, fostered by personal vanity and a belief in his indispensability, drove FDR to delay the entry of the United States into the World War, in the process making the war longer and deadlier than it needed to be. As we dissect the interests that propelled America's war presidents, we pause in each chapter to consider what might have been done differently. In doing so we will not ask of any leader to change what he (or increasingly, she) wanted; rather, we identify actions that could have been taken, which would have been consistent with advancing their interests while also producing a less bellicose result for "We, the people." The final chapter probes the general principles that could foster more successful and also less militaristic policies: those that advance both the well-being of our leaders and of the rest of us. It should be remembered that the case made here would be all the stronger if our attention were turned to less democratic societies, a topic we have tackled elsewhere.[7] What is more, the fixes to the problems highlighted here are more easily instituted in the United States or in other mature democracies than in most of the rest of the world. Thus, the greater possibility of improvement in America makes it an ideal subject for our cynical, tough assessment.

War's Mythology

WHAT HAVE OUR RULERS TOLD US THEIR WARS WERE ABOUT? Every leader understands that there are things people will die for and many of them revolve around protecting our homes, family, society, culture, and way of life. Hence America's presidents, like all nations' leaders, have emphasized the threats to hearth and home and other meritorious considerations as the justification for war's death and destruction. Never have they said that war was to be about their advancement at our expense. Woodrow Wilson, seeking a declaration of war against Germany, exhorted the US Congress, saying, "The world must be made safe for democracy."[8] Barack Obama, in speaking of genocide, noted that "We are haunted by the atrocities we did not stop."[9] George W. Bush, echoing Wilson's sentiment, nobly called on US citizens to advance freedom and democracy throughout the world. As he said, "America is a Nation with a mission—and that mission comes from our most basic beliefs. We have no desire to dominate, no ambitions of empire. Our aim is a democratic peace—a peace founded upon the dignity and rights of every man and woman."[10] And how could the United States, the "one nation under God," possibly forget that as venerable a source as Deuteronomy (20: 3–4) calls on us to go to war with no other than God at our side: "Hear, O Israel, ye draw nigh this day unto battle against your enemies; let not your heart faint; fear not, nor be alarmed, neither be ye affrighted at them; for the LORD your God is He that goeth with you, to fight for you against your enemies, to save you."[11]

These are the noble messages that stir us to action. They are the arguments that set the nation to work to combat evil in the world. And yet, inveterate cynics that we are, we doubt that many wars— US or otherwise—are really motivated by these ideals. Spreading democracy, preventing genocide, advancing God's will, doing the right thing—these are all lofty goals and we do not for a moment doubt that America's leaders have been willing to embrace them. And certainly we agree that it is pleasant to think that the righteous prevail; that right makes might; that God is on our side. Indeed as long as there has been war, we humans have been taught to understand it through lofty ideas. We have been educated to believe that foreign affairs are high politics, the stuff that goes beyond petty calculations of personal power and glory. What a pity. A focus on big ideas misleads us from the truth.

Would any leader, however noble a cause, be so foolish as to plunge a country into the devastation of war without first thinking through what the consequences are likely to be? Who would want a leader, who would keep a leader, who would reelect an incumbent so foolish as not to look ahead, just like any decent chess player, before making a move that could prove to be catastrophic? Surely no American president, having survived the torture of campaigning, can be accused of such naïveté as to plunge the nation into war without careful calculation of the anticipated costs and benefits, without working out the expected results of his or her choices, and adjusting strategies to make those choices work out as well as possible.

But when leaders do look ahead, what are they looking for? There really can be no doubt that a big part of their calculations concern whether things will go well for *them*.[12] If that means things will also go well for the nation, so much the better! That is icing on the cake; it is not the essential ingredient that decides between war and peace. This, as we will see, is true even of our greatest wartime presidents. Indeed, it is especially true of them.

To explain war and peace we have to look no further than to what works best for egotistical politicians. To understand the workings of foreign affairs, we have to be ready to put aside the lofty ideas that we have been taught to believe govern what our leaders do. We have to realize that talk of nations and their policies is metaphor. Nations don't have policies; nations don't wage war; nations don't pay a price for failure: people do! The founding fathers understood this message. They set out to design a government that would protect "We, the people" from their own cynical pursuit of power and glory. In that they succeeded better than many countries have, but they did not succeed as well as any of us dare to hope. They designed a government to limit their personal discretion in plunging us into war and they figured out how to thwart that design. That, we must acknowledge, is a lesson not lost on their successors. It is, however, a dual lesson from which we should learn to restore the intent—rather than the practice—of their design: to make war so unattractive for leaders that it is never their first resort and, likewise, to ensure that it is not delayed when other means to promote peace, prosperity, and justice have failed. Let us consider how the founders saw the danger of personal ambition as a defining motivation for war and then we can dissect the history of American presidents at war.

The Founders Fathomed the Dangers We Forget!

UNEASY WERE THE FOUNDING FATHERS AS THEY CREATED THE POWERS of the president. They worried, and rightly so, that the office might fall captive to the avarice, ambition, and personal aggrandizement of those elected to it. War, and the potential for presidents to wage it for their own benefit, was foremost on their minds. James Madison, addressing the decision to grant sole authority over the declaration of war to Congress, observed that

War is in fact the true nurse of executive aggrandizement. In war, a physical force is to be created; and it is the executive will, which is to direct it. In war, the public treasures are to be unlocked; and it is the executive hand which is to dispense them. In war, the honours and emoluments of office are to be multiplied; and it is the executive patronage under which they are to be enjoyed. It is in war, finally, that laurels are to be gathered, and it is the executive brow they are to encircle. The strongest passions and most dangerous weaknesses of the human breast; ambition, avarice, vanity, the honourable or venial love of fame, are all in conspiracy against the desire and duty of peace.[13]

Today we look upon the founding fathers as wise and noble men who were eager to avoid in America the errant ways of Europe's monarchies. In large measure we are right to view them so. They had a profound comprehension of the dangers inherent in different forms of government, including the very one they invented in the American Constitution. James Madison and Alexander Hamilton most particularly foresaw many of the political and economic struggles that were likely to befall the new nation. Madison understood that competitive electoral politics would naturally give rise to factions, such as political parties and regional divisions, and that these would conspire to satisfy the interests of each party's or faction's own supporters, sometimes at the expense of everyone else.[14] Today's partisan divide would certainly have been no surprise to Madison and, indeed, might be seen as quite mild compared to the vicious attacks in his day by one founding father against another. Madison himself might, in fact, be described as the dirty-tricks advance man for Thomas Jefferson's own ambitions.[15] Still, that was Madison as a day-to-day politician. However base the politics of the day may have been, we simply can have no doubt that these were deep-thinking, insightful political philosophers as well as practical politicians and revolutionaries.

It is our desire to strike a proper balance in our understanding of the two swords borne by such men as Madison, Washington, Adams, and Jefferson, as well as by their presidential successors. They wielded the sword of ideas. As political theorists and revolutionaries, they wrenched the world away from monarchy and, in the later times of Wilson and Franklin Roosevelt, away from other forms of repressive governance. The other sword they wielded was that of day-to-day politicians. This sword was used in service to the very flaws highlighted in Madison's statement quoted earlier. We pay too little attention to the consequences for war and peace of that second sword, the sword of daily political competition and ambition—a knowledge deficiency we hope to correct.

The art of telling American war history all too often has a way of turning presidents into nearly passive observers and even into victims of events beyond their control. In so much of the common telling, our leaders awaken to a world at war, find themselves thrust into it, and then become heroic giants if they rise successfully to the occasion. Such, as we have intimated, might be the story of Franklin Roosevelt as he confronted the Japanese surprise attack on Pearl Harbor or of Abraham Lincoln as he addressed the attack on Fort Sumter. Other presidents, finding themselves ensnared in wars they did not want, become upon retelling the hapless victims of bad luck or bad timing. Such might be the story of William McKinley. He found himself facing irresistible pressure from the yellow press to declare war on Spain. That pressure was reinforced and encouraged by his ambitious assistant secretary of the navy, Theodore Roosevelt. This may even be the war story of Lyndon Johnson who found himself president upon the assassination of John F. Kennedy and forced to make decisions about Vietnam. He perpetuated America's postwar policy of preventing communism's advance. Kennedy had drawn the line in the sand in Vietnam by placing American military advisers in South Vietnam. The time to fulfill Kennedy's anti-communist commitment in Asia came on Johnson's watch. His presidency was tragically consumed by the ultimately futile effort to push back the Viet Cong and North Vietnamese, as too was the presidency of his successor, Richard Nixon. Yet these accounts of peace-loving presidents plunged into war against their will are inadequate. They attribute too much power to the flow of history and not enough to the individual choices of men who, after all, were so skilled in political competition that they succeeded in defeating one political rival after another, placing themselves in a position to become president of the United States.

Indeed, this somewhat passive account is, of late, too often used to attribute to the uncontrolled flow of history the apparent growth in presidential authority over war and peace choices. The tragedy of 9/11 or, for an earlier generation, the advent of nuclear weapons at World War II's end are identified as circumstances that thrust modern US presidents to center stage in war making. By now there appears to be an emergent consensus that presidential authority over war and peace has grown since 9/11, much as there was a growing consensus that this was true after many earlier American wars, especially the world wars. Some have argued that this alleged growth in presidential war-making power is a good thing.[16] Others, at least as fervently, fear the growth of executive authority and its perceived inconsistency with the intentions of the nation's founders.[17] Either way, whether growth in presidential war-making authority is for the good or bad or whether it is real at all, it is a belief widely shared. We believe that Madison framed the problem of war powers exactly right. Its use and potential abuse was and is dictated by the sometimes sharp divide between "the desire and duty of peace" and "[t]he strongest passions and most dangerous weaknesses of the human breast." These passions and weaknesses are, we contend, human constants, invariant in time or space. They are neither new nor unique to our own time.

Politics, even war politics, is a nasty, personal business that is little informed by high principles. Today we bemoan the lack of integrity in political campaigns and the slanderous charges hurled against opponents. We seem to believe that our contemporary politics have fallen prey to the "most dangerous weaknesses of the human breast" and we wish to harken back to a more civilized time of selfless politicians competing over different ideas about how best to improve the lives of the American people. Yet there is nothing new in today's base campaign tactics. Surrogates for then vice president Thomas Jefferson, campaigning against the sitting president, John Adams, in 1800, described Adams as a "blind, bald, crippled, toothless man," who "is a hideous hermaphroditical character with neither the force and firmness of a man, nor the gentleness and sensibility of a woman." Not to be outdone, Adams's backers described Jefferson as "a mean-spirited, low-lived fellow, the son of a half-breed Indian squaw, sired by a Virginia mulatto father." What did the Adams's team say would happen if Jefferson were elected? That "murder, robbery, rape, adultery and incest will be openly taught and practiced, the air will be rent with the cries of the distressed, the soil will be soaked with blood and the nation black with crimes."[18]

And how about the high-minded presidential struggle of 1860 between Stephen Douglas and Abraham Lincoln, two fine men with different ideas about how best to see the country through its sectional divisions? Here is what Douglas had to say of his opponent: that Lincoln could *ruin more liquor than all the boys in town together.*"[19] Indeed, there is nothing new under the sun. Even these long-ago campaigners were merely following a much older tradition. We forget that even in the time of ancient Rome's Cicero, his brother Quintus Tullius urged him to slander his foes and lie to the people: "Slander your opponents as often as possible, reckon their crimes, their sexual depravity, or their attempts to bribe other candidates—all according to the character of the individual opponent."[20] Just as dirty campaigns remain a constant of political competition over millennia, so, too, does the quest for political advantage through the power to make choices between war and peace.

If presidential power over war has grown, as so many assert, that growth is as likely to be caused by the many members of Congress who do not wish to risk blame for failed foreign adventures as it is due to presidents' seizing that power. It is sometimes expedient for members of Congress, fearing the ever-near-at-hand next election, to surrender the power of war to the president.[21] In contrast, presidents, with four years between elections instead of two, have time to recover electorally from such misadventures as a failed war and so are more willing to exercise war powers, especially early in their term.[22] That, we believe, is a tragic flaw that throws open the door to war in pursuit of all the personal depredations and desires for power that Madison noted all executives were subject to. The president's urge for these powers has not particularly changed with time. The president's urge for laurels, riches, or electoral victory, more than a passion for national security or citizen welfare, has directed the pursuit—or avoidance—of war in America at all times.

Of course, we must recognize a difference between those who found war foisted upon them and those who elected to take the country on foreign military adventures. From the beginning, the founders were mindful of the importance of limiting any individual from propelling the country away from peace and into war. As early as 1787, for instance, James Wilson, one of the nation's earliest legal theorists and an original member of the Supreme Court under President Washington, explained to his fellow Pennsylvanians at their ratifying convention, that "This system will not hurry us into war; it is calculated to guard against it. It will not be in the power of a single man, or a single body of men, to involve us in such distress; for the important power of declaring war is vested in the legislature at large. . . . "[23] To this notion of distributed authority, George Washington added further to the meaning of the power to declare war.

President Washington stated plainly in 1793 what it had meant to him for the nation to declare itself at war: "The constitution vests the power of declaring war in Congress; therefore no offensive expedition of importance can be undertaken until after they shall have deliberated upon the subject and authorized such a measure."[24] For Washington, then, a congressional declaration was not required to fight in defense of the nation, but was necessary when the United States was acting offensively (with the vague caveat regarding expeditions "of importance"). In that sense, a declaration of war against Japan in December 1941, or a congressional authorization—short of a declaration of war—against al-Qaeda and the Taliban government in Afghanistan in 2001, was not so much a necessity as a natural reply to the offense of Pearl Harbor and the destruction of the World Trade Center Towers. In these cases the United States plainly took defensive actions and did not engage in Washington's idea of an offensive expedition. The country was attacked and attack called for the president as commander in chief to defend the nation's security.

Interestingly, and contrary to Washington's apparent expectation, US declarations of war were neither purely in support of a president or the country's desire for an offensive expedition "of importance" nor were they purely defensive replies to foreign assaults. That should not surprise us. The lines between offense and defense are so easily blurred—and so susceptible to being blurred by a president who sees advantage in doing so. Was the 2003 Iraq war an offensive foreign adventure? It seems so. The United States was not retaliating for an attack against it or against its diplomatic facilities abroad. But President George W. Bush apparently believed that Saddam Hussein's government in Iraq possessed weapons of mass destruction and that Iraq's government had designs on using them against the United States or at least against some of our closest allies. Is that not an offensive threat that is so severe as to warrant a defensive, preemptive war to nip the enemy's potential in the bud? Is a constitutional declaration of war required in the latter case or only in the former? Washington seemed to think defensive actions—ill-defined as they are—were not covered by the sole authority of Congress to declare war. Indeed, the founders did not provide adequate answers to questions like these, perhaps as an oversight, or perhaps to assure their own discretionary authority. We do not know. What we do know is that the constitutional limitations on the declaration of war have proven too vague and too easily thwarted to prevent the array of privations Madison believed executives were inclined toward.

Since the founding of the nation, Congress has exercised its war declaration authority in the War of 1812, the Mexican-American War, the Spanish-American War, World War I, and World War II (declaring war separately against Germany, Japan, Italy, and Romania).[25] Certainly James Madison's War of 1812 involved an American offensive adventure against Britain's Canadian colonies even though Britain had largely abandoned its impressment policy against American sailors before war was declared, as we will demonstrate in Chapter 2. Still, the fledgling nation arguably was defending its independence against an alleged British effort to reassert control over America.

The Mexican-American War was portrayed by President James Polk in similar terms as a defense of the nation against a Mexican assault. Yet, then congressman Abraham Lincoln, who opposed the declaration of war, argued in Congress in 1848, even as that war was winding down:

> Now, sir, for the purpose of obtaining the very best evidence as to whether Texas had actually carried her revolution to the place where the hostilities of the present war commenced, let the President . . . remember he sits where Washington sat; and, so remembering, let him answer as Washington would answer. As a nation *should* not, and the Almighty *will* not, be evaded, so let him attempt no evasion, no equivocation. And if, so answering, he can show that the soil was ours where the first blood of the war was shed . . . then I am with him for his justification. In that case I shall be most happy to reverse the vote I gave the other day. . . . But if he *cannot*, or *will not* do this—if, on any pretence [sic], or no pretence [sic], he shall refuse or omit it, then I shall be fully convinced . . . that he is deeply conscious of being in the wrong; that he feels the blood of this war, like the blood of Abel, is crying to Heaven against him; that he ordered General Taylor into the midst of a peaceful Mexican settlement, purposely to bring on a war . . . and trusting to escape scrutiny by fixing the public gaze upon the exceeding brightness of military glory—that attractive rainbow that rises in showers of blood—that serpent's eye that charms to destroy—he plunged into it, and has swept *on* and *on*, till disappointed in his calculation of the ease with which Mexico might be subdued, he now finds himself he knows not where. . . .[26]

While Lincoln felt a declaration of war was justified against Mexico only if its purpose were to defend the United States against a Mexican attack—an attack he doubted had occurred—Congress, for its part, rarely declared war in the circumstances identified by Washington; that is, when engaged in foreign expeditions. Congress, for instance, did not declare war, or was not called upon to do so, in the vast majority of American foreign military engagements ranging from two expeditions against Samoa to the massive wars in Korea, Vietnam, and Iraq. It seems undeniable that modern American presidents have followed the lead of their predecessors in eviscerating the commonsense understanding of what it means to be at war.

Contrary to popular notions, it seems much less clear-cut that presidents going to war today act differently from their earlier counterparts. They engage now, as they did then, in offensive expeditions, often of great importance at least to the targets of the campaigns, without the benefit of a declaration of war. They did so in the countless wars against the Indian tribes who occupied lands that did not make up part of the original United States. These wars spanned the time from the birth of the nation when, in addition to fighting tribes aligned with Britain in the American Revolution, wars were also fought with the Cherokee over lands coveted by America's colonial settlers and land speculators; and wars against the Indians continued up to the 1890–1891 Pine Ridge campaign against the Sioux. Over these many years, the United States managed as well to engage in battles against peoples as widespread as in Granada (1856), Cochin (1858–1862), Korea (1878), Samoa (1898–1899), and elsewhere. None of these undertakings could be justified as being required to defend the nation against threats to its security nor did any president seek congressional authorization through a declaration of war for these adventures.

By better understanding the reality of American presidents at war, perhaps we can advance in our society and in all societies an urge to reward those leaders who are best at promoting peace and prosperity rather than those whose success and glory is evaluated in the shedding of blood. Sadly, as we are about to see, the more US deaths occurred in a war overseen by a president, the greater that president's odds of reelection and the greater the esteem in which he is held in the hindsight of history. Sad as that fact is, it is even sadder that advancing the welfare of the average US citizen by improving prosperity has had no beneficial bearing on a president's legacy or, indeed, his reelection prospects.

Political Laurels and the Urge for Power or for Peace

FIGHTING WARS HAS BEEN GOOD FOR PRESIDENTS. REVOLUTIONARY WAR hero George Washington is perhaps unique among American presidents in not having manifested any great desire for political power, although he did not shrink from accepting it. He alone—with the possible exception of James Polk—stepped aside even though his reelection was all but assured.[27] Of course, being first in the office of president, he had little idea of what the job entailed. In any event, his lifetime pursuit was the acquisition of land, not political power (as we will discuss in the next chapter).[28]

With hindsight, we can see that war was good for Franklin Roosevelt's reelection prospects and for many other American leaders who engaged in it. Consider Figure I.1, which compares how historians collectively rate US presidents against the number of Americans who died in wars fought during those presidents' respective term(s), taking into account the nation's population and the number of years a president served.[29]

The dotted line running across the graph reflects a statistical estimate of the average response of the ranking of presidents to war deaths during their time in office. The line slopes upward, showing that the

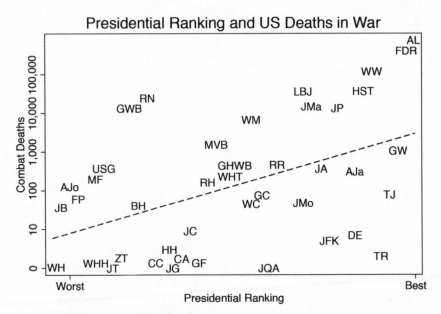

Figure I.1. Presidential Rankings and War's Grim Reaper

more war deaths per year in office, after taking the growing American population into account, the more highly the president is regarded in hindsight by historians; that is, the more deaths, the better the president ranks in the collective judgment of historians. The worst-regarded presidents (such as Warren Harding, denoted by his initials, WH) are clustered around low levels of war deaths. We can see the initials of each president, revealing that the top-rated presidents—such men as Abraham Lincoln (AL), Franklin Roosevelt (FDR), Woodrow Wilson (WW), Harry Truman (HST), and James Polk (JP)—all presided over major wars (the Civil War, World War II, World War I, the end of World War II and the Korean War, and the Mexican-American War, respectively). Their purposes in waging war may have been different— that remains to be seen as we examine many of America's wars in the chapters to follow—but there can be no real doubt that Madison's concern—"the honourable or venial love of fame, are all in conspiracy against the desire and duty of peace"—is at least amplified by this striking graph. Who got the laurels of historians? Those who oversaw death and destruction!

Most of the top presidents, those who have enjoyed the greatest fame and honor among historians, indeed gained fame and honor during times of war. Correlation, of course, is not the same as causation. Just because many died in wars during the time of the best-rated presidents is not proof that war deaths are good for presidents or are even the source of the high regard in which historians hold them. That is what the rest of this book investigates. For the moment, however, we should acknowledge that while correlation most assuredly does not equal causation, the presence of correlation at least encourages the search for an explanation that can rise to the level of a causal account, the task in the chapters that follow.

It is noteworthy that among presidents who presided over heavy US losses in wartime, only George W. Bush ranks in the bottom ten. He apparently believes that history will judge him more kindly than do his contemporaries. If history, as reflected in our graph, is accurate, he may well be right. The remainder of the bottom group is made up of men who, on average, oversaw the deaths in war of less than ninety Americans each. Four were president during a time that zero Americans died in war and only one of these can be explained by an utter lack of opportunity (William Henry Harrison died just one month after taking office). Despite their records of successfully avoiding many American war deaths during their time in office, only two of the bottom ten presidents in ranking were reelected: George W. Bush and Ulysses S. Grant. Bush, as we have already noted, is the exception in this bottom group—he did preside over a lot of war deaths. Grant's fame and rise to the presidency was, of course, on the back of his policy of throwing his own soldiers into the Civil War's death cauldron on the principle that the Union had a bigger population, and so could afford more losses than the Confederacy. While Grant had few war deaths during his presidency to bolster his standing, we must acknowledge that but for the vast war deaths to his account, he surely would never have been president. The rest of the bottom-ranked presidents got one term or less, some having inherited the presidency and having failed to win election on their own.

Among the top presidents, there are exceptions to the pattern the graph shows of deaths translating into high regard by historians. George Washington (GW), Thomas Jefferson (TJ), Andrew Jackson (AJa), Teddy Roosevelt (TR), and Dwight Eisenhower (DE) rank among the ten most highly regarded American presidents and yet they all fall below the projected line of expected deaths associated with their ranking. Among them, however, only Teddy Roosevelt and Thomas Jefferson were not famous US generals who presided over many deaths in war *before* becoming president. Jefferson, of course, was a revolutionary leader during the American Revolution. And, let's be honest, Roosevelt was a prime mover and shaker behind the United States' decision to go to war against Spain in 1898. Not only was he a big promoter of that war; he also went to fight in it and, being a wealthy man positioned to garner attention, he became hugely popular because of the exploits of his "Rough Riders" and their charge up San Juan Hill. Without those "heroics" (and the desire to neutralize his expected future political impact), McKinley might never have chosen him to be his vice president. Washington and Eisenhower are part of a very exclusive club of military officers in America's history to be ranked as general of the army (in Washington's case, the rank not having existed in his lifetime, he was elevated to that rank posthumously in 1978). Both, of course, presided over lots of war deaths in their prepresidential years. Their role in war, like Grant's, is how they got to be president.

We should not be in the least surprised to learn that more highly regarded presidents were more likely to win a second term in office. That, after all, is what elections should produce. Those deemed most

successful should be retained the longest. Perhaps more surprisingly—
certainly more depressingly—those who oversaw more deaths on an
average annual basis, even taking population growth into account,
were particularly likely to be rewarded with a second term. Having
avoided deaths in wartime practically guaranteed that the president
would not get a second term. Of the ten presidents who oversaw no
US deaths in war (several of whom were famous generals who, doing
their jobs faithfully, presided over plenty of deaths before rising to
the presidency), only one managed to be in office for more than four
years. That was Calvin Coolidge, a president barely thought of today
except, perhaps, as the butt of a Dorothy Parker joke: on learning that
Coolidge died, she exclaimed, "How can you tell?"[30] Depressingly, we
seem to have so little regard for presidents who give us peace that those
who oversaw US deaths in war averaged more than six years in office,
whereas those who oversaw no deaths averaged fewer than three years.

Contrast Figure I.1 on rankings and war deaths to Figure I.2. Here
we see the effect—or rather the lack of effect—that presiding over prosperity has on a president's standing among historians. In this figure,
the dotted line reflects the statistically predicted response of ranking
to annual per capita income growth under each president. We would
like to think that presidents who preside over growth in prosperity are

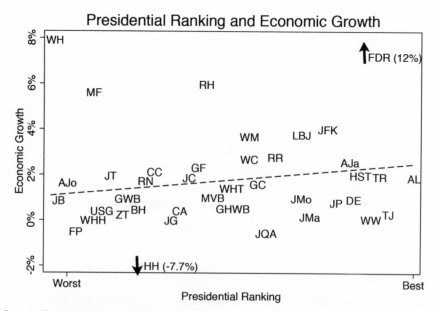

Figure I.2. Presidential Rankings and American Prosperity

especially well regarded and likely to win reelection. Alas, that is not the case. Presiding over prosperous times has no consequential bearing on where a president stands in the hindsight of history.

The second figure reminds us that FDR, who, after inheriting the Depression, restored prosperity through the mobilization for war, not only ranks near the top in annual war deaths during his time in office, but also in annual growth in income. But after him, the next three top presiders over economic growth—we are careful not to attribute growth to or against their economic policies since, after all, all presidents claim credit if the economy does well in their time and cast blame on others if it performs poorly—are Warren Harding (WH), Rutherford B. Hayes (RH), and Millard Fillmore (MF), ranked 43 out of 43, 25th, and 38th respectively. So much for a belief that prosperity produces a great legacy! Apparently it was much better for a president's legacy and his reelection to oversee death than to oversee growth. We will have a look, in the final chapter, at which presidents were best both at minimizing US war deaths and increasing the nation's per capita income.

Yesteryear's Lessons for Today

MADISON'S FEAR OF EXECUTIVE POWER TO MAKE WAR HAS BEEN proven correct. Unbothered by the limitations imposed in Article 1, Section 8 of the Constitution that gives Congress alone the right to declare war, American presidents have often gone about the business of fighting wars on their own, and presenting Congress with a fait accompli. All too often, as we shall see, they did so at least as much because it served their interests as because it served the interests of the nation. That is as worrisome and relevant to the selection of the president and members of Congress in our time as it was throughout US history. Hence, in examining the personal motives of the president and the Congress in past crisis situations, we hope the reader will learn what remains relevant today. To help in that process, we highlight in the concluding chapter what we believe are some important contemporary lessons.

We turn now to an examination of Washington's fervent commitment to revolution and its possible roots in his personal net worth. We then assess presidential choices in several of America's other most important wars, including Madison's decision to turn to Congress and its deeply partisan perspective to design the conduct of the War of 1812; Lincoln's campaign to divide the Democratic Party in 1860 to advance his own personal political fortunes and its readily anticipated consequences for the nation; Franklin Roosevelt's efforts to forge in the United States an arsenal of democracy while avoiding entry into the Second World War; Lyndon Johnson's failed effort in Vietnam, George W. Bush's campaigns against Iraq's Saddam Hussein and Afghanistan's Sheikh Omar; and a comparison of Barack Obama's efforts on the Iraq and Afghan war fronts to JFK's during the Cuban missile crisis. We close finally with ideas about how to promote the importance of peace and prosperity and war, when necessary, to protect the security and well-being of Americans.

Chapter 1

George Washington's Wars:
In Pursuit of Life, Liberty and . . . Avarice!

What Inducements have Men to explore uninhabited Wilds but the prospect of getting good Lands?

—George Washington

O N JULY 4, 1776, FIFTY-SIX AMERICAN REVOLUTIONARIES DECLARED independence from Britain's "absolute Tyranny over these States." In doing so, they formally launched the founding war of the United States. They did so against tremendous odds. Their British adversary was arguably *the* greatest power in the world. Britain's population (estimated at 6.4 million in 1770) was approximately three times the size of the colonial population (estimated at 2.15 million in 1770). At the time of the revolution, Britain's per capita income in today's dollars was roughly equivalent to $1,540, second only to the Netherlands. The comparable figure for the colonies was only $990.[1] Britain had unsurpassed naval strength. The colonists had no navy. Britain had a well-drilled, well-trained, and combat-experienced military leadership as well as the

resources to recruit, provision, and pay a standing army. The colonists
had irregular militias with no professional military training and they
rarely had funds to maintain soldiers in the field. Even the commander
in chief of the Continental Army, George Washington, had no formal
military training and limited military experience. These few men and
their supporters must have been most profoundly aggrieved, believing
that there was no other path open to them to protect and improve their
future than to fight such a desperate war against so great an adversary.[2]

With hindsight we know the War for Independence turned out well
for the colonists, although only after long years of suffering and depri-
vation. Beginning with the Boston Massacre, the Boston Tea Party, and,
in 1775, the Battles of Lexington and Concord, it did not end until 1783.
Tallies of American fatalities vary, with twenty-five thousand dead from
combat and war-related exposure to disease being a modest estimate.[3]
Some calculate the death toll ran to almost three times this. The revolution stands out as unusual on almost every front. Most wars last months.
The length of the American War for Independence surpassed that of either of the two World Wars and was about equal to that of the Vietnam
War. Relative to population size, it was one of America's deadliest fights.
It was expected to be—and proved to be—a long, costly, and difficult
war entered into as a last resort and with significant long-term consequences. The revolution's importance to American history is so far reaching that it demands our attention. Our revisionist attention it shall get.

After more than two centuries in which details of the war have
been recounted to each new generation, average Americans are imbued
with confidence that they know the particulars behind the tyranny of
Britain's King George III (1738–1820) and the courage and integrity
of the founding fathers in freeing the colonies to follow a new and
remarkably successful form of government, one that has become an
exemplar for much of the world.

The standard accounts of the War for Independence as a great
struggle between colonists and Britain, endowed as they are with many
important but only partial truths, miss an appreciation of critical elements that turn our attention from the founding fathers' heroism to
their prosaic pursuit of their own personal interests. That they were
self-interested should not surprise us—who isn't? Self-interest is, after
all, a crucial ingredient in innovation, whether in the arts, the sciences,
or government. That they were demonstrably self-interested should not
detract from their remarkable ideas and accomplishments. However,

America's founders were real, flesh-and-blood aristocrats with, to borrow again from William Shakespeare, all the ills that flesh and blood is heir to. They were hardly the sort of people one stereotypically thinks of as revolutionaries. They were not political or social outcasts, the downtrodden yearning to be free; they were not the religiously oppressed seeking freedom of conscience; nor were they men craving government "of the people, by the people, for the people." They were, in fact, exceptionally rich and influential men: community leaders and political figures elected to the governing bodies of their colonial governments—the colonial elite, the privileged few in a rising society. As such, for the most part they disdained the idea of democracy, which was, as they saw it, government by the mob. In a time and place of great opportunities and great ambition for advancement, these were men hungry to secure their own substantial fame and fortune.

If today we were to observe a comparably small group of enormously wealthy and powerful men conspiring to overthrow their government, we would refer to them suspiciously, maybe even derisively, as oligarchs. We would surely wonder at how they were using their personal power and wealth for their own personal gain and how that affected everyone else. That we do not probe these concerns when assessing the founding fathers means that we risk glossing over their flaws and thereby constructing a distorted understanding of the first defining event in American history. It means misunderstanding what drives political elites to wage war. It perpetuates the mythology of war and revolution as a noble endeavor, the last resort of the righteous against the unrighteous. To begin to rectify the varnished account of American history, we will try to modify the general understanding of the causes of the American War for Independence.

To do so, we focus on two critical aspects of the conditions that produced the American Revolution: what the revolutionaries were after, and why they needed a war to achieve their objectives, as they explained unabashedly within the Declaration of Independence.

We will see that, in addition to possessing high ideals, the founders, or at least many of them, were keen to protect their personal wealth. For some signatories of the Declaration, such as Virginia's Carter Braxton, this meant resisting war until its resistance had clearly become a politically losing cause. For others, such as the Lee brothers, Thomas Jefferson, and for many of the Declaration's supporters, including George Washington, it meant having to rid themselves of two groups of people who threatened their fortune and their future prospects: the British and the Indians. They could get rid of neither without a revolution. Indeed, the immediate postrevolutionary history of the United States is a history of expulsion of the British followed by more than a century of war aimed at the expulsion or destruction of the sovereign Indian nations of North America.

George Washington: The Rise to Prominence

GEORGE WASHINGTON'S IMPORTANCE HARDLY NEEDS COMMENT. LONG before July 4, 1776, and the declaration of war against Britain, he had achieved the status of an American hero. He first came to public attention after being sent into the Ohio Valley wilderness in December 1753 as a representative of England's King George II (1683–1760). Serving in both a military and diplomatic capacity, Washington—then only twenty-one years old and with the rank of major in the Virginia militia—was to seek out the French on a mission designed to ensure their departure. The French were establishing forts, exploiting fur-trading opportunities, and forging ties with local Indian tribes. More to the point, they were asserting control over land that the British king claimed was his, a view Washington fully shared. He came to Fort Leboeuf (located in what is now Erie County, Pennsylvania), one of the French strongholds in the Ohio Valley, and there presented George II's case for the withdrawal of the French to Captain Jacques Legardeur de Saint-Pierre. The captain, with the utmost politeness, assured Washington that he would pass the proposed withdrawal on to his commanding officer, the Marquis Duquesne. But he also made clear his view of the proposal Washington had conveyed: "As to the summons you send me to retire, I do not think myself obliged to obey it."[4] With this news in hand, Washington set out in the dead of winter on an arduous, life-threatening journey back to Williamsburg, then Virginia's capital. Upon arriving, he wrote an impressively detailed account of his experience and of the French fortifications, including important military information about the number of canoes at the disposal of the French, the quantity of artillery they had, and other equipment with which the French and their Indian allies might assert control over territory. The account was widely published and attracted considerable attention to the young irregular military officer, giving him his first public exposure.

While much of the attention Washington got was flattering, not all of it was. He had not only been sent into the Ohio country on behalf of the English king, but also as an agent of the Ohio Company of Virginia—about which we will have much more to say. Many of his fellow Virginians suspected that he had simply concocted a story designed to advance the interests of the Ohio Company. In describing the reaction to his report, Washington wrote bitterly that "after I was sent out in December, 1753, and brought undoubted testimony even from themselves [i.e., the French] of their avowed design [to control the land in the Ohio Valley that was also the object of English ambitions], it was yet thought a fiction and a scheme to promote the interest of a private company, even by some who had a share in the government."[5]

Washington's fame—or infamy, depending on which side one was on—rose further, thanks to his leading, and often disastrous, part in the initiation of the French and Indian War just a short time later. A few months after his encounter at Fort Leboeuf, now having attained the age of twenty-two, Washington, elevated to the rank of lieutenant colonel, led about forty of his men overnight in heavy rain to attack a contingent of thirty-five French soldiers in the wilderness. Although his orders were to use force only defensively against the French, he instead initiated a military strike that ultimately killed ten, including French military commander Joseph Coulon de Jumonville. Jumonville did not die in the immediate engagement. Rather, he was taken prisoner and then assassinated, according to the French, by one of Washington's Indian allies known as Half-King. Although there is controversy over the details, it is clear enough that from the French perspective the incident was an atrocity. As historian James Flexner notes, the French accused Washington "of murdering ambassadors. The Frenchmen, it turned out, had carried diplomatic credentials with instructions to find the English, express a desire for peace, but warn them off lands belonging to the king of France."[6] Washington, of course, did not know that Jumonville came in peace because he and his forty men fell on the French without warning.

Washington was dismissive of French claims to the Ohio country and viewed the outcome of what came to be known as the Jumonville Affair as a military triumph. So did many of his fellow Virginians. However, from a broader perspective it was a monumentally consequential diplomatic and political disaster. As Voltaire described the one-sided battle, "Such was the complication of political interests that a cannon shot [a gross exaggeration of the arms possessed and used by Washington's troops and their Indian supporters] fired in America could give the signal that set Europe in a blaze."[7] Washington's first drawing of blood, the one-sided fight led by the lieutenant colonel, was, in fact, the beginning of the French and Indian War and the much larger and deadlier Seven Years' War. It was followed by other significant military engagements and some defeats, culminating slightly more than two decades later to his leading the Continental Army.

Throughout the French and Indian War, and indeed, ever after, despite his rising prominence as a soldier Washington was mindful of his own limitations as a commanding officer, although rightfully proud of his personal bravery in battle. Especially in later years as the press for revolution mounted, he was a man of measured temperament rather than a fiery revolutionary. Indeed, the young James Madison was highly critical of the Tidewater landed gentry, of which Washington was a part, because of their reluctance to fully embrace revolution. Washington's reserved, cautious approach to the rising threat of war against England differed markedly from the bellicose views of such men as Madison and Patrick Henry. In Washington's reluctance to plunge the country into war, he was probably more closely aligned with the views of the broader body politic.

The average colonist probably was filled with a mix of enthusiasm for the colonial cause and extreme foreboding in taking on so momentous an adversary as George III's Britain. Washington was likely to have been filled with similar foreboding, albeit motivated by different considerations. If the war were lost, he contemplated establishing himself on his extensive lands in the wilderness, prepared to fight off the British in a fantasy that foreshadowed just such efforts by disaffected southerners following defeat in the Civil War.[8] For Washington, the truly great problem was that defeat might cost him his enormous fortune, whereas a failure to fight seemed, under the king's policies, nearly certain to do so.

George Washington's Economic Ambition

WASHINGTON WAS HIS FATHER'S FOURTH CHILD. HE WAS BORN IN 1732 into a comfortable, but not rich, propertied family. When his father died, eleven-year-old George inherited only a small portion of the approximately 5,000 or so acres his father owned. The great bulk of his father's estate went to George's beloved half brother Lawrence, who was nearly fifteen years older than him. The little Washington did inherit was managed by his mother (she would live a long life, surviving into his first term as president), who ran his inheritance into the ground. As a result, Washington started out in life with few resources and a deeply ingrained, lifelong attentiveness to counting every penny he spent. Born into moderate comfort, George Washington died one of the richest men in America—by one estimate, the fifty-ninth wealthiest man *in all of American history*.[9] Yet despite his almost unimaginable wealth, he spent much of his life cash-poor. He sank almost everything he had into land acquisition and diverse business undertakings ranging from innovative farming to mills to fisheries to canal building. By the time he died, Washington owned about 60,000 acres of land encompassing tracts in Virginia, Pennsylvania, New York, Kentucky, Maryland, and West Virginia. Clearly he lived a life of remarkable accomplishment, achieved through his industriousness and skill. He benefited from good fortune in his brother's connections, aggressiveness in his pursuit of wealth, and his own advantageous marriage.

In telling the political story behind his success and its ties to the American Revolution, we want to be emphatic that Washington was a man of his times and, as such, he pursued success as best as he could in the context of his times. We do not wish in the slightest to diminish the commendable life he lived. Indeed, we believe that his life is arguably the most remarkable and successful life lived by any American. This is not hyperbole; it is grounded in impressive evidence. In George Washington we have a man who was preeminent as an entrepreneur, a land developer, a devoted family man, a military man, a politician, a leader, and a nation builder. Who else can claim to have accomplished so much in so many fields with such long-lasting and beneficial consequences? Still, with the greatest respect for what he achieved, we do wish to move him from the pedestal on which his memory resides to the solid ground of reality, where he can be seen as a remarkable flesh-and-blood person who successfully exploited life's opportunities.

George Washington was the least schooled of American presidents. He did not go formally beyond elementary education. His expectation of following his older brothers to England to continue his schooling was cut short by their father's untimely death. Despite the lack of formal education, Washington was a studious man who read and worked hard to improve his ability to speak and write well and who relied on books to instruct him in practical matters, such as better ways to farm and, critically, in better ways to comprehend the military arts and sciences. Despite his great efforts, his lack of education in some regards made him stand out as a black sheep among his fellow revolutionaries. Some of the leading lights of his time were not shy to criticize his lack of education. John Adams, always jealous of the public affection bestowed on Washington, noted, "That Washington was not a scholar was certain. That he was too illiterate, unread, unlearned for his station and reputation is equally past dispute."[10] Still, Washington was ambitious in everything he did. Leaving school behind, he trained as a land surveyor, then a demanding occupation requiring both good skills in mathematics and in withstanding the trials of the wilderness. He was good at both.

The story of Washington's many successes and many of his reasons for supporting revolution begin indirectly with the marriage of his brother Lawrence to Anne Fairfax. Anne was the daughter of William Fairfax who, in turn, served as a land agent for his powerful cousin, Thomas, sixth Lord Fairfax. William Fairfax, a wealthy and influential man from an impeccable family, took a great liking to George Washington. Fairfax's affection and family tie to Washington were manifested in opportunities for Washington while he was still in his teens. It was Fairfax, for instance, who gave Washington his first real opportunity to survey land. More crucially, because of his ties to Lawrence, whose own opportunities owed a great deal to his family tie to William Fairfax, George gained the chance to learn to be a military leader, as well as the opportunity to acquire land and familiarize himself with valuable tracts of land that he would gain ownership over in the future, thanks to his military service.

The Ohio Company and George Washington's Prospects

GEORGE'S EARLY OPPORTUNITY FOR A MILITARY CAREER, BEGINNING when he was a scant twenty-one years old, derived from family ties. He was, as we saw, sent west over the Allegheny Mountains to the Ohio Valley both to survey land and help oust the French. The territory west of the Alleghenies was, in the mid-eighteenth century, difficult to access, nearly impassible, and, consequently, of scant interest to most colonists. There were almost no English settlers. Instead, there were but a few scattered, thinly populated German settlements, as well as the French aspirations to control the area to which we have already referred.

The eighteenth-century Ohio Valley, which spans portions of today's West Virginia, Pennsylvania, and Ohio, had great untapped economic potential. Its land was fertile, well endowed with waterways and a temperate climate. If it could be settled by hard-working, productive farmers, it could become a great asset to whoever controlled it. What is more, there were navigable rivers that flowed together, providing the opportunity for large settlements. The Forks of the Ohio, in today's Pittsburgh, was but one such example and one that was well known to George Washington as he was involved in its survey as well as in a great, unsuccessful battle against the French at Fort Duchesne, which they built at the Forks.

To those who had an eye for investment opportunities (such as Washington, Benjamin Franklin, Thomas Jefferson, and a great many other founding fathers), land in the American frontier, the hinterlands beyond the Alleghenies, was a great attraction. We should not be surprised to find that such gentlemen as had the interest and the means, either in money or in hard labor, to acquire and develop this land would challenge alternative settlers, be they French or Indian or anyone else who might impose restrictions on their own opportunity to do so. As we shall see, those like George Washington, who embraced revolution on the grounds that the king was restricting their opportunities for land acquisition, were making arguments very much aligned with their self-interest in accumulating a fortune, perhaps more so than with their concern for the king's alleged tyranny against the average colonist.

King George III's Proclamation of 1763 imposed the threat of tremendous financial losses on land speculation organizations, such as the Ohio Company, which had been founded in 1747 with the idea of developing the frontier in the Ohio Valley. Indeed, the Ohio Company had received a royal grant in 1749 of up to 500,000 acres (200,000 at first and an additional 300,000 acres later) north of the Ohio River, if it met two conditions: the establishment of a fort and settlement by at least one hundred families within seven years; that is, by 1756. As for meeting the requirement of a fort and garrisoning it, Washington built Fort Necessity (recall the charge that his activities in the Ohio country were "a scheme to promote the interest of a private company") near to where the Jumonville battle occurred. He then lost Fort Necessity on July 3, 1754, on the one and only occasion when he was compelled to surrender to his enemy, in this case the French.

As we know, Washington's military actions in 1754 helped precipitate the French and Indian War. With the war in full swing, it proved all but impossible to attract settlers to the land and so, perforce, the Ohio Company found itself unable to meet the land grant conditions within the seven years it had been allotted. Matters went from bad to worse for the company. Following the death of King George II in 1760, George III adopted new policies, including the Proclamation of 1763. The proclamation prohibited the colonists from settling on land in the Ohio Valley, which meant that neither the Ohio Company nor any other colonial land speculation enterprise—the opportunity for land acquisition remained open to English investors—could capitalize legally on the land development opportunity it believed made investment in the Ohio Valley so attractive.[11] We mention "legally" because, as will become evident, George Washington did not have serious qualms about violating the king's proclamation.

Back in 1747, all of the harmful circumstances that were to arise for the Ohio Company lay in the unknown future. At its outset, the company provided an opportunity for great enrichment. Its original founders were Thomas Lee (1690–1750), John Mercer (1704–1768), and Lawrence Washington (1718–1752). Thomas Lee was a wealthy landowner, the manager of Lord Fairfax's estate (Northern Neck), and briefly the governor of Virginia, as well as a longtime member of the House of Burgesses and the Council of the State of Virginia on which he served until his death in 1750. He was also the father of two signers of the Declaration of Independence, Richard Henry and Francis Lightfoot Lee, both also members of the Virginia House of Burgesses. His was a wealthy, powerful, and important family that continued to exert a strong influence on American politics for over a century, counting, for instance, among its later members, General Robert E. Lee.

John Mercer was a prominent, highly influential Virginia lawyer, as well, of course, as an investor in land. He was, by marriage, George Mason's uncle. Mason, a wealthy and influential Virginia revolutionary, was a neighbor and friend of Washington's in later years. Mercer himself grew close to George Washington, serving later as his lawyer and investment partner. The relationship was apparently not only about business. Mercer's second son, John Fenton Mercer (1735–1756), was commissioned as a captain in 1755 under George Washington. Sadly, John Fenton died in battle in 1756.

Like fellow founding member Thomas Lee, Lawrence Washington was a member of the House of Burgesses. Their two families were more than close. Remember that Lee managed the Fairfax estate and Lawrence was married to Anne Fairfax. When Lawrence died of tuberculosis in 1752, Anne remarried into the Lee family, eventually leaving Mount Vernon, which she had inherited from Lawrence, to George who had rented it from her for many years after she remarried and moved elsewhere. So, the founders of the Ohio Company were powerful figures in Virginia's government who were as well interlinked to one another by close family ties and shared business interests.

The interlocking ties of the Ohio Company did not end with its three primary founders. Virginia's lieutenant governor, Robert Dinwiddie, was another shareholder in the Ohio Company. It was Dinwiddie who gave twenty-one-year-old George Washington an exceptional opportunity to play a part in the unfolding tensions between France and England, thereby launching Washington's career. Dinwiddie, with the backing of the King's Council, was the person who recommended and appointed Washington as the king's emissary to confront the French and "require of them peaceably to depart"; and failing that, George II stated that "[we] do strictly command and charge you to drive them out by force of arms."[12]

Robert Dinwiddie had two critical interests in that mission. He was lieutenant governor of Virginia; that is, the operational government manager of the Virginia Colony. And he also was one of the wealthy, influential shareholders in the Ohio Company, concerned with advancing the firm's value through land acquisition in the very area to which Washington was sent to stop the advance of the French. By making George Washington into Major Washington, Dinwiddie advanced his own governmental and business interests, as well as those of Lee, Mercer, and L. Washington. He gave the king a totally inexperienced, but well connected, officer as his emissary, but one who happened to have two great virtues—Washington knew how to survey land as well as pick and register (*patenting*, in the vernacular of the times) desirable property, and he was a means for the lieutenant governor to curry favor with the founders of the Ohio Company, in which Dinwiddie was an investor. Hence, the seemingly well-grounded charge against George Washington on publication of his report following his encounter at

Fort Leboeuf in the winter of 1753: "a scheme to promote the interest of a private company."

The investors in the Ohio Company were never reluctant to use their influential political connections in Virginia to advance government policies that were beneficial to their personal investment interests. Today we might see that as a scandalous conflict of interests; then, it was how business was done. Consider, for instance, how Lawrence Washington and his associates used their political clout to advance personal and company interests in the commercial development of the Potomac River (on which, as an aside, we noted Lawrence's—later George's—Mount Vernon sits). This development proved later in life to be of the greatest importance to George Washington. The investors who started the Ohio Company hoped to acquire vast amounts of land and hoped to link those lands to a port on the Potomac River from which they could then ship goods, especially tobacco, to London. The company—that is, Lee, Mercer, L. Washington, and Dinwiddie—sought control over a facility known as Hugh West's tobacco warehouse on the Potomac. That part of the river was well suited to the accommodation of commercial ships from England and so it was a perfect location for an entrepôt (a shipping center) from which export and import trade would flow. Lawrence Washington led the effort in the Virginia House of Burgesses to secure the desired site. The successful effort resulted in the creation of the then new town of Alexandria, Virginia, advancing the company's interests at the expense of local farmers who had opposed the plan. Even today, a stroll through Alexandria brings tourists to sign after sign reminding them—benignly—that they are traversing land that belonged to George (and earlier, Lawrence) Washington.

Few tourists today, passing the historic remains of canal locks designed to make the river navigable in the eighteenth century, are likely to know that George Washington later exploited the successful imposition of Ohio Company interests in Alexandria in 1785—long after that firm was defunct—when he became a founder, shareholder, and president of the Potomac Company. The latter built several canals along the Potomac to circumvent its waterfalls and to make it into a major gateway for the shipment of goods not only abroad but also to the rest of the country. The goods, in turn, were in many cases to come from lands that, as it happened, were owned by and leased out to farmers by George Washington. Although the canal company was to fail in the nineteenth century, well after Washington had died, under the pressures of the Erie Canal (an interest of Alexander Hamilton) and the emergence of railroads, Washington, a mere two years before becoming president of the United States, saw this as his most important investment. Indeed, this remained true through the rest of his life. In his will, written in 1799, Washington instructed his executors as follows:

> I recommend it to my Executors not to be precipitate in disposing of the landed property (herein directed to be sold) if from temporary causes the Sale thereof should be dull; experience having fully evinced, that the price of land (especially above the Falls of the Rivers, & on the Western Waters) have been progressively rising, and cannot be long checked in its increasing value.—And I particularly recommend it to such of the Legatees (under this clause of my Will) as can make it convenient, to take each a share of my Stock in the Potomac Company in preference to the amount of what it might sell for; being thoroughly convinced myself, that no uses to which the money can be applied will be so productive as the Tolls arising from this navigation when in full operation (and this from the nature of things it must be 'ere long) and more especially if that of the Shenandoah is added thereto.

Although the Ohio Company opened the door to Washington's military career and to his own later acquisition of vast amounts of land, he was not himself an investor in the company. Hence, he did not stand to gain directly from its success, or to suffer directly from its failure. For Washington, however, all future paths, whether as a landowner, a canal builder, or a military hero, lead back to the benefits he derived from his personal ties to the Ohio Company. It was the catalyst for his success. As Willard Rouse Jillson has noted of Washington, "he had occasion to observe and philosophize upon the lands on the western waters as was the privilege of no other landed gentleman in America."[13]

The Ohio Company's prospects were in awful shape in 1763 when King George III restricted colonists from settling in the Ohio Valley. Any remaining prospects for the company were shattered by 1767 when the British government announced that all the land to the west of the Alleghenies belonged to the king, a command to be countered directly in the Declaration of Independence. The economic implications of the 1767 declaration were, in fact, a crucial casus belli; that is, a justification for going to war in 1776.

While the Ohio Company slipped into oblivion, George Washington's prospects were decidedly on the rise. Already a wealthy man from his own efforts to plow almost everything he earned back into land acquisition, in 1759 Washington married, and married very well. Martha Custis was a very wealthy widow who brought 17,000 acres to the union as well as nearly one hundred dower slaves.[14] Although Washington apparently courted only women from wealthy families and was rebuffed at least once by a father who thought him of too middling a family for his daughter, still we should not overemphasize the importance of Martha's fortune. Make no mistake: Martha Custis and George Washington had a love match. That said, her deep pockets helped further advance Washington's opportunity to accumulate land and fame.

Back in February 1754, on the eve of war with France in America, Robert Dinwiddie, in his capacity as lieutenant governor of Virginia and acting explicitly on behalf of the king, declared:

> for the security and protection of his majesty's subjects in his colony;
> and as it is absolutely necessary that a sufficient force should be raised
> to erect and support the same; for an encouragement to all who shall
> voluntarily enter into the said service, I do hereby notify and promise,
> by and with the advice and consent of his majesty's council of this col-
> ony, that over and above their pay, two hundred thousand acres, of his
> majesty the king of Great Britain's lands, on the east side of the river
> Ohio, within this dominion, (one hundred thousand acres whereof to
> be contiguous to the said fort, and the other hundred thousand acres
> to be on, or near the river Ohio) shall be laid off and granted to such
> persons, who by their voluntary engagement and good behaviour in
> the said service, shall deserve the same. And I further promise, that
> the said lands shall be divided amongst them, immediately after the
> performance of the said service in a proportion due to their respective
> merit, as shall be represented to me by their officers, and held and
> enjoyed by them without paying any rights and also free from the
> payment of quit rents, for the term of fifteen years. . . . [15]

This grant of land to Virginia veterans of the campaign against the French and Indians proved of tremendous value, and not a little controversy, for Washington, who had been raised to the rank of colonel by Robert Dinwiddie. With the war well over, Washington petitioned in 1769 for the 200,000 acres promised to him and his soldiers. The petition was granted with the proviso that the land to be granted not infringe on prior settlements. Washington then accomplished a feat that in hindsight appears both prescient and incredibly audacious: he met with his former soldiers and reached agreement that he would secure the 200,000 acres of land on his and their behalf, and that they would pay their share of his expenses to handle their affairs.[16] In doing so, however, he took the best land for himself, leaving them with the dregs. As historian Ron Chernow has observed, Washington "felt an acute sense of urgency, since settlers were already flocking to the Ohio and Great Kanawha Rivers, and he feared they might preempt the most productive soil. He also got wind of a huge scheme by English investors to obtain 2.5 million acres and inaugurate a new colony, Vandalia, whose borders might further curtail the bounty lands."[17] English investors, favored by the king, were a growing threat to Washington's land acquisition ambitions, a fact that was also true for others among the nation's founders, such as Benjamin Franklin and Thomas Jefferson, who were using their wealth to speculate in land. All of these gentlemen, other than Washington (who had resigned from the Continental Congress upon being designated as commander in chief of the as yet nonexistent Continental Army), were signatories to the Declaration of Independence; that is, the declaration of war against Britain. Like Washington, they were all fabulously wealthy individuals—in today's dollars, holding assets between a hundred million dollars and, in Franklin's case, perhaps billions of dollars apiece. A new British colony could mean the loss of their massive accumulated wealth and investments.

Washington had maneuvered to ensure that his friend and business associate William Crawford would carry out the land surveys that would allocate acreage to Washington and his former comrades in arms. Crawford secured for Washington "the cream of the country,"[18] which meant the best waterfront lands Crawford could find, doing so in violation of a Virginia statute of 1712 that imposed restrictions on the dimensions of land tracts—legislation presumably intended to avoid the very unfair advantages that Washington was seeking at the expense of his former comrades.[19]

This did not go unnoticed by his former soldiers. As John Ferling writes, "Washington ultimately acquired 20,147 acres. Within two years some of the men began to feel they had been duped." He goes on to quote Crawford's communication to Washington to the effect that they are "a good deal shagreend [chagrined]" to discover that "you have all the bottom . . . Land"—that is, the best land in the valleys and near the rivers and streams. Crawford went on to state that none of the land "in the country is so good as your Land."[20] Washington was unsympathetic, even disdainful of those among his former soldiers who complained. He had the land he wanted, which, in the end, was his true objective. He did nothing to redress their complaints.

Crawford was new neither to surveying on Washington's behalf nor to controversy surrounding the work he did for the future president. Following the Proclamation of 1763 that prohibited colonists from settling in the Ohio Valley, Washington sent Crawford to scout out land in the prohibited area, telling him, "I can never look upon that proclamation in any other light (but this I say among ourselves) than as a temporary expedient to quiet the minds of the Indians which must fall, of course, in a few years, especially when those Indians are consenting to our occupying the lands. Any person, therefore, who neglects the present opportunity of hunting out good lands and in some measure marking and distinguishing them for their own (in order to keep others from settling them) will never regain it." Aware of the risks, Washington went on to say, "I would recommend to you to keep this whole matter a profound secret . . . because I might be censured for the opinion I have given in respect to the King's proclamation."[21] Obviously he knew his actions were against the king's orders, hence the need to keep the matter secret, but that did not deter his avaricious desire to beat others to land claims in the area formerly explored by the Ohio Company.

Through tough business dealing, prudent spending, and a superb eye for opportunities in land acquisition and other businesses, George Washington turned himself into a phenomenally wealthy man. And then the economic world around him was turned topsy-turvy by new policies emanating from Britain. These policies and the threat they represented to his, and many other founding fathers', personal interests were a great impetus for revolution. Indeed, the threat to Washington's fortune was, in our view, at least as momentous for American history as any worries about taxation without representation or about the alleged tyranny of the king.

Washington's Pre-Revolution Challenge

S TARTING WITH THE DEATH OF GEORGE II IN 1760 AND GEORGE III's Proclamation of 1763, the economic prospects for America's richest colonists were increasingly in doubt. The new king seemed interested in opening investment opportunities to British speculators at the expense of the colonists. Further, he showed an interest in steering settlements by colonists north into Canada, to help control the French, and south to Florida, to keep the Spaniards at bay, rather than in the Ohio Valley, which by the late 1760s he made clear he believed was part of his frontier.

In addition to these constraints, the king decided to fundamentally alter the economic circumstances in his American colonies. He did so in large measure to get the colonists, especially the wealthiest among them, to pay their share in their own defense. He was, after all, presiding over a government that was nearly bankrupted by the French and Indian War and the larger and largely concurrent Seven Years' War.

The colonies had variously begun issuing their own currency in 1690. Now, at the behest of George III, Parliament passed the Currency Act in 1764. The act stated simply and clearly enough the problem created as a consequence of the colonies' undisciplined printing of money, reminiscent of modern-day debates over whether such issuance makes currency cheap. And it stated an equally simple and clear remedy. It is useful to quote the text of the act so that there is no confusion over Parliament's stated intent:

> WHEREAS great quantities of paper bills of credit have been created and issued in his Majesty's colonies or plantations in America, by virtue of acts, orders, resolutions, or votes of assembly, making and declaring such bills of credit to be legal tender in payment of money: and whereas such bills of credit have greatly depreciated in their value, by means whereof debts have been discharged with a much less than was contracted for . . . for remedy whereof . . . may [it] be enacted . . . by and with the advice and consent of the lords spiritual and temporal, and commons, in this present parliament assembled, . . . no act, order, resolution, or vote of assembly, in any of his Majesty's colonies or plantations in America, shall be made, for creating or issuing any paper bills, or bills of credit of any kind . . .

and every clause or provision which shall hereafter be inserted in any act, order, resolution, or vote of assembly, contrary to this act, shall be null and void.

Parliament, with the king's acquiescence, forbade the colonies from printing their own currency or using it to pay for pretty much anything. In doing so, Parliament was seeking to restrain runaway inflation—resulting from the excessive production of currency—so as to prevent the value of debts from being wiped out. To do otherwise would have damaged the English economy. Now, of course, this was a devastating economic blow to those who relied on bills of credit or other means of settling debts, public or private. Suddenly such colonists found their debts expensive rather than cheap; the price of goods and services much costlier as they had to pay with "real" money, meaning English money, which was in short supply; and the credit they had given others had become unrepayable.

Imagine how any of us would react today if we were told that by order of Congress and the president, all of our money was no longer legal tender. Imagine, instead, that we would have to pay for goods and services with some other currency of which we have little or none. Surely there would be outrage, with protests against the policy led by the richest among us whose wealth was being wiped out. Having failed to convert their now useless paper bills or bills of credit into real money, they would be faced with economic disaster. It is not hard to imagine that some among them would start to whisper about rebellion to overthrow the government.

The Currency Act had been in force but one year when the British government issued another economic affront to the (wealthiest) colonists: the Stamp Act of 1765. This act was the first direct tax levied by the Crown on the colonists. Although it was a broad tax that required every legal document, every piece of paper, even playing cards and dice to have a government stamp, the burden of the tax fell much more heavily on "men of wealth and standing in the community and some of the most influential people in society."[22] Once again, the wealthiest members of colonial society—large landowners and successful lawyers—found their personal economies imposed upon by the Crown. Now, the Crown had a perfectly sensible reason for issuing this tax. The French and Indian War had been fought to defend the English settlements in America from the threat of being overrun by the French with the help of Indian tribes whose own lands were put at the greatest risk by the spread of colonial ambitions. Defense was a heavy economic burden and Parliament saw fit to have the colonists share in that burden.

The colonists—again, the wealthy colonists at the forefront—did not take the tax lightly. Such men as George Washington, George Mason, and many others put together a plan to boycott British goods, much as Mahatma Gandhi was to do in another English colony nearly two hundred years later following the introduction, in that case, of a tax on salt. The colonial resistance proved effective. The tax was repealed one year later but its issuance was the occasion for some colonists, assembled in the Stamp Act Congress in 1765, to make clear their objections. Further, they made clear that, in their view, the only possible remedy to their objections was to remove any tax on them, regardless of the heavy financial burden suffered in England in defense of the colonies. The participants in the Stamp Act Congress were seemingly unconcerned that Britain's defense of the colonies, as in the French and Indian War, may have been necessitated by the actions of the colonists themselves. They set out a set of detailed points of such import in understanding the origins of the American Revolution that we repeat them here. The Stamp Act Congress's grievances were to reverberate over the next decade, leading to specific arguments in the Declaration of Independence and to war:

> The members of this Congress, sincerely devoted, with the warmest sentiments of affection and duty to His Majesty's Person and Government . . . and with minds deeply impressed by a sense of the present and impending misfortunes of the British colonies on this continent; having considered as maturely as time will permit the circumstances of the said colonies, esteem it our indispensable duty to make the following declarations of our humble opinion, respecting the most essential rights and liberties of the colonists, and of the grievances under which they labour, by reason of several late Acts of Parliament.
>
> I. That His Majesty's subjects in these colonies, owe the same allegiance to the Crown of Great-Britain, that is owing from his subjects born within the realm, and all due subordination to that august body the Parliament of Great-Britain.

   II. That His Majesty's liege subjects in these colonies, are entitled to all the inherent rights and liberties of his natural born subjects within the kingdom of Great-Britain.

  III. That it is inseparably essential to the freedom of a people, and the undoubted right of Englishmen, that no taxes be imposed on them, but with their own consent, given personally, or by their representatives.

  IV. That the people of these colonies are not, and from their local circumstances cannot be, represented in the House of Commons in Great-Britain.

   V. That the only representatives of the people of these colonies, are persons chosen therein by themselves, and that no taxes ever have been, or can be constitutionally imposed on them, but by their respective legislatures.

  VI. That all supplies to the Crown, being free gifts of the people, it is unreasonable and inconsistent with the principles and spirit of the British Constitution, for the people of Great-Britain to grant to His Majesty the property of the colonists.

  VII. That trial by jury is the inherent and invaluable right of every British subject in these colonies.

VIII. That the late Act of Parliament, entitled, An Act for granting and applying certain Stamp Duties, and other Duties, in the British colonies and plantations in America, etc., by imposing taxes on the inhabitants of these colonies, and the said Act, and several other Acts, by extending the jurisdiction of the courts of Admiralty beyond its ancient limits, have a manifest tendency to subvert the rights and liberties of the colonists.

  IX. That the duties imposed by several late Acts of Parliament, from the peculiar circumstances of these colonies, will be extremely burthensome and grievous; and from the scarcity of specie [that is, due to the currency act], the payment of them absolutely impracticable.

   X. That as the profits of the trade of these colonies ultimately center in Great-Britain, to pay for the manufactures which they are obliged to take from thence, they eventually contribute very largely to all supplies granted there to the Crown.

  XI. That the restrictions imposed by several late Acts of Parliament, on the trade of these colonies, will render them unable to purchase the manufactures of Great-Britain.

XII.   That the increase, prosperity, and happiness of these colonies,
        depend on the full and free enjoyment of their rights and liber-
        ties, and an intercourse with Great-Britain mutually affectionate
        and advantageous.

XIII.   That it is the right of the British subjects in these colonies, to pe-
        tition the King, Or either House of Parliament.

    Lastly, That it is the indispensable duty of these colonies, to the
best of sovereigns, to the mother country, and to themselves, to en-
deavour by a loyal and dutiful address to his Majesty, and humble
applications to both Houses of Parliament, to procure the repeal of
the Act for granting and applying certain stamp duties, of all clauses
of any other Acts of Parliament, whereby the jurisdiction of the Admiralty is extended as aforesaid, and of the other late Acts for the
restriction of American commerce.[23]

In essence, the colonists said they could not be taxed by Parliament
without being represented in Parliament and then, lest the British resolve this complaint by granting them representation in Parliament,
that "from their local circumstances [they] cannot be, represented in
the House of Commons in Great-Britain." What a beautiful catch-22
they attempted to construct if the British government were gullible
enough to buy it: no taxation without representation but, given their
great physical distance from Britain, they asserted that they could not
be granted representation and hence, no taxation! They then went on
to say, in clear reference to the Currency Act of 1764, that the accumulated costs of the defense of the colonies could not be borne directly by
the colonists "from the scarcity of specie," arguing that their commerce
with Britain, to Britain's great advantage, was the means by which
the colonists had contributed to their defense. The leaders of colonial
America—the very rich, landowners, such as George Washington—
had agreed that they could not be made to shoulder any part of the economic burden of their own defense unless it were done by their own
legislatures (which such men as Washington, from influential families,
largely controlled). They would not tolerate their wealth being diminished by either the Currency Act or the Stamp Act. How remarakably
and narrowly self-interested were these complaints.
    On top of the actions of Parliament, George Washington found the
representatives of the British monarch threatening to his own fortune in

other ways. The land grants he had gained from his military role in the French and Indian War were at risk over a technicality. It was arguably the case that the award of land was aimed only at His Majesty's regular soldiers and not militiamen whose commissions, like his, had no status in the English army. Indeed, Washington had complained throughout his early military career that he, as a colonel, was nevertheless susceptible to being commanded by a regular English captain; that is, a regular soldier of nominally lower rank. Likewise, he routinely objected that officers in colonial militias were paid much less than regular English officers of the same rank. He chose to overlook the fact that he had been commissioned by Robert Dinwiddie, who had no such legal authority. All this came to a head when the last royal governor of Virginia, John Murray, the fourth Earl of Dunmore, with whom Washington had a poor personal relationship, invoked the "technicality," stripping Washington of his Kanawha lands in the Ohio Valley, lands that he was particularly attached to and that he believed would have great value, as they were at the fork of the Kanawha and Monongahela Rivers.[24]

Washington, like so many other wealthy, ambitious colonial leaders, found that British policy was creating an insufferable threat to his future prospects. His Virginia money was diminished in value; his lands were being heavily taxed by the Stamp Act, whereas heretofore they had been subject to no tax whatsoever from England; and now his acquisition of property was constrained by British policies that favored English investors and friendly Indian tribes over men like him. Something had to be done to remove the threat all these British actions represented. And something, indeed, was done: the Declaration of Independence.

The Justification for Revolution

THE SIGNATORIES TO THE DECLARATION OF INDEPENDENCE, BEING pragmatic politicians about to engage in a great and extremely risky war, did not limit themselves to philosophical arguments about social contracts and the rights of men, though the likes of Locke, Rousseau, and Montesquieu certainly provided a valuable intellectual framework. Nor did America's revolutionaries constrain their thinking to historical examples. Rather, and quite practically, they justified the ensuing

War for Independence on the basis of an itemized list of grievances against the British Crown and its agents in the American colonies. These grievances reflected what some colonists saw as a fundamental break from their inalienable rights, a break that had arisen, as we saw, most particularly following the end of the Seven Years' War (1756–1763) and especially its North American manifestation in the French and Indian War (1754–1763).

Almost every American can recite, or at least paraphrase, the Declaration's premise: "We hold these truths to be self-evident, that all men are created equal, that they are endowed by their Creator with certain unalienable Rights, that among these are Life, Liberty and the pursuit of Happiness." Too rarely do we read carefully beyond this glorious portion of the document. Yet, the justification for war is in all that follows, the import of much of which may be surprising to today's reader. However, it was surely transparent to those who heard the Declaration read aloud in their town squares in July 1776, as well as to the fifty-six men who signed it.

Those who signed or supported the Declaration had a subtle, nuanced understanding of what justified rebellion. They knew that revolution, being extremely risky and costly, should not be entered into lightly. None knew this better than George Washington, a veteran and local hero of the French and India War who found himself called upon in 1775 to lead his fellow colonists' war effort as commander in chief of an army against Britain. Washington, like the authors of the Declaration, understood that living under an unjust government was not by itself a sufficient justification for rebellion, but he slowly and reluctantly came to agree that the Crown had gone too far. As the Declaration states, "Prudence, indeed, will dictate that Governments long established should not be changed for light and transient causes; and accordingly all experience hath shewn, that mankind are more disposed to suffer, while evils are sufferable, than to right themselves by abolishing the forms to which they are accustomed. But when a long train of abuses and usurpations, pursuing invariably the same Object evinces a design to reduce them under absolute Despotism, it is their right, it is their duty, to throw off such Government, and to provide new Guards for their future security.—Such has been the patient sufferance of these Colonies; and such is now the necessity which constrains them to alter their former Systems of Government."

In a point-by-point assessment that followed, reminiscent of modern-day cost-benefit analysis, the Declaration's signatories concluded that rebellion was warranted by the intolerable conduct of the British government. And yet, a mere decade earlier, responding to the Stamp Act, many of these same colonists had seemed overjoyed with their good fortune in having such a marvelous sovereign. Remember the opening statement in their petition to the king: "The members of this Congress, sincerely devoted, with the warmest sentiments of affection and duty to His Majesty's Person and Government, inviolably attached to the present happy establishment of the Protestant succession . . . " It seems that their "long train of abuses and usurpations" can have occurred in no longer than a decade and surely, if we are to take their earlier and later claims as sincere, must have been shorter. The king, after all, repealed the Stamp Act within a year of its issuance as well as withdrew his Proclamation of 1763 not long after issuing it. True, in 1770 he then imposed a small tax on tea in an effort to establish no more than the principle that he, as sovereign over the colonies, had the right to exact some tax from them. But in these acts it is hard to see oppression and despotism verging on tyranny . . . unless one happened to be a wealthy landowner who suffered severely from the Currency Act and from the king's declaration of sovereignty over the very Ohio Valley in which such speculators as Washington were aggressively engaged.

What, then, did the Declaration's signatories enumerate as the abuses that warranted their break from the past? What were the particulars that made their grievances neither light nor transient? What had the British done to cross the line from sufferable to insufferable oppression? The document answers these questions, justifying rebellion with a detailed list of grievances against the Crown. The first six grievances can be joined together as a complaint that the king neither agreed to laws passed by the people's legislatures nor respected the legislative process in the colonies, interfering with its good works however he could. These matters were an implicit part of their earlier complaint against the Stamp Act. Recall point five of the Stamp Act Congress, "That the only representatives of the people of these colonies, are persons chosen therein by themselves, and that no taxes ever have been, or can be constitutionally imposed on them, but by their respective legislatures." So, starting at least in 1765, the powerful colonists had already proclaimed that only their own legislatures could tax them; their legislatures—which they controlled—and no others.

Ten items later in the sequence of the list of grievances is the complaint we all remember: that the king was levying taxes on the colonies without their enjoying the benefits of representation ("For imposing Taxes on us without our Consent"), a deliberate reemphasis of the earlier allegations. Collectively, these were tough charges, carefully crafted to leave no room for a remedy deemed acceptable by the British government.

The subsequent complaints, with one notable collective exception—which forms the heart of our assessment of the casus belli for Washington, and perhaps for Jefferson and other founding fathers—are profound objections to the absence of an independent, honest judiciary and the compulsion to quarter British soldiers in private homes. Before we explore the fundamental grievance from which all these others follow, we should, however, pause to understand the historical foundations of the colonists' complaint about taxation without representation.

Taxation Without Representation

THE COMPLAINT THAT THE COLONIES WERE TAXED WITHOUT representation itself had its foundation in long past history, as well as in contemporary complaints about the same thing in Ireland. Thanks to the fact that Edward I agreed in 1297 that new taxes could not be levied without the approval of all Englishmen represented in the House of Commons, everyone subject to the British Crown could argue, as the Americans did, that they had a right to participate in Parliament in making decisions about their taxation. In the colonists' day, the issue was straightforward. The British government had learned through hard experience that the defense of the colonies was extremely costly. King George III and his Parliament—truly he acted as a constitutional monarch, deferring to Parliament on policy in exchange for their support of his lifestyle—wished to tax the colonists for their own defense and not for his own profit. They, however, objected to being taxed by a government that did not include representatives of their choosing in Parliament even as they contended that they could never be represented in Parliament, a claim we will contend later that the king could readily have overcome.

Whether born in England or on American soil, the colonists considered themselves to be English, subject to the rules of governance long established in English history and, to a lesser degree, practice. The question of the moment was whether the king or his prime minister, or, for that matter, the people in England, thought of the colonists as English. If the government in England saw the colonists as English, then, in keeping with centuries-old commitments, the colonists were as entitled to representation and a say in any new taxation as any other Englishman.

Apparently, at least to the colonial leaders, the Crown either did not consider them Englishmen or it did not feel bound in their case by the ancient promise by Edward I to consult even the commons before levying new taxes. To be sure, that promise had often been breached, but by the time of King George III's constitutional form of monarchy it seemed fairly well established. Provided these assumptions were true, then these violations of their rights and interests might well have been viewed by the colonists as a justification for war. Yet, right above this complaint was a completely different objection to the Crown's policies, one that we believe was at least as crucial to the decision to revolt.

The Right to Land—Not in the Colonies

BURIED AMONG THE GRIEVANCES OVER THE COLONIAL LEGISLATURES, the lack of judicial independence, the quartering of soldiers, and the tyranny of taxation without representation was a complaint that was more attuned, we believe, to personal rather than to general abuses of the public good by the Crown. It states of the king that

> He has endeavoured to prevent the population of these States; for that purpose obstructing the Laws for Naturalization of Foreigners; refusing to pass others to encourage their migrations hither, and raising the conditions of new Appropriations of Lands.

The signatories resented the king's interference in these three related areas, particularly as concerned their entrepreneurial zest for acquiring income-producing real estate situated beyond the colonies.

Of course, without additional settlers, the opportunity to profit from land that could then be sold or, as in Washington's case, leased to new settlers for profit, would be diminished. Here, indeed, was a grievance that George Washington felt most keenly. The Proclamation of 1763 and the king's actions in 1767 were designed to thwart the new appropriation of land by colonists. These appropriations were a big part of the foundation of Washington's fortune and of his self-image. Here was a threat to his way of life that one can readily see would have lit the flame of revolution in his breast.

In the great divide between light and transient offenses and insufferable abuses that warranted rebellion, this challenge to just a few private interests suffering economic damage at the king's hands was given a prominent place in the Declaration of Independence. In addition to Washington, Thomas Jefferson—whose father, Peter, founded a land speculation company in competition with the Ohio Company—stood to suffer grievously from the Crown's restrictions on population growth, naturalization, and land acquisition. Did these three measures harm the greater public good? Perhaps in the long run they would have, but most assuredly this grievance was about the immediate economic harm done to a few prominent private interests who led the movement for revolution. We should not be surprised to learn that short-run personal losses may have been at the forefront of the thinking of the leading colonial revolutionaries. We all live in the moment, in the short run, more emphatically than in the long run.

Certainly we would understand our colonial forefathers' being exercised in the extreme if the king willy-nilly began to confiscate their homes, their farms, or their factories—but that was not the complaint. He was doing no such thing. The grievance was that George III was imposing limits or conditions on new acquisitions; that is, he was restricting the incentives for land speculation! Why did this prominent, specific issue constitute so dire a deviation from painful but tolerable practices that it warranted rebellion? Because it was the dividing line between great wealth and power for the revolution's leaders and their diminishment at the hands of the Crown!

The complete list of grievances is, as one would expect, extensive. It culminates with this complaint:

He [the King] has excited domestic insurrections amongst us, and has endeavoured to bring on the inhabitants of our frontiers, the merciless

Indian Savages, whose known rule of warfare, is an undistinguished
destruction of all ages, sexes and conditions.

This final grievance is, as well, worthy of our reflection for it
speaks to the earlier one that the king was "raising the conditions of
new Appropriations of Lands." This connection is apparent in two
seemingly unimportant words: "our frontiers."

How remarkable a choice of language! How audaciously the signatories chose to view the vast frontier beyond their borders as *their*
frontier, as opposed to Britain's frontiers in North America as King
George III had declared it. Moreover, by the use of such language,
they completely overlooked the further claims of the French, the
Spaniards, and, most notably, the territories controlled by the "Indian
Savages" who were, after all, the original and rightful settlers on these
lands (and recognized as such in later years by the Supreme Court). It
seems implicit in their declaration about "our frontier"—despite there
being almost no English settlers yet present in that frontier—that the
revolutionaries already had some nascent notion of manifest destiny, a
concept we normally associate with the attitudes of US citizens in the
time of President James Polk more than a half century later. Indeed, so
eager were the founders to seize the frontier for themselves that they
reprised the claim to "our" frontier verbatim as a justification for the
War of 1812.

Perhaps, in defense of the founding fathers, we might argue that the
idea that the "Indian Savages" had a rightful claim to these lands is an
anachronistic application of modern-day standards. But were their own
claims rightful? Many wealthy individuals besides Washington and the
Ohio Company—for there were many other land speculation companies
up and down the frontier—were actively and aggressively engaged in
land acquisition at the expense of the Indians living in territories beyond the control of the signers and their supporters. Indeed, although
Washington's interest in the Ohio Company had been familial, and not
as an investor, he was an investor in the Dismal Swamp Company, the
Walpole Grant, the Mississippi Company, and other land speculation
companies. He was an avid and well-diversified land holder. As Stanley
Elkins and Eric McKitrick have reported, Washington "was obsessed
with the idea of amassing land in the West, tremendous amounts of
it, putting it all under cultivation and bringing commerce and people
there. This cycle of acquisition and development began very much

as the expression of a 'private' self, of private ambition and private interest. He was fully determined that it should bring him wealth, possessions, and status. He would in fact expend much time and effort on this, revealing considerable executive capacities in the course of it, while some of his dealings—especially with men who seemed to get in the way of his projects and ambitions—were exceedingly sharp and even ruthless."[25] The British and the Indians were among the "men who seemed to get in the way of his projects and ambitions."

What might the founding fathers have known about the legitimacy of the "Indian Savages" and their claims from reading history or from their own experiences? The history of Western thought at the time certainly includes ideas that run contrary to those expressed in the Declaration, and which might have been known to its authors, including especially Thomas Jefferson, a widely read and well-educated man.

They might have known the writings of Francisco de Vitoria, who, in 1532, had argued against the Spanish Crown's usurpation of the rights of the Indians ("barbarians," as he refers to them) to their land and their lives. And perhaps the Declaration's signatories were familiar with the writings, or at least the ideas, of Adriaen van der Donck (ca. 1620–ca.1655). A prominent leader of New Amsterdam, as the head of the city's governing body, the Board of Nine, under Governor General Peter Stuyvesant, Van der Donck was the author of what remains in large measure the fundamentals of the Charter of the City of New York, as well as the first to argue for many of the distinct freedoms that characterize the American melting pot and that were captured in so many of the Declaration's grievances and the Constitution's Bill of Rights. Furthermore, he was the author of a highly successful "best seller" that described the quality of life in New Netherlands. In this amazing work he made very clear that the Indians, including Indian women, are as smart and civilized as Europeans, they learn quickly when they are schooled, and they had much to offer in terms of superior knowledge of agriculture in the soil and weather conditions of New Netherlands.

How about George Washington's personal, firsthand knowledge of Indian concerns and practices? Remember when young George Washington, at Robert Dinwiddie's behest, went into the Ohio Country to confront the French? In the course of carrying out his orders, he had occasion to align with the local Algonquin Indians. An agreement had been reached between the Ohio Company and the Logstown Algonquins, led by a man known to Washington as Half-King. Half-King, who you may recall was the person who killed the French commander in the Jumonville Affair, was a key local chief and the designated representative of the Onandaga Council, the legislative body of the Iroquois nation.[26] As such he represented an important and sizable body of Indian interests. From Washington's perspective, the agreement between the Logstown Algonquins and the Ohio Company meant that Half-King, and the tribes for which he was essentially proconsul, were allied with the English.

With that understanding and with his orders to remove the French in mind, Major Washington called upon Half-King to relate his recent interactions with the local representatives of France. The response, written in George Washington's own hand, with his original emphases noted here, is most instructive. Half-King related how he had told the French to leave, and went on to tell the French, as Washington reported,

> If you had come in a peaceable manner, like our brothers, the *English*, we should not have been against your trading with us, as they do; BUT TO COME, FATHERS, AND BUILD HOUSES UPON OUR LAND AND TO TAKE IT BY FORCE IS WHAT WE CANNOT SUBMIT TO. . . . the Great Being above allowed it to be a place of residence to us, so, Fathers, I desire you to withdraw as I have done [desired of] our brothers the *English* . . . I lay it down as a trial for both, to see which will have the greatest regard for it, and that side we will stand by.[27]

It is evident that the young George Washington understood that Half-King's allegiance depended on who respected his people's claim to the land. It is also evident that he viewed Half-King as a legitimate interlocutor and not as some monstrous Indian Savage. If nothing else, we know he recognized that he needed to cooperate with Half-King and he clearly anticipated a quid pro quo—Half-King would honor his commitments as long as Washington and the British did the same. However, Washington's overall mission was not to respect that land claim but rather to expel the French and to open the way to the English without regard to Indian rights.

Washington's experience notwithstanding, you may still object on the grounds that he, after all, was not a signatory to the Declaration of Independence, nor a man with great knowledge or understanding of the Indians, at least not at the time just related, and so his understanding of the Indians may have been entirely different from the experiences of the actual signers. Then, let's go to the writings of Thomas Jefferson. He, after all, was not only a signatory but was an author of the Declaration, including "the merciless Indian Savages" passage. Jefferson wrote in 1785, "I beleive [sic] the Indian then to be in body and mind equal to the whiteman."[28] On another occasion, Jefferson, writing about the settler practice of retaliatory, disproportionate slaughter of Indians, noted that their "known rule of warfare, is an undistinguished destruction of all ages, sexes and conditions, . . . " Here is his description, in his own words, from page 37 of his handwritten *Notes on the State of Virginia*:

> In the spring of the year 1774, a robbery and murder were committed on an inhabitant of the frontiers of Virginia, by two Indians of the Shawanee tribe. The neighbouring whites, according to their custom, undertook to punish this outrage in a summary way. Col. Cresap, a man infamous for the many murders he had committed on those much-injured people, collected a party, and proceeded down the Kanhaway in quest of vengeance. Unfortunately a canoe of women and children, with one man only, was seen coming from the opposite shore, unarmed, and unsuspecting an hostile attack from the whites. Cresap and his party concealed themselves on the bank of the river, and the moment the canoe reached the shore, singled out their objects, and, at one fire, killed every person in it.[29]

Unlike the Declaration's description of Indians as being "merciless savages," here Jefferson, describing an event that occurred but a scant two years before the Declaration, reports that they were "much-injured people." And in his *Notes*, he further described Colonel Cresap in terms reminiscent of his condemnation of Indians in the Declaration: as a man "whose known rule of warfare, is an undistinguished destruction of all ages, sexes and conditions."

We have articulated the verbatim description of Indians, their expectations, and the ways they were maligned, as offered by two of the most important of America's founding fathers. We could offer many more such accounts but we believe the point is made. The Declaration offered an exceedingly ugly view of the Indian tribes and linked their maliciousness to the Crown's decision to protect their access to land coveted by the colonists, or at least some of them. Now we wish to pull the argument together. The king's actions from 1763 to 1769 put the wealth and future ambitions of the founding fathers at risk. They needed to be rid of British rule and its threat to their welfare. The king furthermore, for his own short-term political interest, was aligning with the Indians at the expense of the colonists. The Indians were the fundamental on-site, ongoing threat to the interests of the land-speculator founders, and in the view of our great leaders, they needed to be tamed to do as the land speculators wanted, or they needed to be removed from the scene. As George Washington emphasized in all-capital letters, in relating Half-King's message: "TO COME, FATHERS, AND BUILD HOUSES UPON OUR LAND AND TO TAKE IT BY FORCE IS WHAT WE CANNOT SUBMIT TO." That, at least as much as the fear of taxation without representation, seems to have been the motivation for revolution and the ouster of the English and oppression of the Indians.

What If?

W̲E HAVE SEEN THAT GEORGE WASHINGTON AND MANY OF THE other leaders of the American Revolution were men of extraordinary wealth who had good reason to fear the loss of that wealth under the prevailing policies of the British government. We have also seen that many of the founding fathers were at each other's throats, sometimes due to personal strains, more often due to policy differences. Washington and Jefferson had strained relations, as did Hamilton and Jefferson, Adams and Jefferson, Adams and Washington, Madison and Hamilton, Madison and Washington, and so forth. These strains provided an opportunity that was poorly exploited by the king and his prime ministers, especially between 1763 and 1776 (that is, by George Grenville,1763–1765, Charles Watson-Wentworth, 1765–1766, William Pitt, 1766–1768, Fitzroy, 1768–1770, and Lord North, 1770–1782). To borrow a later description of British colonial policy, George III had an opportunity to divide and conquer or, either failing that or in conjunction with it, to mollify. The opportunity to do either was squandered. With hindsight that seems eminently to the good of the United States, but back in 1776 when there was no United States, everyone might well have judged a different approach by the king as being a wiser, more beneficial policy.

The Seven Years' War, and its subsidiary, the French and Indian War in North America, greatly increased Britain's indebtedness, prompting the government, which was near bankruptcy, to seek new ways to raise revenue. When Grenville's government introduced the Stamp Act, the British, as we have noted, imposed a great cost on the wealthiest colonial leaders, especially those either with large landhold-ings (such as George Washington) or those with lucrative law practices (such as Mercer and Adams). The outcry against the Stamp Act led to its repeal under Watson-Wentworth, clearly signaling the colonists that they could exert enough pressure on the British government to convince it to change course, a dangerous precedent for any sitting government. No sooner was Watson-Wentworth out than Pitt came in and imposed new taxes under the Townsend Acts. And so it went, with the pressure for revolution mounting in the colonies as its leaders saw their wealth and station put at risk by a British government that, from the colonial leaders' perspective, sought to exploit them.

What might the king and his first minister have done differently to secure revenue from the colonies and diminish the threat of rebellion? Recall that the colonial Stamp Act Congress famously declared that no Englishman could be taxed without representation in Parliament. This was a well-established legal precedent since Edward I signed *Confir-matio Cartarum* in 1297. True, as in the case of George III, the legal precedent was often violated in practice but still, there it sat as a tool used against the Crown by the colonists. The Crown, instead, could have turned it into an advantage.

It was important to many of the colonial leaders to be seen to be and treated as Englishmen. One of George Washington's great sources of resentment, for example, was that in the 1750s and 1760s he was not given the same respect—or the same salary—as a regular British officer of his rank. Recall also that he and many of the other leading revo-lutionaries were reluctant to choose rebellion over an accommodation with the British government. The more radical Madison, as we have noted, accused the Tidewater gentry—Washington, the Lee family, George Mason, and many other leading lights of Virginia—as being too soft toward the king because they looked for compromise, while such men as Patrick Henry and James Madison promoted revolution.

Imagine that the king, rather than going back and forth on tax-ing the colonists, had instead decided to pay down the national debt with a general tax on all Englishmen. Imagine further that he treated the colonists as if they were Englishmen every bit as much as anyone living in England. He could easily have done so by granting represen-tation in Parliament to the colonists in a manner proportionate to their population relative to the population in Britain. Indeed, in the *Wealth of Nations* published in 1776, Adam Smith recommends just that, stating that "there is not the least probability that the British constitution would be hurt by the union of Great Britain with her colonies."[30] That would have translated into 25 percent of parliamentary seats filled by representatives chosen by the colonists who, in turn, might have apportioned those seats according to the population of each colony or by whatever other means they might have agreed to.

Such an action would have mollified the more reluctant rebels among the founding fathers (perhaps including George Washington), providing a means to protect their investment interests by spreading any tax for the defense of the colonies among all of the British represented in Parliament, rather than by concentrating the burden on the colonists, isolating the more radical colonial leaders. George III might have averted the war while such men as George Washington could have been satisfied that they had a say in protecting their investments from arbitrary rule by Parliament and the king. As Smith stated, "[The colonists'] representatives in parliament, of which the number ought from the first to be considerable, would easily be able to protect them from all oppression. The distance could not much weaken the dependency of the representative upon the constituent . . . It would be the interest of the former [representative], therefore, to cultivate that good will by complaining, with all the authority of a member of the legislature, of every outrage which any civil or military officer might be guilty of in those remote parts of the empire."[31] With the representation that they had said was not possible because of their "peculiar circumstances" having being granted, they would have been in a strong enough position to forge coalitions, making themselves pivotal in significant governmental matters. Doing so would have allowed the American colonial leaders to create political checks against a rapacious desire among others to limit the colonists' land acquisition and to protect their sources of revenue. Since the king by this time tended to defer to Parliament and Parliament was already divided over how to deal with the colonies, it is not difficult to imagine that by the simple expedient of representation proportional to population the king's interests and the interests of many founding fathers could have been satisfied. Too bad none had the patience to construct such a simple solution.

Had the colonists been given proper representation in Parliament, we might not have had the American Revolution or, at least, not in the

1770s. What might that have meant for the future? Parliament banned slave trade in 1807 and passed the Slavery Abolition Act in 1833, which made slavery illegal throughout almost all of the British Empire.[32] If the American colonies were then an integral part of Britain, slavery would have been abolished nearly thirty years before the Civil war. Perhaps the southern "parliamentary districts" would have rebelled, but then they would not only have had the northern "parliamentary districts" in America, including the Canadian colonies, against them; they would have had the British Empire opposed to them. Civil war would have been that much less attractive an option and so, perhaps, just perhaps, slavery would have been eliminated earlier and in a less wrenching way than was the case in the 1860s. Against that, remaining part of Britain—but with full representation—would have meant that the US Constitution as we know it, especially its explicit Bill of Rights and its detailed institutions to ensure separation of powers, would not have existed. Rather, the colonies that became the United States might have looked more like the Canadian colonies that secured independence nearly a century after the American Revolution. What that might have meant is the domain of speculation that we invite readers to undertake on their own.

Coda

THE AMERICAN REVOLUTION PROVED A GREAT EXPERIMENT IN THE introduction of a new, representative form of government. As we have seen, it was to a consequential degree motivated by the interests of a small group of wealthy, elite colonists. Although we focused on George Washington, we could just as easily have made the same case for John Hancock (America's 54th-richest man ever), Benjamin Franklin (America's 86th-richest man ever), Thomas Jefferson (the third-wealthiest president, after Washington and Kennedy), Robert Morris, Alexander Hamilton, and others. One charge we have not addressed head-on was the tyranny of which George III was accused. He, too, of course, was a product of his times and not strongly inclined to what we might deem to be democratic, accountable government. Still, tyranny is a harsh charge, and while here is not the place to address it in depth, it is worth looking at a tad of evidence by way of a natural experiment.

Tyrannical governments generally run their economies into the ground as they focus on securing as much of society's wealth for themselves and their cronies as possible, always at the expense of their subjects who are not a threat to their hold on power.[33] In the case of George III we can compare growth in per capita income in America and Canada as a first-blush indicator of how tyrannical and exploitative his rule was, or wasn't. Figure 1.1 shows Angus Maddison's estimates of per capita income in the United States and Canada beginning in 1700 and until it became independent in 1867. Canada lived under George III's "tyranny" until the king died in 1820. Despite the claim of tyranny, it is pretty hard to see that Canadians suffered terribly compared to Americans. Indeed, the wedge between American and Canadian per capita income does not really start to grow until after George III died and is more likely due to the colder, less hospitable climate in Canada and the paucity of labor, given Canada's then small population.

Of course, tyranny might have taken many different forms so per capita income—one of the few indicators for which data are available going back that far—is certainly not the only way to assess the alleged oppression of the king. Still, we do well to remember that what we now think of as the early Canadian colonies were given the opportunity to be part of the United States by ratifying the Constitution—and they

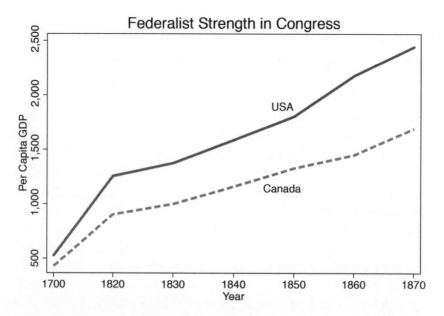

Figure 1.1. Per Capita Income, United States and Canada, 1700–1870

declined.[34] And equally we do well to remember that the revolutionaries were actively supported by about 40 percent of the population, while about 20 percent supported the British. The remainder tried mostly to stay under the radar, if you will forgive the anachronism. It does not seem that the vast majority of people shared the view of the very rich elite whose wealth was at risk from Britain. For most, it seems the king's rule was not tyranny.[35]

Chapter 2

Congress's War of 1812: Partisanship Starts at the Water's Edge

The truth is that all men having power ought to be mistrusted.
—James Madison

THE FIRST DECLARATION OF WAR BY THE UNITED STATES CAME ON JUNE 18, 1812. In keeping with the stipulations of the Constitution, it was Congress that declared this war against Britain. The decision was not an easy one. Both the House of Representatives and the Senate were deeply divided on the question, with the House voting 70 for and 49 against. The vote in the Senate was 19 yea and 13 nay. The division within each chamber of Congress followed along partisan lines, a fact crucial to understanding the causes and conduct of the war.

Especially by President James Madison's Federalist opponents, this war came to be referred to as "Mr. Madison's War." An equally strong case might be made for thinking of the War of 1812 as "Congress's War." Whatever the label and the implied responsibility behind it, we believe that the war had relatively little to do with its frequently attributed causes. It was, instead, largely about two matters. First was the quest for American territorial expansion, particularly, as others have also noted, expansion into what is today's Canada.[1] Second and too infrequently noted, it was about the partisan interest of a segment of the majority party in Congress—the War Hawks. The evidence will show that the War of 1812 was at least as much driven by Madison's desire to be nominated and reelected as it was by a desire to defend the United States against the threats of Great Britain and its allies.

Very much in keeping with the ambition addressed in the Declaration of Independence to rid "our frontiers" of the British and the Indians, at the outset, the president and the War Hawks created an intentionally inaccurate rendering of the war's true purpose in the hopes of creating bipartisan support. When that effort failed, then, like any group of self-interested politicians, they unabashedly followed policies designed both to satisfy their quest for territorial gains and to secure, through the war effort and war propaganda, electoral advantage at the expense of their Federalist opponents. The war failed in its expansionist purpose, but it was a great success for those whose partisan interests were tied to the War Hawk faction in Congress, including President Madison. The Federalists' opposition to the declaration of war proved a short-lived boon followed by the collapse of their party and a realignment of American political competition along lines favored by the War Hawks.

To begin, what was the War of 1812 ostensibly about? We say "ostensibly" because the causes of the war have been much debated and seem to us only partially related to the causes offered up by the president and Congress at the time. On June 1, 1812, President Madison wrote to Congress, outlining the disagreements between the United States and Britain. Although he did not explicitly call for a declaration of war, the purpose of the letter quite clearly could have been none other. But then, the pressure on him to declare war was well established and already long argued in Congress before he sent his list of grievances. Those advocating war were, in fact, a faction within Madison's own political party, sometimes known today as the Democrat-Republican Party but then known as Republican (albeit unrelated to the Republican Party of today that came into existence in 1854). This faction, called the War Hawks, was led by two freshman congressmen who would go on to remarkable careers: Henry Clay of Kentucky and John C. Calhoun of South Carolina.

The grievances Madison highlighted fell into four categories: that the British were violating the rights of American sailors; that the British were unlawfully, and solely for their own economic and political purposes, infringing the right to free trade; that the British, in a reprise of the Declaration of Independence's complaint, were working with the Indian tribes on the northwestern frontier of the new nation to foment war against American settlers to the benefit of Indian and British traders; and finally, that the British lacked seriousness and good faith in dealing with US proposals for a peaceful settlement of their differences, thereby precluding diplomacy as a solution to the problems. It is useful to quote the most critical portions of Madison's message to Congress, as we will draw a sharp distinction between the complaints he leveled as the ostensible cause of war and the reality behind the war and Congress's interest in it:

> British cruisers have been in the continued practice of violating the American flag on the great highway of nations, and of seizing and carrying off persons sailing under it, not in the exercise of a belligerent right founded on the law of nations against an enemy, but of a municipal prerogative over British subjects. . . .
>
> The practice, hence, is so far from affecting British subjects alone that, under the pretext of searching for these, thousands of American citizens, under the safeguard of public law and of their national flag, have been torn from their country and from everything dear to them. . . .
>
> British cruisers have been in the practice also of violating the rights and the peace of our coasts. They hover over and harass our entering and departing commerce.
>
> It has become, indeed, sufficiently certain that the commerce of the United States is to be sacrificed, not as interfering with the belligerent rights of Great Britain; not as supplying the wants of her enemies, which she herself supplies; but as interfering with the monopoly which she covets for her own commerce and navigation. . . .
>
> In reviewing the conduct of Great Britain toward the United States our attention is necessarily drawn to the warfare just renewed by the savages on one of our extensive frontiers, a warfare which is known to spare neither age nor sex and to be distinguished by features peculiarly shocking to humanity. It is difficult to account for the activity and combinations . . . among tribes in constant intercourse

with British traders and garrisons without connecting their hostility with that influence and without recollecting the authenticated examples of such interpositions heretofore furnished by the officers and agents of that government. . . .

Our moderation and conciliation have had no other effect than to encourage perseverance and to enlarge pretensions. . . .

We behold, in fine, on the side of Great Britain, a state of war against the United States, and on the side of the United States a state of peace toward Great Britain.

Whether the United States shall continue passive under these progressive usurpations and these accumulating wrongs, or, opposing force to force in defense of their national rights . . . is a solemn question which the Constitution wisely confides to the legislative department of the government. In recommending it to their early deliberations I am happy in the assurance that the decision will be worthy the enlightened and patriotic councils of a virtuous, a free, and a powerful nation. . . . [2]

Congress had been discussing the possibility of and justifications for war for many months before receiving the president's letter. It declared war less than three weeks later. As John C. Calhoun argued on the floor of Congress in response to the call to arms,

If a long forbearance under injuries ought ever to be considered a virtue in any Nation, it is one which peculiarly becomes the United States. . . . But the period has now arrived, when the United States must support their character and station among the Nations of the Earth, or submit to the most shameful degradation. Forbearance has ceased to be a virtue. War on the one side, and peace on the other, is a situation as ruinous as it is disgraceful. The mad ambition, the lust of power, and commercial avarice of Great Britain . . . have left to Neutral Nations—an alternative only, between the base surrender of their rights, and a manly vindication of them. Happily for the United States, their destiny, under the aid of Heaven, is in their own hands. . . . [3]

The "injuries" were clearly set forth both by the president and his party's leaders in Congress. Yet, before we can properly assess how these grievances fit into what the war really was about, we must first reflect on the way the dispute was framed in Madison's letter (and equally, in Calhoun's reinforcement of it) and how that framing sat against the established understanding of the purpose of a war declaration under the international law of the time. As we will see, while the true purpose of the war indeed did require a constitutional declaration, the ostensible purposes of the war, as set out by the president, did not; those reasons for war could easily have been addressed within the legitimate and exclusive powers of the president as commander in chief. Madison, however, having been reluctant to wage war and understanding what the true objectives of the War Hawks were and deferring to them, chose—in today's parlance—to kick the can down the road and let the congressional leadership take responsibility for their ambition. His decision to do so was, arguably, the great tragic decision of that period in US history.

When to Declare War

PRESIDENT MADISON STATED IN HIS LETTER TO CONGRESS THAT BRITAIN was acting aggressively in impressing American sailors into the British navy; blockading American ports and restricting American commerce; and fomenting Indian tribes to commit aggression against American settlers. He summarized all of this in the telling defensive phrase, "We behold, in fine, on the side of Great Britain, a state of war against the United States, and on the side of the United States a state of peace toward Great Britain." That is, he turned to Congress in the hope of eliciting a declaration of war because, in his opinion, Britain was already at war with the United States despite the state of peace that the United States was pursuing vis-à-vis Britain.

Madison was a lawyer thoroughly familiar with the international law of the time regarding questions of war and peace. Of course, he would also have been thoroughly familiar with George Washington's interpretation of the power to declare war that had been granted to Congress in the Constitution that Madison had helped craft. Recall that George Washington understood that war needed to be declared constitutionally not for self-defense, but when the government intended to pursue an offensive expedition of some importance. Washington had been echoing Hugo Grotius, whose teachings on international law were central to Madison's legal training.

Grotius, in his *The Law of War and Peace* (1625), noted that "In a case where either an attack is being warded off, or a penalty is demanded from the very person who has done wrong, no declaration is required by the law of nature."[4] Thus, contrary to Madison's letter but fully consistent with what we believe was the true foreign policy purpose of the War of 1812; that is, as an offensive expedition of some importance, there was no need to declare war to defend against British abuse. Defense falls within the purview of the commander in chief; defense does not require a declaration of war. Hence, the president, well informed in the law, provided what amounted to an appealing public relations justification for Congress to declare war, rhetoric seemingly designed to appeal to the pro-Federalist New England states that were exposed to Britain's naval interference—and to insulate him politically if the war went badly.

The Official Account

IN 1812 THE BRITISH WERE IN THE MIDST OF THE NAPOLEONIC WARS with France. Following the French Revolution (1789) and the beheading of King Louis XVI (1793), France had fought on and off with its European rivals. From 1803, under Napoleon's leadership, France had defeated in battle the major continental powers, including Austria, Prussia, Spain, and Russia. But Napoleon, while dominating continental Europe, could not defeat the British at sea. With the British unable to confront the French army directly on the Continent (although they introduced Wellington's army into Spain following an uprising in 1808) and with the French unable to invade Britain, given the latter's naval supremacy, economic warfare became a major component of the struggle between these two nineteenth-century superpowers. The United States' merchant shipping became a bit player in that struggle.

In the early 1800s the United States was an important supplier of raw materials and a market for manufactured goods, but it was far from a major economic, let alone military, power. Both Britain and France had far more important issues to worry about—especially each other—than US sensibilities to how it was treated by either. Indeed, American complaints to the British government largely fell on deaf ears, just as President Madison noted they did. Even when the situation deteriorated into a state of war, for the British the war with the United States was but a minor sideshow compared to its struggle with France. In fact, having grown up in Britain, one of us was completely unaware that there had been a British-American War of 1812 until after having lived in the United States for several years. To the average Brit, the year 1812 certainly conjures up images of war, but the war it conjures up is Napoleon's ultimately disastrous invasion of Russia. As William Kingsford writes in his *History of Canada*, "the events of the War of 1812 have not been forgotten in England for they have never been known there."[5]

To Americans at the time, in contrast, it was an event of some significance, although that significance has faded with the passage of time, the experience of bigger wars, and the close ties that have emerged between the United States and Britain. The War of 1812 cost the lives of about fifteen thousand Americans.[6] The British lost close to one third of that. The US national debt shot up from $45 million in 1812 to $127 million after the war, making the United States virtually bankrupt by the end of 1814. The nation's capital city, Washington, DC, including the White House, was torched by the British, with US officials having to flee for their lives. Thus, its effects were substantial at the time and important to understand if we are to avoid other crises that seem momentarily important in their own time and that then shortly after fade into oblivion.

The Impressment Grievance

BRITAIN'S OVERRIDING FOCUS ON DEFEATING FRANCE ACCOUNTS FOR most of Madison's complaints in his letter to Congress. Britain needed 140,000 sailors to man its vast navy. Conditions in the navy were appalling, casualty rates were enormous, and the pay was a pittance. Little wonder then, that many experienced sailors preferred service on American merchant vessels. However, the British did not recognize American naturalization and claimed the right to impress into service anyone they judged to be a British subject. To reclaim their sailors, the British navy boarded American ships to seize sailors they believed were British. The 1807 *Leopard* and *Chesapeake* incident is an often cited example of this kind of behavior. The HMS *Leopard* fired on the unprepared USS *Chesapeake* as it left Norfolk, Virginia. After the American ship's surrender, four sailors were taken as deserters and one was subsequently hanged. Estimates suggest that perhaps as many as ten thousand US sailors were victims of such impressment. Indeed, the standard American high school account of the War of 1812 is that it was a war to stop the British from impressing American sailors, which, as we have seen, is certainly a part of the story. Whether it is the main story, however, is a quite different matter.

Although the British did impress thousands of American sailors, the impressment policy was on the way out before war was declared. In the fall of 1811 the British returned the two surviving men who had been impressed from the *Chesapeake* (the third having died in hospital) and they paid reparations. Further, in 1812 the British admiralty ordered the British navy to take extra care not to antagonize American shipping and "to contribute . . . to that good understanding which it is his Royal Highness's most earnest wish to maintain."[7] Much of the fleet was ordered away from the US coast to prevent incidents. The impressment issue was therefore much diminished if not completely resolved before the war began.

The Free Trade Grievance

DURING THE NAPOLEONIC WARS, BRITAIN CERTAINLY WANTED TO STOP supplies from reaching France, which likewise wanted to cut off Britain's access to goods. Trade by neutral nations, such as the United States, stood in the way of each side's objectives, and so each did try to restrict and control American trade just as President Madison's letter to Congress indicated. As the superpowers of the day, neither Britain nor France had much need to accommodate demands for fairness from a backwater like the United States. They seemed to have thought that weak nations need to know their place, in much the same way that the United States shows scant regard for the wishes of small, weak nations today. As Daniel Sheffey, a Virginia Federalist, observed in a speech on the eve of war, "We have considered ourselves of too much importance in the scale of nations." Such a view, he went on to contend, "has led us into great errors. Instead of yielding to circumstances, which human power cannot control, we have imagined that our own destiny, and that of other nations, was in our hands, to be regulated as we thought proper."[8]

As reported on June 3, 1812, by the Congressional Committee on Foreign Relations (headed by Calhoun), Britain's Orders in Council were that "neutral powers are prohibited trading from one port to another of France, or her allies, or any other country with which G. Britain might not freely trade. . . . "[9] As commented on in the US House of Representatives, Congress inferred that "the British government evidently disclaimed all regard for neutral rights."[10]

The British government justified its restrictive trade policy based on the Rule of 1756, which indicated that neutrals should not engage in trade with the enemy if that trade did not exist before the war. Although such British restrictions were perceived as the primary problem, probably because the British had the naval power to enforce its policies, French policy was equally problematic and equally illegal. In his letter to Congress, Madison also complained about French conduct but left open the question of whether the United States should also do something about it. In his letter he noted, "It will have been seen also that no indemnity had been provided or satisfactorily pledged for the extensive spoliations committed under the violent and retrospective orders of the French Government against the property of our citizens seized within the jurisdiction of France. I abstain at this time from recommending to the consideration of Congress definitive measures with respect to that nation."[11]

That Britain's actions were perceived to be the greater burden should not come as a surprise. As Albert Gallatin, Madison's secretary of the treasury, reported, US trade with Britain and her allies was $38.5 million. Trade with France and her allies was only about $1.2 million.[12] Clearly, British trade policy was the more salient consideration, although both protagonists imposed restrictions that the United States deemed illegal. The free trade grievance certainly had a strong foundation that one could well imagine a nation dependent on such commerce would see as a casus belli. As it happens, however, the British repealed the Orders in Council on June 23.[13]

Given the slow speed of transatlantic communication at the time, the British were unaware of the American declaration of war and the US government did not know that Britain had relaxed the trade restrictions imposed on American exports. It took a little time for each side to learn of the other's actions. Yet, before a single shot was fired, by mid-1812 news reached America that the Orders in Council were repealed. With that knowledge in hand the second grievance was irrelevant. Hence, at least two of the three primary justifications for war identified by Madison had been largely resolved before fighting commenced.

The British Ignore America's Maritime Grievances

A S THE BRITISH WERE ACTIVELY RECTIFYING AMERICAN COMPLAINTS against them, Madison's concern that the British ignored American efforts to resolve their differences would also have diminished, if not evaporated altogether. To be sure, his June 1 complaint that the British government dealt with the US government in bad faith had good justification, relating to his own experience with the British as early as 1809: in April of that year, David Erskine, Britain's then ambassador to Washington, appeared to negotiate an agreement under which the British would remove the Orders in exchange for the US repeal of the Non-Importation Act—the trade embargo against British goods implemented by Madison's presidential predecessor, Thomas Jefferson, in the hope of forcing just such an agreement. Unfortunately, Erskine promised more than the British government had given him permission to do. The offer was withdrawn and Erskine eventually replaced. This, not surprisingly, left a legacy of mistrust. Once the Orders in Council were repealed, impressment was essentially over, and hence Madison's argument that the British ignored US complaints, especially regarding impressment and maritime trade, had become difficult to sustain.

The Second War of Independence: "Indian Savages" Reprised

J OHN C. CALHOUN PORTRAYED THE AS-YET UNDECLARED WAR OF 1812 as the second war of independence. Speaking in Congress on May 6, 1812, regarding the proposed repeal of the trade embargo with Britain, he stated, "I assert, and gentlemen know it, if we submit to the pretensions of England, now openly avowed, the independence of this nation is lost—we will be, as to our commerce, re-colonised. This is the second struggle for our liberty; and if we but do justice to ourselves, it will be no less glorious and successful than the first."[14] We believe this notion is what he wanted people to understand the war to be, but that it is also a piece of historical mythology far removed from the truth. Rather, we believe that Madison's third point—about the British conspiracy with the "savages"—was a rhetorical flourish intended to cover the true motivation behind the call for war: to take the frontier—"our frontier"—from the Indians and their British patrons and make it part of the United States, with credit going as much as possible to the president and the War Hawk faction in the Republican Party.

Madison's third grievance was a familiar one, both in its content and wording, almost perfectly echoing a similar one in the Declaration of Independence thirty-six years earlier. Once again, in 1812, the leadership of the now independent United States complained that, ostensibly with the support of the British, Indian "savages," specifically those in what is today's Midwest, were again—or still—waging "a warfare which is known to spare neither age nor sex and to be distinguished by features peculiarly shocking to humanity."[15] Just as the Virginia founding fathers needed to rid themselves of the British and the Indians in the American Revolution, so, too, did America's early nineteenth century leaders. They needed a "second war of independence" to advance their interests at the expense of the British and the Indians. This was especially true in such places as the Louisiana Territory, purchased from France by President Jefferson, and in such relatively new states as Kentucky and Tennessee. These were on the frontier, confronting the ongoing alleged threat from the English and the Indians.

Remember, the American Revolution had succeeded in driving the British from the original thirteen colonies, but not from the continent and not from their alignments with Indian tribes. The removal of the British was one of the most deeply held concerns in early American history. We forget today, but back then Evacuation Day—November 25—was celebrated, most especially in New York, as a holiday of as great importance as July 4. It commemorated the withdrawal of the last British troop from Manhattan on that day in 1783. Massachusetts and Illinois continue even now to observe variations of Evacuation Day. Back in 1812, as the threat of war was being stirred up in the United States, British colonial power persisted in Canada and in "our frontier" where the British and Indians worked hand in hand and often against the interests of expansionist Americans. The British were far from having evacuated North America!

British relations with Indian tribes were motivated both by economic opportunity and shared military interests. The latter resided in protecting the territory each held from the encroachments of American settlers. In fact, hoping that a strong confederacy of tribes would provide an effective buffer between the expanding United States and Britain's Canadian colonies, the British supported and traded with

Indian tribes, including those associated with Tecumseh and the confederation he formed. They also provided supplies to stop the Indians
from starving. But there were frequent assertions, usually without any
evidence produced, that the British were conspiring with the Indians
to threaten the security of American settlers.[16] Yet it was much more
clearly the goal of American settlers to expand their settlements and
colonize land held by sovereign Indian nations and the British than it
was of either of these groups to recolonize the lands that constituted
the United States of the time.

In reality the Indians had much more to fear from the Americans
than the American settlers did from them. As noted by Ellmore Barce,
an early twentieth-century historian whose approach was extremely
sympathetic to such American Indian fighters as William Henry Harrison, later ninth president of the United States:

> It is needless to say that no fine sense of right and justice existed
> either in the mind of the white land-grabber or in that of his red
> antagonist. Many unlawful invasions of the Indian lands were made.
> Moreover, many of the fur-traders along the Wabash were of the
> lowest type of humanity. They employed any and all means to
> cheat and defraud the Indians by the barter and sale of cheap trin-
> kets and bad whiskey and often violated every principle of honesty
> and fair-dealing. This kind of conduct on the part of the settlers and
> traders furnished ample justification in the mind of the ignorant sav-
> age for the making of reprisals. Many horses were stolen by them
> and often foul murders were committed by the more lawless element.
> This horse-stealing and assassination led in turn to counter-attacks
> on the part of the whites. In time, these acts of violence on the part
> of the vicious element in both races spread hate and enmity in every
> direction.[17]

William Henry Harrison, the son of Benjamin Harrison, signatory
to the Declaration of Independence, was the governor of the Indiana
Territories, appointed to this post originally by second president John
Adams and renewed in it by Presidents Jefferson and Madison. While
he also speculated in land himself, his job was to acquire rights to as
much Indian land as he could as an agent of the US government. He
proved a master at taking advantage of—or recognizing that—the Indians had scant notion of themselves as landowners. In 1805, for instance,

he secured control over an astounding 51 million acres, constituting a substantial portion of what are today Illinois, Missouri, and Wisconsin.

Harrison, a lifetime soldier, frequently went out of his way to stir up fear regarding the threat posed to prospective settlers by the combined interests of the Indians and the British. His role in acquiring land on behalf of the government played a central part in the instigation of President Madison's expressed concern about the Indian "savages" that was crucial to the US declaration of war in 1812.

To see the linkage between Harrison's land acquisition, western settler interests, and the War of 1812, it is useful to take a look at the Treaty of Fort Wayne concluded in 1809 between Harrison and the alleged chiefs of several Indian tribes. In exchange for the nearly 3 million acres of Indian land handed over in this treaty and in keeping with a policy first established by President Jefferson, "the said United States being desirous that the Indian tribes should participate in the benefits to be derived . . . hereby engage to deliver yearly and every year for the use of the said Indians, a quantity of salt not exceeding one hundred and fifty bushels, and which shall be divided among the several tribes in such manner as the general council of the chiefs may determine." This annuity, in the terms of the time, meant that the US government agreed to annual payments of $500 to the Delaware, Miami, and Potawatomie tribes as well as $250 to the Eel River tribe.[18]

Harrison apparently was unconcerned whether the chiefs who signed the treaty represented the Indians who actually lived on the land in question. This would not be the first or last time he exploited Indians, although he stated, "This is the first request that your new Father [Madison] has ever made of you and it will be the last, he wants no more of your land."[19] Tecumseh, a Shawnee leader, rejected Harrison's treaty on the grounds that those who signed it were not the chiefs of those whose land was covered by the treaty. He formed a confederation of tribes to resist the growing pressure of settlers. In response, Harrison took about a thousand troops to destroy the Indian's principal village, known variously as Prophetstown and Tippecanoe. Forewarned of Harrison's intention, Tecumseh attacked with his much smaller force of about five hundred warriors and succeeded in destroying about one fifth of Harrison's force. Still, Harrison succeeded in sacking the village. Later Tecumseh and his confederation fought alongside Britain in the War of 1812. He was killed in the Battle of the Thames in 1813. The shattering of his confederacy removed the last serious Indian impediment to US westward expansion and was, therefore, a critical contributor to the interest of the leaders of America's second war of independence in ridding themselves of the Indian "savages."

The 1812 Second War of American Expansion

ONCE CONGRESS HAD DECLARED WAR, BY ALL APPEARANCES PRESIDENT Madison did not actually want to fight the war he had asked for. No sooner had war been declared than he sent a delegation to negotiate peace. The British representative to the United States, Augustus Foster, reported, after visiting Madison following the declaration of war, that

> the President was white as a sheet and very naturally felt all the responsibility he would incur. He was, too, believed by many to have been much disappointed at the Senate's decision. A day or two afterwards, as I affected to know nothing of the Declaration, I received an invitation to call on Mr. Monroe [Madison's then secretary of state and later his secretary of war and the fifth president of the United States] when he put it into my hands with many expressions of regret and of hope that matters would soon be again arranged, which I believe for his part he very sincerely desired. He also intimated to me that Mr. Madison would be glad if I would call upon him which I immediately did; he assured me that he would use his best endeavours to prevent any serious collision and appeared to wish to impress me with an idea that the war would be but nominal.[20]

Naturally, given both Madison's reluctance and the reality that the United States possessed woefully inadequate military capabilities compared to those of the British navy and army, the British thought that actual hostilities were unlikely.[21] Nevertheless, fighting ensued and the war was on.

Given his reluctance, why did Madison support and why did Congress declare war on Britain? We begin our answer speculatively and then, in the remainder of this chapter, work our way through the evidence that seems fully consistent with our speculation. As we have seen, while the British may have thought the real issues were impressment and the Orders in Council, both of which were largely rectified before fighting began, the motivation for war among the congressional War Hawks was territorial expansion and removal of the Indians from the frontier, opening the land to exploitation by American settlers. Why, then, did Madison emphasize, at the outset, the maritime griev-ances regarding impressment and interference with trade, grievances that little affected the voters who backed the Republican majority in Congress or that had elected him in 1808?

Madison, as an architect of the Constitution, believed deeply in crafting a strong office of president. His ideas about the executive however were hemmed in by other elements that shaped his thinking, especially regarding questions of war. First, the motivation for struc-turing the Constitution was to escape what he understood to be the inability of the nation to make policy under the crippling Articles of Confederation, the precursor to the Constitution. The president of the first American government, the Continental Congress, was a mostly inconsequential figure with no executive authority. So, on the one hand, Madison sought to create a presidency with substantially more authority than existed under the Articles. On the other hand, he de-cidedly did not want a presidency with such power that the holder of that office would rival an "absolute" monarch in authority. Madison wanted a president who had real authority but was subject to checks and balances as created by the separation of powers. On no subject was this separation of powers of greater significance than in the authority to commit the nation to war. Here Madison insisted on congressional authority—not merely oversight, but genuine and exclusive authority to declare war.

In Madison's view, when it came to a question of war, the natural authority to turn to for guidance as to what policy should be executed was the constitutionally mandated leader of the House of Represen-tatives, the Speaker. When Madison submitted his letter to Congress, Henry Clay was the Speaker of the House—and leader of the War Hawk faction of Madison's own political party, the Republican Party. Clay was, of course, a strong advocate of war. It is reasonable to infer that Madison, himself reluctant to fight the war, deferred to Clay both in calling for a declaration of war and in framing it around the maritime grievances as well as the true concern—national territorial expansion. Why War Hawks like Clay would have wanted such a framing will become evident as we proceed.

Domestic Ambition, Expansionism, and War

THE MAIN POINT OF CONTENTION THAT PROVOKED WAR WAS BRITAIN'S remaining colonies in North America; that is, what is today Canada. In a speech in December 1811, John Randolph, an old-school anti–War Hawk Republican and staunch opponent of war, questioned the motives of those who sought war: "This war of conquest, a war for the acquisition of territory and subjects, is to be a new commentary on the doctrine that Republics are destitute of ambition—that they are addicted to peace, wedded to the happiness and safety of the people." He also questioned the willingness to finance the war: "But it seems this is to be a holiday campaign—there is to be no expense of blood, or treasure, on our part—Canada is to conquer herself—she is to be subdued by the principles of fraternity."[22]

Randolph's concerns were spot-on right on both counts: the war was about land acquisition and the government was utterly unprepared for war. This lack of preparation emanated largely from the president's own decisions, starting with his actions when he was Jefferson's secretary of state. Jefferson and Madison, working together, had reversed the Federalist policies of building up a professional military and a firm fiscal foundation. They had weakened the US's position, yet Madison urged Congress to go to war. As Henry Clay, leader of the War Hawk faction and fellow Republican, declared of his president:

> It is in vain to conceal the fact—at least I will not attempt to disguise with you—Mr. Madison is wholly unfit for the storms of War. Nature has cast him in too benevolent a mould. Admirably adapted to the tranquil scenes of peace blending all the mild & amiable virtues, he is not fit for the rough and rude blasts which the conflicts of Nations generate. Our hopes then for the future conduct of the War must be placed upon the vigor which he may bring into the administration by the organization of his new Cabinet. And here again he is so hesitating, so tardy, so far behind the National sentiment, in his proceedings towards his War Ministers, that he will lose whatever credit he might otherwise acquire by the introduction of suitable characters in their places. . . . On the part of the Legislature never was there a body assembled more disposed to adopt any and every measure calculated to give effect and vigor to the operations of the War than are the Members of the 12th Congress.[23]

And so it was that Clay and his War Hawk colleagues took the lead in planning the war, empowering themselves through Congress's authority to declare war and then using the power of the purse to serve their partisan interest at the expense of their Federalist rivals. Even in their partisan zeal, however, they used the power of the purse remarkably ineptly. Their fear of negative political fallout seems to have dominated good judgment about how a war alleged to be over maritime issues was to be fought! They were strong on rhetoric and ambition, and naive or, as Clay accused others, pusillanimous in their expectations of what was to come and what it was to cost. In fact, lacking a strong military with which to challenge Britain, Congress relied on amazingly wishful thinking: it presumed the nation would face no meaningful resistance. Clay led the charge in the contention that the United States was more than adequately prepared for war. He claimed,

> But it is said that we are not prepared for war, and ought therefore not to declare it. This is an idle objection, which can have weight with the timid and pusillanimous only. The fact is otherwise. Our preparations are adequate to every essential object. Do we apprehend danger to ourselves? From what quarter will it assail us? From England, and by invasion? The idea is too absurd to merit a moment's consideration. Where are her troops? . . . Can any one believe, that . . . the British government could be so infatuated, or rather mad, as to send troops here for the purpose of invasion? . . . Have we cause to dread an attack from her neighboring provinces? That apprehension is still more groundless. Seven or eight millions of people have nothing to dread from 300,000. . . . Nor is any serious danger to be apprehended from their savage allies. Our frontiers may be easily protected against them. . . . But our coast and seaport towns are exposed and may be annoyed. Even this danger, which exists in a certain degree, has been much exaggerated. No land force can be brought to bear against them, because Great Britain has none to spare for such a service; and without a land force, no great impression can be made. . . . [24]

The facts at the time should have led any thoughtful person to believe that Clay's argument was pure fancy. The United States certainly did not have a military establishment to put fear in the hearts of British leaders: The American military officers who were to lead the fight, for instance, were a mix of aged veterans of the Revolutionary

War or untrained greenhorns. Further, the United States relied heavily on state militias, which on occasion fought well but in general performed miserably and often refused to cross state borders (even the term "United States" was plural, not singular, back then). Plus, crucially, the new nation essentially had no navy with which to go head-to-head against the world's greatest naval power, Britain.

The Congress's Sectional Interests: O Canada . . . With glowing hearts we see thee rise

WITH THE PRESIDENT RELUCTANT AND THE COUNTRY ILL-PREPARED, how is it that Congress was gung-ho for war? The answer resides in the sectional differences across the country. Sectional considerations lay at the heart of the real aims of the congressional leadership that pushed to declare it, why the war was fought in the manner it was, and why the Jeffersonian Republicans ultimately could claim victory.[25]

Following the 1810 congressional elections, the House was dominated by the Republicans, who had won 107 seats, up 13 seats from 1808 when the unpopularity of the Non-Importation Act had harmed them. In comparison, the Federalist Party held only 36 seats in Congress. Its strength was somewhat greater than these numbers alone implied, however, because the Federalists consistently voted as a bloc against the administration. The Republicans, in contrast, were divided into factions, including Old Republicans, the Invisibles, the Clintonians, and the War Hawks, each holding quite different ideas about important policy matters, including relations with Britain. The Old Republicans, led by John Randolph, believed in traditional Jeffersonian policies of small government in support of citizen farmers. Their members came primarily from southern agricultural states. Invisibles and Clintonians fell politically between the main Republicans and the Federalists. The Invisibles favored greater war preparedness, while the Clintonians, who came predominantly from states with strong commercial interests, were against trade restrictions, such as Jefferson's Non-Importation Act. The most influential faction was the War Hawks, composed of about a dozen young representatives from southern and western states; that is, about one ninth of the Republican congressional delegation. For them, the most pertinent issues were the "savage" Indians on the frontier, territorial expansion, and increasing their future political influence.

Henry Clay, leader of the War Hawk faction, was a first-term congressman in 1811, but he was not an inexperienced legislator. He had previously served in the United States Senate, his first term having begun in 1806 when he was actually below the constitutionally stipulated age to serve in that body. After five years in the Senate, Clay entered the House, where he was elected as Speaker in his freshman year, a feat that has never been repeated. He used that position to great political advantage by packing congressional committees with fellow War Hawks, thus ensuring committee reports favorable to his prowar position and giving the War Hawks an influence over policy—and leverage with the president—well beyond what their small number in Congress suggested. In explaining his, and implicitly War Hawk, advocacy of war, Clay observed, "No man in the nation desires peace more than I. But I prefer the troubled ocean of war, demanded by the honor and independence of the country, with all its calamities, and desolations, to the tranquil, putrescent pool of ignominious peace."[26] Although Clay was extremely hawkish when it came to arguing for war, he turned out to be much less belligerent when it came to paying for the war.

Support for the war and for the various political factions that made up Congress differed enormously across regions. After John Adams's single term as president and the death of the Federalist Party's intellectual leader, Alexander Hamilton, following a duel with Vice President Aaron Burr, the Federalists remained strong only in New England. Hamilton's policies were for a strong central government with a strong fiscal capacity, internal taxes, a national bank, a strong navy, and a mercantile focus. When Jefferson's Republican Party came to power, it reversed many of these programs. Expenditures were cut, the army and navy were allowed to dwindle, internal taxes were abolished, the national debt was paid down, and the National Bank's charter was not renewed when it expired in 1811. The Jeffersonian agenda was popular in the South and in the western, more agrarian states. Indeed, the difference in the popularity of the Federalist and Republican agendas could not have been more starkly demonstrated than in the congressional election of 1812. War, you will recall, was declared in June. The November election five months later produced a surge in Federalist seats in the House of Representatives. The party won 68 seats in 1812, an increase of 32 over the 1810 election. The increase in representation, however, came almost entirely from the Northeast; the Federalists gained almost nothing in the South and exactly nothing in the West where they had zero congressional seats to begin with.

The New England states, Federalist all, were the states in which industry, commerce, fishing, and shipbuilding were especially important. Given these interests, one might expect New Englanders to have had much to gain from the protection of sailors' rights and from free trade; that is, Madison's first two grievances. It is likely that he (and Henry Clay), seeking bipartisan support for the war of expansion he contemplated, emphasized maritime grievances in the hope of eliciting Federalist backing. Yet, the New England states, like Federalists elsewhere, stubbornly refused to support the war. New England provided few soldiers or militia units and New England banks generally refused to purchase bonds to help finance the war. Indeed, when Treasury secretary Gallatin could sell only $6 million of an $11 million bond issue, with New Englanders taking very few of the bonds, France's representative in Washington, Serurier, wrote to the French foreign minister Maret on May 4, 1812, explaining that "they had counted on more national energy on the opening of a first loan for a war so just. This cooling of the national pulse, the resistance which the Northern States seem once more willing to offer the Administration, the defection it meets every day in Congress, all this, joined to its irritation at our measures which make its own system unpopular, adds to its embarrassment and hesitation."[27]

The absence of Federalist backing for the war agenda almost certainly resided in two realizations. First, the Federalists likely understood that the War Hawks had little interest in taking actions—such as strengthening the capability of the navy to defend the American coast—that would be beneficial to the Federalist states. Second, seeing how unprepared and unrealistic the War Hawks were with regard to the ease of achieving their territorial goals, the Federalists probably made the correct political assessment by opposing the war, improving their own electoral odds for the 1812 election.

It makes sense for a foreign policy, such as waging war, to garner bipartisan support when it is expected to succeed. Opposing a victorious war effort is unlikely to win many seats for the opposition, as all the kudos go to the party that backed victory. But if the war is expected to fail, then the opposition—the Federalist Party in this case—is more likely to enjoy electoral gains by opposing rather than supporting the war.[28] By the November 1812 election, New England voters exposed to the maritime aspects of the war would not have cared about territorial expansion nearly as much as voters in western states did. The upshot was that with the war going badly, as predicted by Federalists, those voters for whom the maritime issues were salient were likely to be anti-Madison, Federalist voters. Only several years later, when the fortunes of war turned, did the voters begin once again to abandon the Federalists. Figure 2.1 shows the rise and decline of Federalist support as a percentage of the Congress to illustrate the partisan swings. Just to the right of the dotted vertical line we see the substantial Federalist gains in the November 1812 election. In 1816, after everyone knows the outcome of the war, the Federalists—having ultimately backed the wrong position—go into a tailspin, ceasing to exist less than a decade later.

The Republican effort to achieve bipartisan support for the declaration of war was a failure. How, then, did the Republicans respond to the lack of Federalist support? They responded by accusing them of being unpatriotic and even of being traitors. In Baltimore such disagreements turned into riots. Federalist newspaper publishers and other prominent Federalists became the objects of mob violence. For their protection, authorities placed Federalists in jail, but the mob broke into the jail and beat, humiliated, and even killed some Federalists.

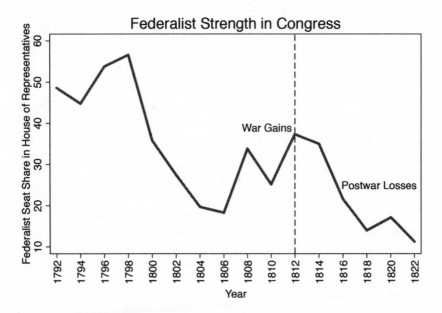

Figure 2.1. Partisan Swings in Federalist Support

Note: The dotted vertical line denotes the June 1812 declaration of war.

The War Hawks publicly pressed for war on the moral grounds of protecting sailors' rights and free trade, issues presumably designed to garner support among New Englanders. These issues were less relevant to the War Hawks' constituents; that is, the people living in the South or on the country's frontier in such states as Clay's Kentucky. Having failed to win bipartisan support, the War Hawks turned their emphasis to opportunities for their empowerment that was reminiscent of the motives of the Revolutionary War, namely to rid North America of the British and to remove "savage" Indians from "our frontiers." Additionally, the War Hawks now had little political incentive to worry about impressment and maritime trade arguments. Speaking in a debate following a Foreign Relations Committee Report on December 9, 1811, War Hawk congressman Felix Grundy of Tennessee set the tone of future argumentation: "This war, if carried successfully, will have its advantages. We shall drive the British from our Continent. . . . I therefore feel anxious not only to add the Floridas to the South, but the Canadas to the North of this empire."[29] Presaging Clay's arguments for the Missouri Compromise nine years later, Grundy also made an appeal to the need for a balance between North and South. He noted that with the South's enlargement by acquisition of Louisiana (and, he expected, Florida), the North would be disadvantaged. "I am willing to receive the Canadians as adopted brethren. It will have beneficial political effects; it will preserve the equilibrium of the government. When Louisiana shall be fully peopled, the Northern States will lose their power; they will be at the discretion of others; they can be depressed at pleasure, and then this Union might be endangered."[30] Indeed, he may well have hoped that the appeal to include Canada would be better received by the New England Federalists, who traded with Canada, than the general War Hawk call for war, but he did not emphasize how the war would protect Federalist New England's maritime concerns!

War Hawk Richard Johnson of Kentucky similarly presaged later Manifest Destiny arguments: "I shall never die contented until I see her [Britain's] expulsion from North America and her territories incorporated with the United States. . . . In point of territorial limit the map will prove [conquering Canada's] importance. The waters of the St. Lawrence and the Mississippi interlock in a number of places and the Great Disposer of Human Events intended those two rivers should belong to the same people."[31]

Clearly for some, the acquisition of Canada was an essential goal in itself. For many others, it was described as a bargaining chip to gain British concessions on trade. As Henry Clay put it, "Canada was not the end but the means, the object of the War being the redress of injuries, and Canada being the instrument by which that redress was to be obtained."[32] However, Clay goes on to say, "But it has ever been my opinion that if Canada is conquered it ought never to be surrendered if it can possibly be retained." Just before the declaration of war, John Randolph would declare, "Ever since the report of the Committee on Foreign Relations came into the House we have heard but one word,—like the whippoorwill, but one monotonous tone,—Canada, Canada, Canada!" Clay may have believed what he said when pointing to the war as the means to redress injuries, but his actions when it came to support for a stronger blue-water navy belied his claim. Of the leading War Hawks in Congress, only William Lowndes voted in favor of legislation to significantly expand the navy—Clay did not, Calhoun did not, Cheves, Williams, Grundy, Johnson, and Porter did not. Once they knew the Federalists were not with them on the declaration of war, they had no more reason to take actions that were designed to redress the issue felt most keenly by Federalists; that is, the maritime grievances.[33]

For the War Hawks, the idea of expanding the country by seizing Canada was seen to be an attractive possibility that could be easily fulfilled. Many in the United States assumed it would be a simple "matter of marching" to take Canada and that its citizens would gladly throw off the British yoke as the Americans had decades earlier. Clay stated, "I trust I shall not be deemed presumptuous when I state, what I verily believe, that the militia of Kentucky are alone competent to place Montreal and Upper Canada at your feet."[34] In response to claims that the United States was not ready to commence hostilities, Calhoun declared, "So far from being unprepared, sir, I believe that in four weeks from the time that a declaration of war is heard on our frontiers the whole of Upper and a part of Lower Canada will be in our possession."

Contrary to such expectations, the land war did not go well for the unprepared and unrealistic United States. The first engagement was testament to the fact that victory would not be just a walkover. Having advanced into Canada, US commander Hull fell back to Fort Detroit and after a brief siege surrendered to the numerically inferior forces

led by General Brock and Tecumseh. A big contributor to the difficulty
in achieving success against Canada lay at the feet of those who were
reluctant to recognize that war cannot be fought without cost. Indeed,
reluctance to learn this lesson is a crucial problem that must be reme-
died if we are to diminish presidential or congressional inclinations to
wage wars without regard to their expense. This theme, so prominent
in 1812, remains fundamental to understanding George W. Bush's Iraq
War nearly two hundred years later, as we show in Chapter 5.

Paying the Costs of the War

UNDER WAR HAWK LEADERSHIP, CONGRESS PROVED UNWILLING TO
adequately finance the war. Particularly reluctant to pay for the
army, although more willing to pay for naval expansion, and sensitive
to the sectional divide between their interests and those of the War
Hawks, the Federalists wanted to know how the war was to be paid
for. As Federalist New York congressman Harmanus Bleecker inquired,
"Where are your armies; your navy? Have you money? No, sir! Rely
upon it, there will be, there can be, no war."[35] John Randolph echoed
a similar sentiment: "Go to war without money, without men, without
a navy! Go to war when we have not the courage, while your lips utter
war, to lay war taxes! when your whole courage is exhibited in passing
Resolutions! The people will not believe it!"[36]

As it turns out, and as we might expect from self-interested politicians, the War Hawks ultimately were prepared to pay to increase
the army but not the navy. That is, they were willing to support the
costs—and even then to a limited degree—of Madison's third grievance, against the conspiracy of the British and the Indian "savages"
on "our frontiers," but not to fund the naval requirements of those
(Federalist) states with strong commercial interests and little desire for a
fight, especially over Canada or the frontier.

Of course, there were those on all sides of the issue who were
concerned about how the war would be paid for. It was one thing to
dream of territorial expansion and quite another to face the hard political reality of needing to raise taxes to pay for the effort required by
war. Federalist James Bayard hoped the difficulties of financing the war
would cool the War Hawks, as he stated in a letter on January 25, 1812:

Nothing has depressed the war spirit here more than the frightful exhibition made by Gallatin of War taxes. Many who voted for the army will not vote for the taxes and I much doubt whether any one proposed by the Secretary can be carried thro both Houses of Congress. They are not such fools at the same time as not to know that war cannot be carried on without money. And when they have arrived at the point—no money, no war—even they who are now panting after war if they cant have it without taxing the people and of course ruining their popularity will abandon the object.

I shall consider the taxes as the test, and when a majority agree to the proposed taxes, I shall believe them in earnest and determined upon war, but till then I shall consider the whole as a game of juggling in which the presidency and the loaves and fishes belonging to it are the objects they are contending for.[37]

Bayard rightly saw that the earnest desire for war depended strongly on not taking any actions that would affect the welfare of War Hawk politicians by "ruining their popularity." Perhaps to the surprise of men like Bayard, the War Hawks, under the guidance of Clay, in fact managed to pass a series of bills through Congress in preparation for war. For instance, the army was theoretically increased by twenty-five thousand men—although as John Randolph predicted, it was an "army on paper only"[38] as few of the men had actually been recruited. Congress was less adept at funding the rebuilding of the navy, which is difficult to reconcile from a "national interest" perspective if the real objectives of the war were primarily maritime, as stated in the president's letter of June 1, 1812. But if viewed, as Bayard did, in terms of what might ruin a politician's popularity, it should have been clear that for War Hawks a strong army with which to gain territory was of paramount interest, while the maritime issues were at very best secondary and, after all, more of concern to Federalist constituencies than Republican ones.

In December 1811, War Hawk Langdon Cheves proposed a bill to fund the building of ten additional naval ships and to repair others.[39] Fellow War Hawks, however, feared that naval expansion would divert funds from the army—which, after all, was the military arm most needed if Canada were to be added to the territory of the United States—and so they opposed the measure, asserting that the United

States should not have a permanent navy. Often their opposition to funding a blue-water navy is explained benignly as a realistic assessment that the nation could not build a navy of such a size as to compete with the thousands of ships in the British navy. We must realize there are two devastating objections to this argument. First, if the members of Congress and the president thought it was hopeless to compete against the British navy and they were sincere that a main purpose of the war was to alleviate trade restrictions, then they were on a fool's errand in going to war and they knew it. Second, the objection to ship building was almost exclusively limited to Republicans with expansionist interests; Federalists were all for building a larger navy to defend their vulnerable coastal towns and cities.

The naval bill was defeated 59–62. It is worth reiterating that few of the War Hawks' constituents would be harmed by British naval raids on the coast. The burden of such raids would fall overwhelmingly on the residents of northeastern coastal cities, bastions of Federalist, not Republican, support. The House debates in January 1812 were explicit in providing costs of equipping an adequate navy and argued that $80 million, vast amount though it was, would be a small price compared to the losses if the British raided coastal cities.[40] Yet the members of Congress were predictably unmoved by concerns over such raids.

We can compare actual congressional support for a strong navy with support for the war by examining how congressmen voted on the declaration of war and how they voted on an amendment to the navy bill for the completion of seventy-four gun frigates.[41] A vote for this amendment reflects support for the building of a blue-water navy. We use this amendment rather than the final naval bill because that bill was watered down and contained little support for a permanent navy.

The votes on these two bills highlight the differences between the support for the war and its stated goals. No Federalist voted in favor of declaring war; yet 25 of them voted for an improved navy. Although 15 Republicans opposed the war, 78 supported it.[42] Most interesting, only 5 of the 78 Republicans who voted for war also voted in favor of strengthening the navy. This evidence belies the contention that the war was about impressment or about the infringement of free trade on the high seas, both of which could only be defended against with a navy, not an army! Far from being what today we think of as a bipartisan foreign policy effort, the War of 1812 most clearly was about advancing Republican interests at the expense of Federalist ones—a partisan struggle between frontier territorial expansionists and representatives of the exposed seaports of America. It was a war in which the partisan divide started at the water's edge!

Congress did approve new loans to pay for armaments. However, to the chagrin of Treasury Secretary Albert Gallatin, but as predicted by James Bayard, Congress refused to vote for new taxes to pay for the war. Gallatin, acutely aware of how difficult financing the war would be, responded to an inquiry from the Committee of Ways and Means, by laying out the finances of the United States and the implication of incurring $50 million in debt to fight the war.[43] Gallatin believed his cost estimate was conservative. Rather than support the secretary's measures, the War Hawks turned on him. For instance the *Aurora Magazine* ran stories under the title "The Rat—In the Treasury."[44] Until late in the war, Congress resisted calls for direct taxation. As war expenses rose, the much maligned Gallatin proposed some creative means for generating revenue but the War Hawks struck down his proposals. War Hawk congressman Langdon Cheves, chairman of the Ways and Means Committee, stated, "I would rather see the objects of the war fail. I would rather see the seamen of the country impressed on the ocean and our commerce swept away from its bosom, than see the long arm of the Treasury indirectly thrust into the pocket of the citizen through the medium of a penal law."[45] Avoiding higher taxes apparently trumped paying for the war among electorally vulnerable politicians, again as Bayard had anticipated when he observed that "even they who are now panting after war if they cant have it without taxing the people and of course ruining their popularity will abandon the object."

We should be in awe of how politically adept the War Hawks were. By rejecting internal taxes and relying instead on revenue from tariffs, they ensured that the economic cost of the war fell on those states most engaged in foreign commerce; that is, the Federalist strongholds. As Congressman Bleecker asked in the debate over how to finance the war, "Is it just and fair to abandon the internal taxes and impose so much of the burden of the war upon the people of the Northern and Eastern States, the majority of whom are known to be opposed to it; whose hearts and souls are not in the business; who are driven, and dragged, and forced into a war, in which they will go with you no further, nor any longer, than a patriotic obedience to the Constitution and laws of the country requires; a war which they consider unwise, impolitic, inexpedient, and ruinous; a war which must annihilate their commerce . . . "[46]

The Republicans—the president's political allies—provided few assets to rectify the maritime issue upon which the war was nominally based. Federalist New England and seaboard states were most at risk from the British navy and chafed at paying for a war of expansion that they did not want. Meanwhile, Clay's Republican backers in Kentucky, who stood to gain from expansion on the frontiers, were geographically beyond the reaches of the British navy and engaged in little foreign commerce that could be disrupted by blue-water warfare. No wonder the partisan divides were so deep. By the fall of 1814, Federalist opposition to the war was so intense that representatives of numerous New England states met in Hartford to discuss secession from the Union.

Following the December 24 Treaty of Ghent, the Republicans at last could denounce the traitorous behavior of the Federalists.

Political Winners and Losers

THE PRESIDENTIAL ELECTION OF 1812, WHICH TOOK PLACE ABOUT FOUR months after the start of hostilities, reflected clearly who stood to benefit from the war and who bore its economic and financial costs. The Federalist candidate, De Witt Clinton, gained 89 Electoral College votes from seaboard states ranging from Delaware and Maryland up to New Hampshire. All other states returned electors for Madison (128 Electoral College votes), who had locked in the South and the West, the very places where the War Hawks were strongest. He had thrown his lot in with them and it had paid off even though his popular vote margin was less than 3 percent.

Historian Henry Adams summarized the war as "a conflict that had commenced without its participants having clear understanding of why it had done so while its conduct illustrated both an abundance of human folly and the unintended, and often irrelevant, consequences of such folly."[47] What eventually saved the United States was that the British simply did not care that much. Following the defeat of Napoleon, the British increased their presence in America, a consequence contrary to Henry Clay's expectations. However, they utilized only a fraction of the resources freed up by their victory in Europe. At the end of the day, the British were happy just to secure their Canadian colonies, as they were far more concerned with negotiating the Treaty of Vienna and constraining future French ambition. North America had been a sideshow during the Napoleonic Wars, and even after Napoleon's defeat it remained a sideshow.

The course of the war was almost farcical. Britain was mistress of the ocean and yet the United States did surprisingly well in its maritime engagements despite the failure of Congress to pay for a naval buildup. Privateers—this being the last war in which they were regularly used—proved particularly successful against British merchantmen. Of course, how much more could have been achieved with a real navy will never be known. In contrast, the war on land—for which the Republicans were less reluctant to pay—went very poorly. Canada remained British, although the Indian threat to western expansion was severely curtailed.

The United States had gifted political leaders, some of whom were sent to negotiate with the British. The British also had gifted men, but they were not sent to negotiate an end to the hostilities with the former colonies. The most able British diplomats were more interested in the Congress of Vienna, which negotiated treaties dealing with continental Europe after Napoleon's defeat, and so Britain sent its diplomatic B-team to Ghent. The United States gained on virtually every issue being negotiated. The division of territory was largely a return to prewar boundaries, despite Britain's acquisition of eastern Maine during the fighting. The issues of impressment and trade, although stated as the major causes of the war, were by this time moot points. Britain had already conceded the Orders in Council before hostilities started; and with Napoleon's defeat, the demand for sailors had dropped so much that impressment was practically irrelevant. Tecumseh's confederation had been smashed and the British soon neglected their commitments to their Indian allies. America had achieved little if anything on the battlefield, but made up somewhat for its losses at the negotiating table. The territorial settlement restored the status quo antebellum. All that remained was for Madison to declare victory.

Certainly in a partisan sense, Madison could in fact declare victory. Military success enhances political careers, especially among those affiliated with the winning political party. That was certainly true for the War of 1812. Donald Hickey described the legacy of the War of 1812: "Four statesmen—James Monroe, John Quincy Adams, Andrew Jackson, and William Henry Harrison—were able to parlay their public service during the war into the presidency, and three others—Daniel D.

Tompkins, John C. Calhoun, and Richard M. Johnson—were elevated to the vice-presidency."[48] Of these seven men, all but John Quincy Adams were Republicans during the war and Adams did not have strong party ties. In fact, Republican Henry Clay, upon failing in his own bid for the presidency, was instrumental in Adams's selection as president in the House of Representatives. Adams, son of founding father John Adams, would become the sixth US president, in 1825.

Federalists might have expected to have done well electorally, given so few gains for so much treasure and lives expended. Yet, writes Madison biographer Richard Brookhiser, by "not losing, America had won. . . . Madison made a peace and called it victory, and the nation was so giddy from a combination of relief and pride that no one disputed him."[49] Federalists had borne the brunt of the war's economic costs, but for their opposition to the war, they were labeled traitors.

What If?

J AMES MADISON, BY ALL APPEARANCES, ALLOWED THE YOUNG, RISING party leaders, men like Clay and Calhoun, to lead him by the nose rather than take responsibility for the war. We must ask: why? The answer is not hard to find. Rather than veto the war bill, Madison signed it, recognizing that it came amid discussion over who would be the Republican nominee for president in the 1812 election. As British representative Foster wrote to London, "The reason why there has been no nomination made in caucus yet, by the Democratic [that is, Republican, sometimes then referred to as Democrat and later as Democrat-Republican] members, of Mr. Madison as candidate for the Presidency is, as I am assured in confidence, because the war party have suspected him not to have been serious in his late hostile measures, and wish previously to ascertain his real sentiments. I have been endeavoring to put the Federalists upon insinuating that they will support him, if he will agree to give up the advocates for war."[50] Madison, of course, did not "give up the advocates for war" and he did receive his party's nomination. As noted by Sidney Gray in his history of Madison: "Mr. Madison for years had opposed a war with England as unwise and useless,— unwise, because the United States was not in a condition to go to war with the greatest naval power in the world; and useless, because the end to be reached by war could be gained more certainly, and at infinitely less cost, by peaceful measures. The situation had not changed. . . . But the faction determined upon war must have at their command an administration to carry out that policy. Their choice was not limited to Madison for an available candidate. Whoever was nominated by the [Republicans for the 1812 presidential election] was sure to be chosen, and Madison had two formidable rivals . . . eager for war."[51]

The Federalists recognized that the War Hawks had maneuvered Madison into supporting the war. Speaking in the debate over a bill to provide more resources for the invasion of Canada, introduced in December 1812, Federalist Josiah Quincy III of Massachusetts explicitly pointed to Madison's motives:

> The war was declared. Canada was invaded. We were in haste to plunge into these great difficulties, and we have now reason, as well as leisure enough, for regret and repentance. The great mistake of all those who reasoned concerning the war and the invasion of Canada, and concluded that it was impossible that either should be seriously intended, resulted from this, that they never took into consideration the connection of both those events with the great election for the chief magistracy which was then pending. It never was sufficiently considered by them that plunging into war with Great Britain was among the conditions on which the support for the Presidency was made dependent. They did not understand that an invasion of Canada was to be in truth only a mode of carrying on an electioneering campaign. But since events have explained political purposes there is no difficulty in seeing the connections between projects and interests. It is now apparent to the most mole-sighted how a nation may be disgraced, and yet a cabinet attain its desired honors. All is clear. A country may be ruined in making an Administration happy.[52]

Our line of reasoning follows Quincy's conclusions, that the motivations for war too often are personal and not undertaken for the national good: "Let the American people receive this as an undoubted truth, which experience will verify. Whoever plants the American standard on the walls of Quebec conquers it for himself, and not for the people of the United States."[53]

Madison had correctly diagnosed the pathology of leaders and the ease with which they place personal aggrandizement over the national good. As he had foreseen, he chose retention of the presidency as more important than preventing an unproductive war. Here we can ask what if this brilliant man had acted more courageously—as he had done through most of his career—by standing up to the War Hawks faction. We may well ask what might have happened had he followed his own advice when he noted, "The truth is that all men having power ought to be mistrusted."[54]

The War Hawk faction was but a small portion of the membership in the House of Representatives. The faction's leaders, Clay and Calhoun, were new to the House and keen to build their reputations and power base. In fact, Henry Clay, to whom Madison deferred on the war issue, turned the position of speaker of the house into the powerful position it is today. Still, Madison, not Clay, was president. He could have thrown his backing somewhere between the Invisibles and the Clintonians. That would almost certainly have bolstered their political weight in the House and the Senate and diminished the War Hawks' ability to muster sufficient support to declare war.

Had Madison acted on his instincts to avoid war, what might then have been the consequences? First, however unpleasantly the Indians were being treated, the territorial gains sought at their expense would surely have continued to go forward unfettered by concern for their welfare or for just treatment. Enough Indian leaders were willing to surrender large tracts of their lands at an easily met economic price offered by the US government, that the urge for war against them would have been diminished. With a more generous provision of funds and greater efforts to align with the Indians, it is certainly imaginable that the professional, friendly relations that George Washington experienced early in his career with Half-King might have been achieved much more widely and to everyone's benefit, Indian and settler alike. With regard to Canada, Madison might have turned to Congress to allocate funds equal to a fraction of the eventual cost of the war with the purpose of making defection from Britain and alignment—even incorporation—with the United States more attractive. There were, after all, at the time only about 300,000 Europeans in Canada. The vinegar of war seems a much less productive way to gain their support than the sugar of enrichment. Special privileges and other private benefits are effective means of "buying" support when the number of people whose support is sought is rather small, as was the case in Canada.

The British, to be sure, were keen to retain control over Canada. Their interest, however, was primarily economic and not political.

Chapter 3

Abraham Lincoln and the Pursuit of Ambition

Bring on a war . . . and . . . escape scrutiny by fixing the public gaze upon the exceeding brightness of military glory.

—Abraham Lincoln

ABRAHAM LINCOLN WAS A BRILLIANT POLITICIAN, A FAILED politician, an extremist, a pragmatist; honest as the day is long—and a smoke-filled-room, dirty-tricks operator. The same Abraham Lincoln who wanted nothing more than to preserve the Union also seems to have wanted to be president of the United States at any cost. Each of these descriptions identifies a central feature of Lincoln's character that, contradictory as they may be, taken together made him into such a remarkable figure. Today he is remembered and revered because of what was accomplished in the Civil War. We will see, however, that all of it could have, and in all likelihood would have, been done without war. But had he not exacerbated the risk of war as the price for winning the presidency, his place in history might be minor, and his ambition to matter greatly would have been unfulfilled.

With any figure of Lincoln's stature and nobility, it is tempting to gloss over unpleasant, or at least dissonant, truths about who he was. Yet we argue that those very truths were central—not incidental—to what he achieved. Our interest is in how the Civil War might have been avoided but for Lincoln's personal ambition and the southern leadership's poor decision making. We do so as a further cautionary tale that we hope will help us find future leaders whose path to greatness need not be strewn with blood and gore, but with the promotion of peace and prosperity for all. Once again it will be evident how profoundly right James Madison was in worrying that unfettered presidents would wage war for their own benefit and all-too-often at the expense of "the desire and duty of peace."

We admire Abraham Lincoln today, as well we should, because we know, in ways his contemporaries did not, that he set into motion the transformation of America's moral standing before the world. Most of us believe, and we are almost certainly right in that belief, that but for the assassin's bullet, Lincoln would have proven a great fabricator of peace and reunion. Had he lived to serve out his second term, it seems likely that the century long foray into the "separate but equal" doctrine of segregation and repression might have never occurred. Of course, we cannot know because the assassin's bullet did happen. But what can be known—and shown—is that to fulfill his personal ambition and, incidentally, to fabricate a better America, he needed to raise the risk of a civil war and all the dangers that implied, and therefore he maneuvered to gamble on the dissolution of the Union whose salvation he professed was his foremost ambition. And if we think fairly about him and his times we will see that without the bloodiest war in American history, we would almost certainly barely know his name today.

With or without Lincoln, slavery would have been extinguished long ago. How long it would have taken is a question intensely debated among historians. Whether postponing the moment of liberation for nearly 4 million slaves would have been a better or worse outcome depends on who is answering; it is a question that cannot have a definitive answer. We will return to that issue. For now, we know that Lincoln's presidency cut short the productive lives of more than 700,000 Americans (northern and southern combined); that is, about 2.4 percent of the population of the United States and a vastly higher proportion of the working-age population. However justified in hindsight the cost of the Civil War was, we also need to remember that Lincoln did not contend that ending slavery was his goal.

We will argue that war most assuredly was Lincoln's expedient to defeat the political vision that had come to be the law of the land, replacing it with a national future closer to his own moral standard. The great results he attained, like those of other political leaders, did not and do not require high-mindedness or altruism. Indeed, such achievements may often be precluded by a politician who sets out intent on making selfless sacrifices on behalf of others. Such men or women are unlikely to come to power and if they do they are even less likely to survive in office for long.[1] Lincoln can hardly be said to have been a selfless altruist. He came to power by sowing division and discord. He was an ambitious, calculating man who saw opportunity and seized it when he could. That is certainly not a fault; it is simply a fact!

Great results in politics require leaders with ambition, vision, and a willingness to pay the price in hard work and political maneuvering to fulfill a dream. Lyndon Johnson, for instance, understood that in promoting and signing the Voting Rights Act of 1965 he was turning the southern electorate over to the Republican Party. This was a great political price that had to be paid by future generations of Democrats (and less so, perhaps, by himself) to enable Johnson to fulfill his personal (and laudatory) vision for civil rights in America. The irony must not have been lost on Johnson that the Republican Party was to be the beneficiary of his choice to follow where Republican president Abraham Lincoln had earlier dared to tread. The southern states, after all, had voted against the Republicans (then the more progressive party) for more than one hundred years, starting in 1856. Then they anticipated that the Republican Party (under John Frémont) was committed to undoing the federal deal that, in their interpretation, created a nation that tolerated slavery. With Lincoln's campaign in 1860, and then for a hundred more years, the South continued to vote against the Republican Party out of the realization that its fears had been justified. As Johnson feared, the Republican Party today and for a half century has dominated southern elections probably because of the Voting Rights Act, which expanded the enfranchisement of African American voters but stimulated higher turnout in the South by those opposed to the act, turning the Democrats' former Dixiecrat southern stronghold into Republican territory, as we will explore in Chapter 5.

Lincoln must have asked himself from time to time whether the fulfillment of his political ambition and his vision for America was worth the price to be paid. But did he also ask, as we have suggested all presidents must, whether the price was worth it to "We, the people"? Were candidate Abraham Lincoln here to defend himself, he might well argue, as he did in 1861, that he indeed did ask himself this question and that his answer was yes. He addressed this issue in a letter to Senator John Hale from New Hampshire: "We have just carried an election on principles fairly stated to the people. . . . Now we are told in advance, the government shall be broken up, unless we surrender to those we have beaten, before we take the offices. In this they are either attempting to play upon us, or they are in dead earnest. Either way, if we surrender, it is the end of us, and of the government."[2] Thus, president-elect Lincoln maintained, seemingly quite sensibly, that he was setting the nation on the path desired by "We, the people" as expressed through the ballot box. In his judgment it was others who promoted the idea of national dissolution and the grave danger of war.

Lincoln's electoral defense was a good defense but a tad disingenuous. True, he won the presidential election, but then he did so with the smallest popular vote percentage of any American president except John Quincy Adams. And he won in an election in which the opposition—the Democratic Party—was divided, putting forth three candidates whose very division was fostered, nay instigated, by Lincoln's own political maneuvers in 1858. Hence, the outcome of the 1860 election could readily be said to have masked the true will of the voting electorate, more than 60 percent of whom voted against Lincoln. The remainder of this chapter can be seen as an exploration of that hypothetical debate between Mr. Lincoln and ourselves regarding his extremism or moderation; his political talents and honesty; and the role of his ambition when confronted with his desire to save the Union. To conduct this debate properly, we must understand how slavery was handled by the country's founders, how the Dred Scott decision of 1857 altered that understanding, and how Lincoln built his ultimate political success around the changes wrought in 1857.

Slavery and America's Founding

SLAVERY DEFINED THE GREATEST PHILOSOPHICAL AND POLICY QUESTION that confronted the founders of the United States. To preserve this "peculiar institution," the Constitution was filled with oddities designed to ensure the ability of the slave states, predominantly in the

South, to protect their political power. Even as slaves were deprived of their freedom and despite the Declaration's proclamation that "all men are created equal," slaves—the word is never used in the Constitution—were counted by the Constitution as three fifths of a free person or, for that matter, as three fifths of a person bound to service for a fixed number of years.[3] This created, among many peculiarities, the notion that congressional representation was dictated not by the number of eligible voters in a state or even by the number of citizens, but by a mix of citizens, indentured people (often immigrants), and a vast number of noncitizens who were enslaved. This meant that slave states received greater congressional representation than their free citizen population warranted. So, those interested in preserving slavery were, by virtue of their holding slaves, given increased representation, and therefore increased policy control in the very federal government that was founded allegedly on the basis that all men are created equal. Furthermore, each unfortunate slave's very existence counted toward and contributed to the reinforcement of a regime in which he or she was to be oppressed as a matter of law and without hope of betterment.

The three-fifths rule, of course, also biased the Electoral College and, therefore, the selection of the president in favor of proslavery interests. After all, the number of state electors in the Electoral College was (and still is) determined by the size of the state's congressional delegation, which prior to emancipation was a function of its population, including the disenfranchised slave population.[4] The peculiarity of how political power was distorted in favor of slave states was all the more emphatic as it was increasingly out of touch with how the founding fathers—and the rest of the world—professed to look upon slavery.

Despite having been enshrined in the constitutional processes of election and political representation, slavery was politically contested from the outset. Many of the most prominent founding fathers, even among those who were slave holders, were embarrassed by slavery, or at least professed to be. Thomas Jefferson and George Washington both declared the injustice of slavery even as they persisted in owning and exploiting slaves for their personal gain. In his will, Washington left a modest annuity of $30 to his faithful slave William Lee, who accompanied him throughout the revolution.[5] Further, in that document Washington set out the terms of the liberation of most of his human property.[6] He was the only southern founding father to manumit most of his slaves or to give them the option of choosing to be free. And, we should also note, he was sensitive in his lifetime, as in his will, to prevent the division of slave families in his possession. Since many of his slaves were married to his wife's dower slaves, he kept them on even when it would have been profitable to sell them. Indeed, he acknowledged that he held approximately twice as many slaves at Mount Vernon as would have been profitable, retaining them out of concern to maintain the integrity of their families.[7]

Still, the same George Washington also signed the Fugitive Slave Act in 1793, making it lawful for slave owners to recover their "property" even if the slave had escaped to an area where slavery was banned. Indeed, he pursued one of his own runaway slaves during his presidency. Another escapee apparently found enforced service in the Washington household sufficiently objectionable that he fought against Washington and on behalf of the British during the revolution, while still others of Washington's slaves sought their liberty by supporting the British against the rebels.[8] So, clearly, Washington's relationship to slavery was complex even as he professed his dislike of the institution.

Thomas Jefferson, commenting on slavery and the objectives of the American Revolution, wrote in June 1786, "What a stupendous, what an incomprehensible machine is man! who can endure toil, famine, stripes, imprisonment or death itself in vindication of his own liberty, and the next moment be deaf to all those motives whose power supported him thro' his trial, and inflict on his fellow men a bondage, one hour of which is fraught with more misery than ages of that which he rose in rebellion to oppose."[9] And while he manumitted hardly any slaves of his own, he did propose for the state of Virginia in 1783 that the "General assembly shall not have power . . . to permit the introduction of any more slaves to reside in this state, or the continuance of slavery beyond the generation which shall be living on the 31st. day of December 1800; all persons born after that day being hereby declared free."[10] Unlike the statement in 1786 that we might cynically interpret as no more than rhetoric, the proposal in 1783 was politically bold and likely to cost him support in Virginia and elsewhere in the South. In that sense, it is harder to dismiss the proposal of 1783 as a statement without substance. Although to be sure Washington's and Jefferson's own conduct did not coincide with their rhetoric, still we cannot avoid the sentiment that, however insufficiently the view was expressed, these two powerful Virginia slaveholding founding fathers were apparently embarrassed by the institution even as they profited from it.

Such northern founding fathers as John Adams and Alexander Hamilton were unquestionably more vehement in their opposition to the continuation of slavery. Yet, forging a successful union against Britain meant that they had to live with compromise, and so they compromised by accepting a federal government structure that protected the power and authority of state governments to preserve their own institutions, including slavery. Without the constitutional guarantees given to the South, it is unlikely that the United States could have been formed. Against this backdrop, the nation, from its birth, felt the political pain associated with deep divisions over what came to be called states' rights, not to mention what today we call human rights.

We should not forget that while slavery persisted as an alleged economic necessity in the South and in the Caribbean, it was an institution in its political, if not economic, death throes throughout much of the world.[11] Indeed, slavery in the American colonies was banned by Spain as early as 1542. As early as 1569, the English courts are thought to have judged in the Cartwright case "that England was too pure an air for a slave to breathe in."[12] With the original documentation of that quotation lost in the mists of time, we might equally consider that an English court ruled in 1763 that as "soon as a man sets foot on English ground he is free."[13] The antislavery movement continued its spread across Europe throughout the eighteenth and nineteenth centuries, leaving few governments that tolerated human bondage well before US states fought the bloodiest American war, the Civil War, to resolve the issue.

No one can reasonably dispute that the founding fathers constructed a Constitution and specific rules of representation that favored slaveholders. Yet the slavery question came to a head not during the writing of the Constitution, but later, during the landmark Supreme Court decision made in 1857. That decision had a profound impact on the country, and also on a little-known politician, who before 1857 had bounced from electoral defeat to electoral defeat: Abraham Lincoln.

The Great Divide: Dred Scott

EVERY NATION'S HISTORY IS PUNCTUATED BY EVENTS SO MEMORABLE that the mention of a date is sufficient to invoke the facts of the time. The United States has its share of such dates—July 4, 1776; April 14, 1865; December 7, 1941; November 22, 1963; September 11, 2001.[14]

Unlike other nations, however, the history of the United States also
turns on those few placid days when nine justices of the Supreme Court
hand down technical and yet momentous opinions. May 17, 1954, was
such a day. On that day the court ruled on *Brown v. Board of Education of Topeka*, marking the beginning of the end of segregation, the
undoing of the "separate but equal" doctrine supported in *Plessy v.
Ferguson* (1896). *Brown* tore apart the era of racial oppression that had
been enshrined in the Constitution and then had been expanded upon
in *Dred Scott v. Sandford* (March 6, 1857). The Dred Scott decision is
widely regarded as the worst ruling the Supreme Court ever made. Of
that there seems little doubt. The awful clarity of the court's opinion in
the Dred Scott case, however, was also the making of Abraham Lincoln.
Without that horrendous ruling, would we have had—could we have
had—Abraham Lincoln as president of the United States? We think the
answer is no and we believe Mr. Lincoln would have agreed.

To understand the significance of the Dred Scott ruling, it is useful
to summarize the issues before the court. Dred Scott, a slave, was taken
by his owner, John Emerson, an army surgeon, into the Wisconsin
territory (in a portion later to be part of the state of Minnesota) when
Emerson was assigned to an army fort there. Under the terms both of
the Northwest Ordinance of 1787 and the Missouri Compromise, passed
in Congress in 1820, Scott had been transported into free territory several times in the 1840s. Arguably, once transported to free territory, an
enslaved person was no longer a slave. Nevertheless, Emerson leased
Scott out as a worker. This was arguably a violation of the free-state
designation of the Wisconsin territory. Scott and his wife were moved
again, eventually to the state of Missouri where he, with the help of abolitionist advisers and with financial backing from his original owner,
Peter Blow, sued for his freedom after repeated efforts to purchase his
freedom (and after Emerson had died and Scott's ownership had been
passed on). The basis of his case was that because he had resided in a
free territory, Scott had been emancipated. Missouri seemed like a good
venue for the suit as there were numerous precedents in which state
courts had ruled in favor of slaves who were in fact judged to have
been emancipated by dint of their having been taken to a free territory.
As expected, the Missouri lower court found in Scott's favor but the
Missouri Supreme Court did not. Eventually the case made its way to
the Supreme Court of the United States, where Scott's future—and we
believe, Lincoln's—was determined.

In the Dred Scott decision, the court, in a 7–2 vote, concluded that no black person, whether slave or free, could be a citizen of the United States. And since no black person, whether slave or free, could be a citizen of the United States, then it followed that no such person could have standing to sue in an American court or to enjoy any of the other rights and privileges of a citizen of the United States, and that this was true even if a state or territorial government conferred citizenship on such a person. The chief justice of the Supreme Court, Roger Taney, in expressing the court's majority opinion, observed that all of Europe, and England in particular (the court cases we referred to earlier notwithstanding), considered the people of Africa and their descendants to be "beings of an inferior order, and altogether unfit to associate with the white race, either in social or political relations; and so far inferior, that they had no rights which the white man was bound to respect; and that the negro might justly and lawfully be reduced to slavery for his benefit . . . "

Hence, while slavery was sliding into oblivion in "the civilized portion of the white race," the court ruled to the contrary. Having denied the possibility that Dred Scott could be a citizen and therefore have the right to bring suit, the court nevertheless went on to rule on the rest of the case. While finding against all of Scott's claims, the court then proceeded—only for the second time in US history—to overturn a law passed by Congress on the grounds that it was unconstitutional. Specifically, the Supreme Court overturned the Missouri Compromise of 1820. As Justice Taney opined,

an act of Congress which deprives a citizen of the United States of his liberty or property, merely because he came himself or brought his property into a particular Territory of the United States, and who had committed no offence against the laws, could hardly be dignified with the name of due process of law. . . . [I]t is the opinion of the court that the act of Congress which prohibited a citizen from holding and owning property of this kind in the territory of the United States north of the line therein mentioned, is not warranted by the Constitution, and is therefore void; and that neither Dred Scott himself, nor any of his family, were made free by being carried into this territory; even if they had been carried there by the owner, with the intention of becoming a permanent resident.

And so, voilà, in this one major decision the Supreme Court destroyed the nation's delicate compromise between the divisions of opinion over the multitude of questions related to slavery. It did so by the simple mechanism of concluding that those of African descent were not people, but purely property. The logic was simple. Suppose someone decided to move to a territory of the United States. He would pack his few sticks of furniture, perhaps a bag or two of flour, maybe a horse and some oxen, and perhaps a few slaves and move them all to the territory in which he was going to settle. Now obviously, the sticks of furniture remained the property of the person who packed them and moved them. No one could lawfully take that furniture from its rightful owner. And likewise with the bag or two of flour, the horse and oxen, and, of course, because they were nothing more than property, the slaves! Poof, the Missouri Compromise was gone and so too was the idea that Congress could regulate the spread of slavery.

The Missouri Compromise had been intended to maintain balance between slave states and free states by establishing the principle that for every new slave state to enter the Union there would also be a new free state. In overturning this law, the Supreme Court held that Congress did not have a constitutional right to dictate whether a territory had to be slave or free as a condition of its becoming a state. The decision went still further. The Kansas-Nebraska Act of 1854, promoted by Senator Stephen Douglas of Illinois, advanced the idea of popular sovereignty in the territories as an alternative to the by-then foundering Missouri Compromise. The act granted to the people in each territory the authority to determine for themselves whether their territory was to be free or slave. That is, Douglas advanced the idea that policy decisions, including decisions regarding slavery, should be made through democratic practices—through popular sovereignty—and not by fiat by some remote body of legislators. However, the Dred Scott ruling dictated that the territories did not have the constitutional right to ban slavery, thereby undoing the idea of popular sovereignty. Again, the logic was straightforward. Popular sovereignty violated the property rights and entitlement to due process of American citizens who might move to a free territory with their property, including their slaves, whose ownership remained sacrosanct. Thus, according to the Supreme Court, there was no constitutional restriction on the spread of slavery in the territories of the United States. This opened the floodgates to the spread of that "peculiar institution" throughout the territories, each expecting eventually to become a state.

By striking down the Missouri Compromise, forbidding territories from deciding whether they were slave or free, and expanding slaveholder rights to pursue their slaves or willingly transport them into free areas, the Dred Scott decision seemed to resolve the furious debate over slavery that was central to US politics from the founding of the nation. It opened the door to the possibility that slavery could and would spread across the land and that Congress could do nothing to prohibit it, short of a constitutional amendment. Vilified as an abomination by all who held slavery to be a repugnant institution while seemingly resolving the slavery issue in the South's favor, the Dred Scott decision also proved critical to Lincoln's eventual election as president.

Without the Dred Scott decision, Abraham Lincoln would almost certainly be forgotten by history. Hence, to form a proper sense of Lincoln, we need to understand who he was before March 1857; that is, who he was before the Dred Scott decision came down and Democrat James Buchanan took the oath of office to become the fifteenth president of the United States. And we need to understand what the debate over slavery—and Lincoln's part in it—looked like before and then after the Dred Scott case. We argue that pre–Dred Scott, Lincoln was little more than an aspiring but mostly inept failed politician, although a rather capable, smart, articulate, and successful lawyer. As we will see, after Dred Scott, Lincoln did not hesitate to use the subject of slavery to stoke the engine of civil war as a necessity to advance his political fortune and just maybe his sincerely held beliefs.

Lincoln Before Dred Scott

LINCOLN APPARENTLY HAD A LIFELONG DISLIKE OF SLAVERY. SOME OF his ancestors had been antislavery Quakers and his father, Thomas Lincoln, is reported by Abraham to have left Kentucky for two reasons: (1) because Kentucky had weak property rights laws and so his homestead was at constant risk of being lost; and (2) he disliked slavery, ultimately moving his family to Illinois, where it was prohibited. Although Abraham Lincoln personally found slavery objectionable on moral grounds, still abolition did not occupy a prominent place in his early political career. He addressed his earlier position on slavery in a speech he gave in Chicago in July 1858, a year after the Dred Scott decision, noting that "I have always hated it, but I have always been quiet about it until this new era of the introduction of the Nebraska Bill began."[15] The Nebraska Bill (which we know as the Kansas-Nebraska Act) was the basis of the idea of popular sovereignty, which was strongly supported, especially by northern Democrats like Stephen Douglas.

Although pre–Dred Scott, popular sovereignty was thought to solve the question of how territories would determine whether they were slave or free, as a practical matter it was pretty much a disaster. The idea of popular sovereignty led to a stampede of proslavery and antislavery settlers in Kansas and Nebraska, each trying to tip the popular-sovereignty electoral advantage their way, resulting in extensive violence between the two factions. In any event, however popular sovereignty might have worked given more time, the Dred Scott decision eliminated the legal foundation for the Kansas-Nebraska Act. The people in a territory of the United States simply had no legal right to deprive lawful slaveholders of their property just because a slaveholder moved to the territory.

Prior to Dred Scott and the "Nebraska Bill," as Lincoln said, he was mostly quiet on the subject. Robert Browne, for instance, claimed that Lincoln told him in 1854: "The slavery question often bothered me as far back as 1836–40. I was troubled and grieved over it; but after the annexation of Texas I gave it up, believing as I now do, that God will settle it, and settle it right, and that he will, in some inscrutable way, restrict the spread of so great an evil; but for the present it is our duty to wait."[16] This statement is quite revealing of Lincoln's thinking. It is noteworthy that, as of 1854, he acknowledged that he attached no urgency to the slavery question. He understood his duty as being to wait rather than to agitate. Furthermore, the focus of his concern at that time was not the continuation of slavery per se, but its spread. Indeed, according to Browne, he did not even call upon God to end slavery but only to "restrict the spread of so great an evil." It is exactly Lincoln's disinclination toward activism, as distinct from his apparent personal sentiment, that engendered disdain for him among such abolitionists as H. Ford Douglas, quoted in the introductory chapter, or the more famous Frederick Douglass, who expressed a low opinion of Lincoln's prospects of addressing slavery successfully prior to the firing on Fort Sumter. Lincoln had, after all, stated clearly that as president he would enforce the Constitution, including Article 4, Section 2, Clause 3, which states, "No person held to service or labour in one state, under the laws thereof, escaping into another, shall, in consequence of any law or regulation therein, be discharged from such service or labour, but shall be delivered up on claim of the party to whom such service or labour may be due."

That said, Lincoln was not utterly silent on the slavery question in his early political career. As we learned in the Introduction, during his one term in Congress he introduced a bill that would have ensured the rights of slaveholders to pursue fugitive slaves in the District of Columbia, thereby extending the Constitution's reach to the pursuit of fugitive slaves outside the states. The actual piece of legislation was more complex, however, than the abolitionist's account that simply condemned it for bringing to the district a fugitive slave statute from which it had thus far been immune. The actual bill attempted to find a balance between antislavery interests and the interests of slaveholders in not losing ownership of their slaves by bringing them to the district. This was, of course, of considerable importance to congressmen who traveled with slaves. A bill that protected elected officials' ownership rights was bound to garner their support. But the bill also sought to prevent the spread of slavery to the district by setting a date after which slaves, other than fugitive slaves or those owned by members of Congress, would be freed. This double agenda characterized much of Lincoln's attitude toward slavery before the Dred Scott decision made it irrelevant.

Even in his role as a practicing lawyer, Lincoln pursued a balanced approach between his personal dislike of slavery and his interest in sustaining adequate protection of slaveholder rights under the Constitution. Illinois barred slavery, and also tried to bar the entry of free blacks into the state. Free it was, but hardly a bastion of abolitionism and certainly not a place arguing for equal protection for free blacks under the law. Lincoln joined together in a legal action with Lyman Trumbull, later senator from Illinois, and Gustave Koerner to undermine the legal foundation of the indentured servitude system applied to African Americans in Illinois in what amounted to a reworking of the antislavery law. They succeeded in gaining a court ruling that stated that in Illinois there was a presumption that blacks were free. Despite this good turn, it was also the case that Abraham Lincoln "appeared in so few suits in behalf of negroes . . . because he didn't want to be a party to a violation of the Fugitive Slave law."[17] Of the more than five thousand cases in which Lincoln was involved as a lawyer, only thirty-four concerned the free blacks in Springfield, where he practiced law.[18] And then, too, he also represented slave owners. As with any rising lawyer, he seems not to have turned away business because of personal scruples regarding slavery.

How do we reconcile the Lincoln who professed slavery to be "so great an evil" with the man who put forward a bill to promote the spread of a fugitive slave law into the District of Columbia? Reconciliation is not difficult. Lincoln's personal views, not only on slavery, but also on the rights, of "negroes" under the Declaration of Independence were extremist views in the context of the times. Lincoln believed that the Declaration correctly stated that "all men are created equal" and that "they are endowed by their Creator with certain unalienable Rights, that among these are Life, Liberty and the pursuit of Happiness." Today it is difficult for us to imagine how extreme a view this was seen to be when applied to nonwhites. Chief Justice Taney, in writing the majority opinion of the Supreme Court in the Dred Scott matter, did address this question and concluded, "In the opinion of the court, . . . the language used in the Declaration of Independence, show[s], that neither the class of persons who had been imported as slaves, nor their descendants, whether they had become free or not, were then acknowledged as a part of the people, nor intended to be included in the general words used in that memorable instrument." Thus, the law of the land, as stipulated by the Supreme Court, differed dramatically from Abraham Lincoln's opinion. So, too, did the view of Stephen Douglas, generally regarded in his own time as a moderate on the slavery issue. He mocked Lincoln and the rest of the "black Republicans" for contending that the founding fathers had "Negroes" in mind, suggesting that Lincoln even favored—shockingly at the time—intermarriage. In Douglas's opinion, "This Government was made by our fathers on the white basis . . . made by white men for the benefit of white men and their posterity forever."[19]

Douglas questioned the very idea that slaves could be considered as "persons," let alone as people with rights. They were to him, as they were in Taney's interpretation of the Constitution, simply property like any other property, with no rights. Hard as it is today to tolerate his statements about blacks and about Lincoln, we must remember that he really was a moderate on the slavery issue—so much so that the southern perception of Douglas as a moderate translated into his being seen as too antislavery to be acceptable to southern Democrats, who abandoned him in the presidential election of 1860.

So, on the one hand, Lincoln, the extremist, rather courageously argued that the Declaration of Independence referred to all people and that therefore slavery was an abomination. On the other hand, being a pragmatist, he chose to remain silent before the Dred Scott decision promised the spread of slavery throughout the territories and future states of the United States. The Supreme Court decision persuaded Lincoln to speak out against slavery. It provided the context for his political advancement.

Lincoln: A Failed and a Fulfilled Politician

THAT ABRAHAM LINCOLN WAS AMBITIOUS IS NEITHER IN DOUBT NOR A criticism. Few people do great things without trying to. That he did great things is, as well, not in doubt, but exactly how and why he did them needs deeper consideration. For one thing, while we might readily accept that Lincoln's time as president produced momentous changes in America, still we might wonder to what extent these changes required Lincoln. And then, even more, why he is often described as our country's most brilliant politician, a man who balanced disparate views within his cabinet, drawing adversaries together and bringing the nation to victory in its most trying time.[20] Indeed, even the notion that building a cabinet of rivals was evidence of good politics is highly questionable, despite its being the received wisdom.

Many people like to think that the best politicians surround them-selves with diverse points of view, listen to arguments on all sides, and then, evaluating the competing arguments, make their decisions. Yet logic and experience instruct us that the opposite is true. Better decisions are likely to be made when leaders surround themselves with yes-men. This is so alien a thought, so contrary to conventional wisdom, that it is necessary for us to pause and elaborate on the logic of the claim. We believe doing so will prove enlightening about what actually makes for good decision making and why being surrounded by rival opinions often translates, as perhaps it did for Lincoln, into unnecessarily prolonged periods of indecision or worse.

Consider the difficult problem a president has in assessing diverse opinions on subjects he—thus far we have only had men as president—knows relatively little about. We must realize that the president's advisers are likely to have their own interests and inevitably some of those interests are likely to differ from his. Overseeing departments that specialize in specific areas, cabinet members are likely to have more direct access to information than the president has on any given topic of debate. But they also have incentives to shade the information they present to the president, so as to favor their own point of view and their own advancement. Thus, the president cannot count on an honest exchange of information across colleagues whose objectives diverge from his own. This well-known and well-studied matter is referred to as the principal-agent problem.

One solution to the principal-agent problem is to have redundant sources of information. Another is to be surrounded by like-minded people, which adds a further benefit for the president. Imagine that someone who has routinely disagreed with the president in the past once again disagrees with him today on an important policy matter related, say, to war and peace. What can the president learn from such disagreement? Nothing really. The president already knows that the "rival" adviser sees the world differently than he does and so is likely to dismiss whatever the "rival" has to say as simply "same old, same old." Now imagine that an adviser who is known by the president to just about always agree with him, tells the president that his approach to an issue is wrong and needs to change. This is "real" information that is likely to lead the president to reconsider his opinion. After all, someone known to see the world the way he does now disagrees—it is not "same old, same old."

Lyndon Johnson had a dissident adviser in George Ball, undersecretary of state in his administration, and he also had his close friend, Clark Clifford, as secretary of defense late in his term. Ball constantly told Johnson that Vietnam was a mistake and Johnson ignored him. It was just more of the "same old, same old." When Clifford, who Johnson understood saw the world pretty much the way he did, told him that Vietnam was a political mistake and he needed to get out, Johnson modified his policy. He listened to the yes-man who suddenly disagreed with him; he ignored the naysayer who always disagreed. There was less benefit from having Ball's council than there was from having Clifford's.[21] A cabinet of rivals is more likely an indication of weak leadership than it is of statesmanship and political acumen. Just as LBJ understood this, so, too, did Abraham Lincoln.

Despite the praise Lincoln receives for having surrounded himself with political opponents, it is noteworthy that he was not eager to do so, and whenever he could, he avoided doing so. His private secretaries, John Nicolay and John Hay, for instance, reported, "We see such frequent allusion to a supposed purpose on the part of Mr. Lincoln to call into his cabinet two or three Southern gentlemen, from the parties opposed to him politically, that we are prompted to ask a few questions. 'First. Is it known that any such gentleman of character, would accept a place in the cabinet? Second. If yes, on what terms? Does he surrender to Mr. Lincoln, or Mr. Lincoln to him, on the political difference between them? Or do they enter upon the administration in open opposition to each other?'" They then noted how Lincoln resolved these questions: "The selection of enemies being out of the question, Mr. Lincoln, in execution of long-matured plans, proceeded to choose his friends, and the best and ablest."[22] What, then, characterized the rivals that he ultimately did bring into the cabinet? The answer as provided by historian Edward Conrad Smith is, "Shortly after the election he determined to give the former democratic element of the Republican party a strong representation in his cabinet, with a view to uniting the North."[23] That is, Lincoln included fellow Republicans whose opposition needed to be mollified or neutralized, much as Barack Obama included Hillary Rodham Clinton, his erstwhile political adversary, in his cabinet—and then he proceeded to pursue the policies and strategies he favored.

So, Lincoln's credit for building a cabinet of rivals and then brilliantly managing it is put into doubt by the statement of some of his closest associates and by the relatively narrow range of views he ultimately chose to accommodate. He was a good enough politician to know it was best to be surrounded by friends, although not good enough to figure out how to keep his own party united while avoiding the pressure to include dissidents. Furthermore, his and the nation's Civil War experience hardly provides a strong basis for concluding that Lincoln was a brilliant politician or a stellar commander in chief. Did he in fact successfully and effectively manage disparate views in his cabinet, Congress, and the country? We think not, and offer evidence to the contrary. Indeed, the view of Lincoln as a consummate politician seems like a very generous interpretation, perhaps driven in part by the knowledge today that the war was won, he was reelected (which no president had managed since Andrew Jackson), and he was murdered.

A less generous, but no less compelling, view is that he was an indecisive leader and a terrible commander in chief. Consider the facts:

Even the most prominent politicians in the Confederacy—such men as Confederate president Jefferson Davis and (late in the war) Confederate secretary of war (and previously James Buchanan's vice president) John Breckinridge—believed the South could not win the war.[24] Lincoln, however, could not figure out how to win it quickly, thereby saving hundreds of thousands of lives. The Confederate leaders were men of experience. Jefferson Davis was a graduate of West Point, a veteran of the Mexican-American War, and had served as secretary of war under President Franklin Pierce. Breckinridge had worked with Senator Douglas to advance the Kansas-Nebraska Act and had a long résumé of political successes. They understood that the North was wealthier, had a thriving industrial economy, manufactured most of the nation's weaponry, and had a much bigger population than the South. Hence, they both opposed secession and then looked for ways to compromise with Lincoln to avoid war. We will have more to say about that later. For now, the point is that Lincoln's leading southern opponents adamantly opposed secession and thought the North would win, and yet the Civil War lasted for all of Lincoln's first term.

How long might we—or Lincoln—have reasonably expected the war to last, given the asymmetry in the capabilities of the two sides? The North, for instance, had about 22 million people; the South, 9 million, of which about 4 million were slaves. As we have noted, the North produced most of the munitions made in the United States at the time. Against the overwhelming manpower and economic advantage, the Confederacy's main advantage was that it would be on the defense and so the venue of fighting would be turf more familiar to the Confederate army than the Union army, but then that also meant the South's infrastructure would take a bigger hit than the North's. With facts like these in mind, it is fortunately straightforward to estimate how long the war might have been expected to last.

We treat the US Civil War as if it were a war between two independent nations, each with its own central government, and each with its own regular army. Hence, we compare it to all other wars fought by nations between 1816 and 1985. The method we use is based on a prominent article on the duration of wars by Professors Scott Bennett and Allan Stam. They examined the duration of war based on the type of governments of each side, the type of military strategies used, the number of nations on each side, the type of terrain, and the total and relative size of military and economic strength on each side. Adapting Bennett and Stam's method to the North and South (see endnote), we find that the Civil War should have lasted only about six months.[25] Yet it went on for a bit over four years. Is that really to Lincoln's credit?

Why was the war so much longer than the difference in capabilities had suggested it would be to Davis or to modern statistical analysis? There could be many answers, of course, but we think the clearest is one people prefer not to address. Lincoln was an indecisive and inept commander in chief. He was unable to find a general to command the Army of Washington (later the Army of the Potomac) and crush its weaker adversary. Why didn't he have a parade of generals coming through his office, interviewing them about how they would fight the war, giving himself a chance to discover a "George Washington" for his time? Instead, he turned to old, tired military men or to those with political ambitions of their own. When the elderly General Winfield Scott failed him, he turned to his political foe, General George McClellan, who had been a staunch backer of Stephen Douglas in 1858 and 1860, to run the war. Lincoln allowed General McClellan to humiliate him (for which, oddly, we laud him today—and conversely we laud Lyndon Johnson because we cannot imagine his ever putting himself in a politically humiliating position). McClellan, for example, willfully kept Lincoln cooling his heels, waiting to meet with him, rather than showing the president (and his office) the respect he deserved. After Lincoln had waited for thirty minutes at McClellan's home, he was informed that the general had gone to sleep for the night![26] And then McClellan, finally having been sacked by Lincoln and returned to civilian life, also pursued a course designed to advance his own presidential ambitions at his former commander in chief's expense, unfettered by Lincoln. Indeed, before the fortuitous fall of Atlanta on September 2, 1864, just weeks before the presidential election, George McClellan, not Lincoln, was expected to win the presidency. Prior to that, the electorate seemed to favor the Democratic Party platform, which called for a negotiated peace with the Confederacy. That, of course, became irrelevant after September 2, 1864, thereby ensuring Lincoln's reelection.

The view of Lincoln as an inept decision maker is certainly out of favor today. But contemporaries thought of him in just that way. Maybe they were blind to his political genius and maybe, just maybe, their experiences with him and especially his failure to bring the war to a rapid conclusion were fully consistent with who he was as a politician and the evidence amassed about him in that role earlier in his political career. Perhaps it is we who with hindsight reconstruct Lincoln's failures into triumphs.

It is easy to overlook the simple fact that Lincoln was a failed politician for much of his career. He was a local Illinois state legislator who managed to win but one term in Congress and then twice lost bids to become a senator, once in 1855 to Lyman Trumbull (who later was to become one of the authors of the Thirteenth Amendment that ended slavery) and once to Stephen Douglas in 1858. True, he did manage to win an election to the state assembly, following his failure to win a second term in Congress, but then he passed up that opportunity to pursue unsuccessfully election to the Senate (then done by the state legislature and not by popular vote) instead. He ran mostly failed campaigns before the Dred Scott decision. With that decision, he had the insight to see how to use it to open the door to a change in his electoral fortunes.

Lincoln's political skill fell in two directions, only one of which can truly be seen as laudable. He was a smoke-filled-room politician, skilled at political machinations, and a superb lawyer capable of using legal-like briefs as campaign instruments to great advantage. Consider how he won his party's nomination for president in 1860.

Going into the nominating convention, William Seward (later Lincoln's secretary of state—foreshadowing the Obama–Rodham Clinton relationship of 150 years later) was the frontrunner. Indeed, the view at the time was that he was practically a sure thing. The main concern expressed about Seward was whether he could win the national election. His strong antislavery stance and his proimmigrant attitude raised doubts about whether he could carry the crucial "swing-states" of Pennsylvania and New Jersey, without which a solid South was likely to defeat the Republican candidate for president. Lincoln was positioned as a more moderate candidate on the slavery question. On immigrants as well, he was more moderate than Seward but still perceived nationally as having proimmigrant views. That he had such views cannot be in doubt.

In an 1855 letter—and not in a public speech—to his friend Joshua Speed, Lincoln addressed his views regarding immigrants and the nativist Know-Nothing Party, which was an offshoot of the Whig Party led by Millard Fillmore, the thirteenth president. Lincoln was quite conscious that, from time to time, he was falsely accused of being sympathetic to the Know-Nothings. Reflecting back on the Declaration of Independence, he wrote, "Our progress in degeneracy appears to me to be pretty rapid. As a nation, we began by declaring that 'all men are created equal.' We now practically read it 'all men are created equal, except negroes[.]' When the Know-Nothings get control, it will read 'all men are created equal, except negroes, and foreigners, and Catholics.' When it comes to this I should prefer emigrating to some country where they make no pretence of loving liberty—to Russia, for instance, where despotism can be taken pure, and without the base alloy of hypocracy [sic]."[27]

Although Seward went in as the expected winner and other prominent candidates presented themselves, including the governor of Ohio, Salmon Chase, and Edward Bates, a congressman from Missouri, Lincoln prevailed. He secured the nomination on the third ballot. How did he do it? Well, it certainly helped that the convention was held in Chicago, Lincoln's backyard, where he could exert the kind of double-dealing influence that would not have been easily available to him had the convention not been in Illinois. The convention venue, the Wigwam, required tickets for entry. Lincoln's campaign team had counterfeit tickets printed and used them to pack the hall with his supporters. Since space was limited, he managed by this means to keep many of Seward's supporters from entering the Wigwam and being present to cast their ballot in his favor. Those who made their way in found that Lincoln's political managers engineered it so that Seward's men were seated in a far corner of the hall where, in a time before microphones, they could not be heard. And then, as the *Chicago Tribune* reported on May 18, 1860: "During the third ballot, with Lincoln tantalizingly close to winning the nomination, [Chicago mayor Joseph] Medill sat close to the chairman of the Ohio delegation, which had backed its favorite son, Salmon P. Chase. Swing your votes to Lincoln, Medill whispered, and your boy can have anything he wants. The Ohio chairman shot out of his chair and changed the state's votes. After a moment of stunned silence, the flimsy Wigwam began to shake with the stomping of feet and the shouting of the Lincoln backers who packed the hall and blocked the streets outside." Thus, through clever maneuvering of the sort that today we might call dirty tricks, Lincoln rose in the Republican political ranks to become his party's nominee. The promise to Salmon Chase was not forgotten. Chase became Lincoln's secretary of the treasury.

It is the second aspect of Lincoln's political ability that is more appealing and that shows him to be the brilliant man we prefer to remember. He manifested his brilliance politically just about whenever he could turn campaigning into an opportunity to argue a lawyer's brief for his preferred point of view. Consider his famous "House Divided" speech in June 1858. We all know the famous, quotable lines, such as "A house divided against itself cannot stand," but too few of us appreciate the stark and belligerent message he conveyed in that great lawyer's brief that essentially called for a war on slavery. It is difficult to imagine how anyone today can read that speech—given when Lincoln accepted the Republican Party's nomination for an Illinois Senate seat—without seeing it as a call for war. It is harder still to imagine that his contemporaries did not understand that he was demanding either war or a surrender of the proslavery parts of the country to a leader bent on getting rid of "so great an evil."

Lincoln gave the "House Divided" speech against the backdrop of the recent Dred Scott decision. The speech and the subsequent Lincoln-Douglas debates were part of Lincoln's political strategy to maneuver his Senate rival, the incumbent Stephen Douglas, into staking out a position on slavery that was sure to divide the national Democratic Party in 1860. By doing so, Lincoln cost himself the Senate seat but improved, as he understood he was doing, his chances of becoming the Republican nominee for president. And he increased the chances of war if he (or any Republican) was elected president in 1860. This, too, he also surely understood. Indeed, he delivered the controversial "House Divided" speech against the advice of his own friends and advisers who had these very fears. In it Lincoln stated (with his own emphasis included):

> We are now far into the *fifth* year, since a policy was initiated, with the *avowed* object, and *confident* promise, of putting an end to slavery agitation.
>
> Under the operation of that policy, that agitation has not only, *not ceased*, but has *constantly augmented*.
>
> In *my* opinion, it *will* not cease, until a *crisis* shall have been reached, and passed.
>
> "A house divided against itself cannot stand."
>
> I believe this government cannot endure, permanently half *slave* and half *free*.

> I do not expect the Union to be *dissolved*—I do not expect the
> house to *fall*—but I *do* expect it will cease to be divided.
> It will become *all* one thing or *all* the other.

This passage reminds us of Lincoln's conviction that the Dred Scott
decision had undone the federal bargain that was necessary to unify
the states under the Constitution. Now, with the Supreme Court's ruling, it became clear to Lincoln that the country would survive only by
being all slave or all free. The message he delivered in that speech was
a strongly argued brief for a free nation, or, at least, that is how it was
interpreted by Douglas, who referred repeatedly to the "black" Republican Party, and it was how it apparently was interpreted by the state
legislators in Illinois who chose Douglas over Lincoln.

Did Lincoln *hope*, as he intimated, to avoid national dissolution
over the question of slavery? Certainly. Did he *expect* that it could be
avoided? That seems doubtful given that he knew the South was not
about to give up slavery voluntarily and the North increasingly found
it intolerable; hence his statement, "it will become *all* one thing or *all*
the other." In this regard it is worth recalling the less often quoted
closing portion of that same "House Divided" speech:

> Two years ago the Republicans of the nation mustered over thirteen
> hundred thousand strong. We did this under the single impulse of
> resistance to a common danger, with every external circumstance
> against us. Of *strange, discordant*, and even, *hostile* elements, we gath-
> ered from the four winds, and *formed* and fought the battle through,
> under the constant hot fire of a disciplined, proud, and pampered
> enemy. Did we brave all *then* to *falter* now?—now—when that same
> enemy is *wavering*, dissevered and belligerent?
> The result is not doubtful. We shall not fail—if we stand firm,
> we shall not fail. *Wise councils* may *accelerate* or *mistakes delay* it, but,
> sooner or later the victory is sure to come.[28]

Most clearly, the "common danger" to which he referred was not
just national dissolution, but the unfettered spread of slavery throughout the states and the territories, a spread promoted by the Dred Scott
decision. All the great political developments of the previous few years
had pointed to a nation that would be all slave and that was an outcome
intolerable to Abraham Lincoln, as well as to much of the population

in the northern states and, of course, to abolitionists everywhere. Lincoln's declaration "We shall not fail" and all the rest of the heated rhetoric in this speech hardly seems the utterance of a man seeking to push the regional differences onto the backburner for the sake of preserving the Union. It sounds much more like the man who declared that the "Republicans of the nation" came together "under the single impulse of resistance to a common danger." It was a radical statement and it was understood as such in its time, just as it was understood by Lincoln to be both an instrument for his eventual rise to the presidency and almost certainly as well a provocation likely to trigger a heightened threat of civil war.

Indeed, Lincoln's law partner, William Herndon, in a lecture delivered on January 24, 1866, reflected back on the writing of the "House Divided" speech and his discussions with Lincoln about its incendiary tenor. Here is an excerpt of the critical portions of Herndon's much lengthier lecture:

> On the evening of the 16th of June Mr. Lincoln came into his office—locked the door—put the key in his own pocket-pulled out of his person the manuscript of the house divided against speech [sic]. He took a seat at his table, and commenced reading the speech to me. When he had finished the first paragraph he stopt—turned to me, and said—How do you like that—What do you think of it? I told him—"I think it is true, but is it entirely politic to read or speak it as written," referring to the House divided sentence. "That makes no difference: that expression is a truth of all human experience . . . and I will deliver it as written. . . . I would rather be defeated with this expression in the speech and it held up and discussed before the People than to be victorious without it." Noble words most nobly said. . . . On the evening of the 17th June the speech was read, or spoken rather, just as it was written, the house divided against itself sentence included. The Hall of the House of Representatives was full to overflowing, and the speech was then and there delivered; and so the sentence spoken of went out into the world to struggle for existence. . . . That speech did awaken and did arouse the People to the think [sic], and though Mr. Lincoln was defeated in that Contest, still it made him President. I thought at the time the speech was read to me, that it was made as it was to take the winds out of Sewards Sales [sic]. . . . These simple

facts are evidences of much meaning—First, that Mr. Lincoln was seized by an idea—Secondly, that he fully calculated and weighed its effects—Thirdly—, That he had a policy—Fourthly, That he had a will—a strong self determination to utter it Fifthly—: That he was willing to suffer political death in the Senatorial Canvass for an idea—Sixthly, that he was secretive—cautious, complex minded and morally courageous. . . . I am fully aware the world holds, that Mr. Lincoln was a simple minded man—that he had no will—no policy, and was all heart. But the great world will distinguish between what it thinks, and what in solid reality is. It is often said of Mr. Lincoln that he was God's prophet, and that the house divided against itself speech is an unanswerable evidence of it.[29]

Anyone who doubts that Lincoln intended the "House Divided" speech as an intense brief in favor of the defeat of the South's ambition to spread slavery across the land would do well to remember Mr. Herndon's statement that "Mr. Lincoln was seized by an idea" and that "he fully calculated and weighed its effects." And then one should also note that deep in the body of the "House Divided" text, where his lawyer's brief is strongest, Lincoln also declared, "Put this and that together, and we have another nice little niche, which we may, ere long, see filled with another Supreme Court decision, declaring that the Constitution of the United States does not permit a State to exclude slavery from its limits. . . . We shall lie down pleasantly dreaming that the people of Missouri are on the verge of making their State free, and we shall awake to the reality instead, that the Supreme Court has made Illinois a slave State." Here Lincoln projects the course, as he sees it, that is inevitable and that only dreamers can fail to see. Dred Scott, for him, was the peak of the slippery slope into universal slavery. In 1857 the Supreme Court ruled on the lack of authority that Congress had to decide for the territories of the United States whether they were to be free or slave. And then he speculates that a future court decision will expand on Dred Scott, concluding that the Constitution does not give any state the right to dictate that it prohibits slavery.

Of course, Herndon's account was based on his recollection many years after the "House Divided" speech was delivered and might, therefore, be seen as politically motivated. But then we can see similar sentiments expressed, albeit a bit more cautiously, as early as August

15, 1855, in a letter written by Lincoln to George Robertson, a lawyer who had represented Lincoln's family. Lincoln, commenting on Robertson's role in a precursor to the Missouri Compromise, observed,

> [Y]ou are not a friend of slavery in the abstract. In that [earlier] speech you spoke of *"the peaceful extinction of slavery"* and used other expressions indicating your belief that the thing was, at some time, to have an end[.] Since then we have had thirty six years of experience; and this experience has demonstrated, I think, that there is no peaceful extinction of slavery in prospect for us[.] . . . That spirit which desired the peaceful extinction of slavery, has itself become extinct, with the *occasion,* and the *men* of the Revolution. Under the impulse of that occasion, nearly half the states adopted systems of emancipation at once; and it is a significant fact, that not a single state has done the like since. So far as peaceful, voluntary emancipation is concerned, the condition of the negro slave in America, scarcely less terrible to the contemplation of a free mind, is now as fixed, and hopeless of change for the better, as that of the lost souls of the finally impenitent. The Autocrat of all the Russias will resign his crown, and proclaim his subjects free republicans sooner than will our American masters voluntarily give up their slaves. Our political problem now is "Can we, as a nation, continue together *permanently—forever*—half slave, and half free?" The problem is too mighty for me. May God, in his mercy, superintend the solution.[30]

By 1858 it appears the problem was no longer too mighty for him! And, as he said, "the peaceful extinction of slavery, has itself become extinct."

How were the proslavery portions of the nation to interpret his words in the "House Divided" speech (and how are we to understand them, given his letter to Robertson and similar documents in his own hand?) other than as an extreme commitment to limit the power of the Supreme Court in such a way that it could not foster the spread of slavery? There was only one constitutional means to achieve that end, especially given the 1857 ruling that Congress had violated the Constitution by passing the Missouri Compromise. The only means available within the Constitution was to amend it. How would he have amended it? Well, he didn't say it directly, but he did state that the country cannot endure half free and half slave and so must be all one or all the other. All one or the other was the course the Supreme Court had put the country on, and that course was "all slave." To alter that course—the idea Lincoln had and the carefully calculated way to achieve his idea—could only mean an amendment to make the nation "all free." And to get such an amendment passed, he needed a nation without the slave states.

While Senate candidate Lincoln certainly did not explicitly call for amending the Constitution to ban slavery everywhere, and surely would not have uttered such words so plainly, still that was likely to be the way his words and his party's position was understood by the electors in Illinois in 1858. Consider what the Republican Party was believed to stand for at the time. Famous journalist Horace Greeley coined the name "Republican Party." He wrote in 1854, "We should not care much whether those thus united (*against slavery*) were designated 'Whig,' 'Free Democrat' or something else; though we think some simple name like 'Republican' would more fitly designate those who had united to restore the Union to its true mission of champion and promulgator of Liberty rather than propagandist of slavery."[31] Obviously the then newly formed Republican Party was understood to be antislavery above all else.

Brilliantly Boxing In Stephen Douglas

THE DRED SCOTT DECISION NOT ONLY BROUGHT ABRAHAM LINCOLN out of his silence on slavery; it also compelled the "moderate" Stephen Douglas, with direct pressure from Senate-candidate Abraham Lincoln, to figure out how to maintain his position in favor of popular sovereignty without going against the Supreme Court. Douglas's solution, set out in reply to a question from Lincoln, was to introduce the Freeport Doctrine. Lincoln's question, as reiterated by Douglas, was, "Can the people of a Territory in any lawful way, against the wishes of any citizen of the United States, exclude slavery from their limits prior to the formation of a State constitution?" To which Douglas, clearly irritated, replied,

> I answer emphatically, as Mr. Lincoln has heard me answer a hundred times from every stump in Illinois, that in my opinion the people of a Territory can, by lawful means, exclude slavery from their limits prior to the formation of a State constitution. Mr Lincoln knew that I had answered that question over and over again. He heard me argue

the Nebraska bill on that principle all over the State in 1854, in 1855, and in 1856, and he has no excuse for pretending to be in doubt as to my position on that question. It matters not what way the Supreme Court may hereafter decide as to the abstract question whether slavery may or may not go into a Territory under the Constitution, the people have the lawful means to introduce it or exclude it as they please, for the reason that slavery cannot exist a day or an hour anywhere, unless it is supported by local police regulations. Those police regulations can only be established by the local legislature; and if the people are opposed to slavery, they will elect representatives to that body who will by unfriendly legislation effectually prevent the introduction of it into their midst. If, on the contrary, they are for it, their legislation will favor its extension. Hence, no matter what the decision of the Supreme Court may be on that abstract question, still the right of the people to make a Slave Territory or a Free Territory is perfect and complete under the Nebraska bill. I hope Mr. Lincoln deems my answer satisfactory on that point.[32]

The idea, put succinctly, was that slavery could not be established in any territory if the people in the territory chose not to pass regulations that facilitated law enforcement on behalf of its establishment. Douglas's solution was consistent with the letter but clearly not the spirit of the law as articulated in the Dred Scott decision. It had two fundamental political consequences. First, it appealed to the Illinois legislature, the body with the constitutional authority at the time to elect members of the Senate. Hence, his Freeport Doctrine was a politically expedient path to defeating Lincoln for the Senate. But, second, it was not well received by the southern portions of the Democratic Party. They saw the Freeport Doctrine for what it was—an effort to thwart the Dred Scott ruling that had opened the territories to the unfettered spread of slavery just as desired by southern politicians.

Lincoln understood that he was putting Douglas in a quandary.[33] Douglas professed the utmost regard for the Supreme Court. He also was a strong advocate of popular sovereignty. The court had ruled against popular sovereignty. What, Lincoln pondered, was Douglas's position on the free spread of slavery into the territories following the Dred Scott decision? The reply he extracted from Douglas practically guaranteed that the Democratic Party, or a substantial—proslavery— part of it, would not support Stephen Douglas for president in 1860. With the Democrats likely to be divided in the presidential election, the door was opened to the election of a Republican and Lincoln had every intention of being that Republican.

Lincoln's maneuver in posing a question to Douglas that could only harm Douglas—either he would answer in favor of the Court ruling and lose his Senate seat or he would answer as he did and lose the bulk of the Democratic Party in 1860—was politically brilliant but also foreseeably dangerous. Lincoln was knowingly dividing the Democratic Party, which meant deepening sectional divisions and a heightened risk of war. This, as we saw in examining the "House Divided" speech and his explicit letter to Robertson on the peaceful extinction of slavery, was surely front and center on his mind. He had options. For instance, he could have chosen not to ask the question, in the process probably still losing the Senate seat to the incumbent (as he did anyway), without precipitating deeper national rancor. Probably the upshot of that course would have been that Lincoln would have faded from the political scene, adding yet another failed campaign to his long list. Or he could, by posing the question and dividing the opposition, increase his odds of becoming president at the price of a heightened risk of civil war. Ambition dictated his course—he asked the question, lost the Senate race, and heightened his prospects for 1860, which he further heightened by adding another lawyer's brief against Douglas and the Southern Democrats in his Cooper Union speech a couple of years later.

Lincoln's own position on the fateful question he put to Douglas, as indicated in the "House Divided" speech, was that the country faced the need to determine if it was to be all slave or all free. He clearly favored the latter position, contrary to the implications of the Dred Scott decision. Not surprisingly, Illinois's Democrats defended their position by characterizing Lincoln and his entire party as extremists who were prepared to reject the law of the land as set out by the Supreme Court with the intent of precipitating a war. Douglas specifically attacked Lincoln's view that the nation could not endure without being all slave or all free. Lest anyone doubt that Lincoln's position was understood to be a call to civil war, here are Douglas's own words on Lincoln's speech, delivered on July 9, 1858, with Lincoln known by Douglas to be in the audience:

> Mr. Lincoln asserts, as a fundamental principle of this government, that there must be uniformity in the local laws and domestic institutions of each and all the States of the Union; and he therefore invites all the non-slaveholding States to band together, organize as one body, and make war upon slavery in Kentucky, upon slavery in

Virginia, upon the Carolinas, upon slavery in all of the slaveholding States in this Union, and to persevere in that war until it shall be exterminated. He then notifies the slaveholding States to stand together as a unit and make an aggressive war upon the free States of this Union with a view of establishing slavery in them all; of forcing it upon Illinois, of forcing it upon New York, upon New England, and upon every other free State, and that they shall keep up the warfare until it has been formally established in them all. In other words, Mr. Lincoln advocates boldly and clearly a war of sections, a war of the North against the South, of the free States against the slave States, a war of extermination to be continued relentlessly until the one or the other shall be subdued, and all the States shall either become free or become slave.[34]

Perhaps this was merely harsh, negative campaign rhetoric and fear-mongering; perhaps it was sincerely believed. Either way, it was a prophetic statement! The lines had been clearly drawn. Lincoln was portrayed as lawless and as advocating dissolution of the Union, as calling for civil war; Douglas as law abiding and willing to try to finesse the difficulties created by the Dred Scott decision.

Divide and Conquer: The Election of 1860

LINCOLN'S ATTACK AGAINST DOUGLAS IN 1858 HELPED FORGE HIS famously slim electoral victory in 1860. To see how his call for a United States that was all slave or all free shaped his electoral victory, it is useful to compare the electoral college maps of 1852, 1856 (that is, the first time the Republicans ran a candidate for president), and 1860, when Lincoln prevailed over a heavily divided field.

We begin with the 1852 election between Democrat Franklin Pierce and Whig Winfield Scott (later Lincoln's first—failed—general in the Civil War). Senator John Hale of New Hampshire, whom we have already met, ran as well, as the candidate of the Free Soil Party, but he won no states and no Electoral College votes. Figure 3.1 shows the division of the Electoral College and the popular vote in that pre–Republican Party election. When we take a look at the 1856 and 1860 elections, we will want to remember what the 1852 map looks like. Before the Kansas-Nebraska Act (1854), the first presidential campaign of

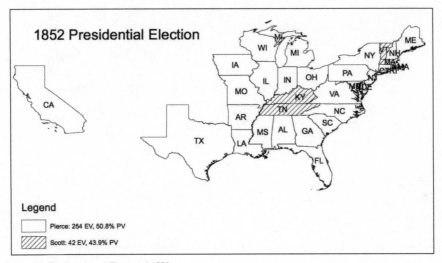

Figure 3.1. The Presidential Election of 1852

the antislavery Republican Party (1856), and the Dred Scott decision (1857), the presidential electoral map was not divided along sectional lines. Indeed, it was barely divided at all.

With the events just enumerated having happened and having reanimated the sectional battle lines that were prominent at America's founding, the unity of the country was in doubt. We have to go back to the Andrew Jackson–John Quincy Adams election of 1828 (when Adams dominated in the New England states and Jackson just about everywhere else) to see anything resembling the clear sectional divide that was presented in the 1856 election, as seen in Figure 3.2.

The Republican candidate, John Frémont, won 33 percent of the popular vote and 38 percent of the Electoral College vote. The entire South went for James Buchanan who, with a plurality of 45 percent of the vote (Millard Fillmore having won 22 percent) was elected president. Needing 149 electoral votes to win, Frémont fell short by only 55. This was a strong showing for a new party whose support was highly sectional. Frémont did not carry all of the North, but every state he won was in the North. To win in the future, the Republicans needed either to attract more votes or to deprive the Democrats of some of their successes. They could do this, for example, by dividing the Democratic Party's vote among many candidates. As we saw, Lincoln's "House Divided" speech coupled with the associated question he posed to Stephen Douglas did just that. This can be seen in the map of the 1860 election (Figure 3.3).

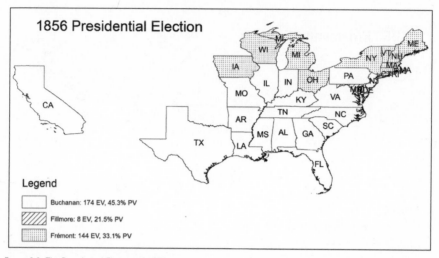

Figure 3.2. The Presidential Election of 1856

The Republican Party captured just less than 40 percent of the popular vote in 1860—better than Frémont had done—and they took 59
percent of the Electoral College vote, a solid majority. Douglas won almost no votes in the Electoral College (12) although he managed to secure
29 percent of the popular vote. This imbalance reflected the inefficient
distribution of his electoral support and his inability to convert popular
support into Electoral College clout because of deep electoral divisions
within some states as well as across sections of the country. Where did
the votes go? They went to Vice President John Breckinridge, who won
the entire Deep South and to antisecession candidate Tennessee senator
John Bell (who secured 13 percent of the popular vote and 13 percent
of the Electoral College vote). This is crucial to reflect on. Breckinridge
secured far fewer popular votes than Douglas and yet secured six times
the Electoral College votes (72 compared to 12). Lincoln's divide-and-
conquer strategy really seems to have worked in 1860. A large portion
of Douglas's vote was dissipated, having been spread out in many states
where he did not win. Furthermore, we can reasonably expect that a
significant number of would-be pro-Douglas voters, seeing that the contest was really between the southern proslavery candidate Breckinridge
and the antislavery Lincoln, voted strategically, giving their vote to
Lincoln, who they would have seen as the lesser of two evils, thereby
turning Lincoln votes efficiently into Electoral College votes.

Lincoln's electoral efficiency was quite remarkable. He won
the presidency with less than 40 percent of the popular vote while

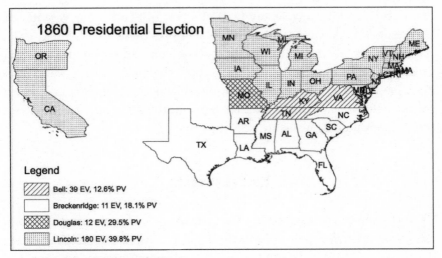

Figure 3.3. The Presidential Election of 1860

securing essentially no votes at all in most of the South where, in fact, he generally did not even appear on the ballot. The relatively moderate candidates on slavery—Douglas and Bell—did well in the border states but nowhere else. Lincoln managed to produce the house divided of which he spoke, a division not seen since 1828. In successfully splitting the national electorate, he dissolved the Democrats' hold on the presidency. To be sure, as the 1856 map shows, the house was already divided electorally as soon as the Republican Party replaced the Whig Party. The difference was that Frémont ran against a united South and moderate antislavery middle that reached up to include such free states as Illinois, New Jersey, and Pennsylvania. Lincoln had made the contest much more sectional and divisive than it had been in 1856. To do so, he ran on a platform punctuated by critical issues that attracted support among antislavery voters, protariff voters, and Democrats disgusted by the divisions within their own party; divisions that Lincoln had worked tirelessly to foster. While some disgruntled Democrats undoubtedly turned to Bell or to Breckinridge, many, as we have noted, were likely to have voted for Lincoln rather than any of the former Democrats. Thus, Lincoln won in a significant number of states that Frémont lost, including the very swing states that party bosses had worried Seward might not carry (Seward being seen as more extreme on slavery and immigration—important questions in Pennsylvania and New Jersey—than Lincoln). Lincoln very narrowly won his home state (and Douglas's) of Illinois (11 Electoral College votes), as well as Indiana (3),

Pennsylvania (27), New Jersey (4), California (4), and the new states of Minnesota (4) and Oregon (3). And he was president!

Lincoln's electoral campaign was accompanied by intensified threats of secession, followed by actual secessions during the lame-duck period when he was president-elect. Hence, it is important now to consider the views he held on secession and the actions he took to keep the Union together, his professed objective!

Views on Secession

THE THREAT OF SECESSION WAS NOT NEW TO LINCOLN'S ELECTION. From the country's very earliest days it was an issue that presidents had to confront. As we saw in the Introduction and in Chapter 2, James Madison faced the threat of secession by the New England states.

As Lincoln the lawyer most assuredly knew, the Constitution of the United States provides for the entry of new states into the Union, but it seemed to be silent on the subject of withdrawal from the Union once a state's people had ratified that document. Perhaps he reflected back on Jefferson's own experience and thoughts. Jefferson, in his own way an extremist on constitutional questions, felt from the outset that the Constitution, like all laws, should be an ephemeral document. He believed that every generation had the right to define for itself the social contract under which it lived. Hence, he believed that

> it may be proved that no society can make a perpetual constitution, or even a perpetual law. The earth belongs always to the living generation. They may manage it then, and what proceeds from it, as they please, during their usufruct. They are masters too of their own persons, and consequently may govern them as they please. But persons and property make the sum of the objects of government. The constitution and the laws of their predecessors extinguished then in their natural course with those who gave them being. This could preserve that being till it ceased to be itself, and no longer. Every constitution then, and every law, naturally expires at the end of 19 years. If it be enforced longer, it is an act of force, and not of right.[35]

As clearly and rigorously as Jefferson argued the case for the replacement of laws every nineteen years, once in the office of president

and Senate accepted the secessionist government of West Virginia as legitimate, seating two senators and their House members in Congress.

Lincoln's position was consistent with the Constitution only if he, an accomplished attorney, accepted that Virginia was no longer part of the United States (as it declared to be the case). In that instance, West Virginia's formation would not have violated the Constitution. However if Virginia was considered still part of the Union, as Lincoln deemed it to be, then West Virginia's admission to the Union was impossible without the agreement of Virginia's legislature—agreement that was not forthcoming.

As we have noted, apart from establishing conditions for the creation of a new state from an existing territory, the Constitution is silent on the subject of secession. In a somewhat remarkable post–Civil War finding, the Supreme Court ruled, in a divided decision, in *Virginia v. West Virginia*, 78 U.S. 39 (1871) that the State had assented to the withdrawal of the counties that formed West Virginia, making that action consistent with the Constitution. Furthermore, in *Texas v. White*, 74 U.S. 700 (1869), again in a divided vote, the Supreme Court judged that the Constitution provided for the "perpetuity and indissolubility of the Union"; that is, the Constitution, previously thought not to address the matter at all, prohibited secession, although it also acknowledged that the Union might be dissolved by "revolution, or through consent of the States."

Thus, in a set of post–Civil War decisions, the court found that the Constitution denied the most sacred right that congressman and legal authority Abraham Lincoln argued for in 1848. We are in no position to question the wisdom of the court in the 1870s. Still, we must note that Lincoln gave the greatest historic weight to his view in support of internal revolt—perhaps we could call it "civil war"—in the sentences that immediately followed the quotation on page 127. He invoked the American Revolution, noting that it had been justified when the local majority rose up against the pro-British colonists: "Such minority was precisely the case of the Tories of our own Revolution. It is a quality of revolutions not to go by *old* lines, or *old* laws; but to break up both, and make new ones."[38]

President-elect Lincoln faced not merely talk of secession but also the votes of virtually all southern states to secede from the Union. He was repeatedly pressed to look for a compromise and he routinely declined. He claimed that the secessionists for their own purposes ignored his clear statements that he meant not to alter the federal bargain and that there was no point in repeating his words to people who chose not to listen. In the same letter to Senator Hale that we quoted earlier, he said in this regard, "There is, in my judgment, but one compromise which would really settle the slavery question, and that would be a prohibition against acquiring any more territory."[39] William Herndon, Lincoln's law partner, summarized Lincoln's view on compromise quite succinctly: "Away—off—begone! If the nation wants to back down, let it—not I."[40]

The South's Great Mistake

LINCOLN'S RELUCTANCE TO COMPROMISE WAS PART PERSONAL conviction; part loyalty to his core Republican constituency; and, in many accounts, an apparent failure to grasp how real the threat of dissolution was. In his 1858 campaign, Lincoln of course understood, as we have emphasized, that a sectional crisis was coming. As he said, "The tug has to come and better now, than any time hereafter."[41] And yet when it came he seems to have believed—or at least we are asked to believe that he believed—that it would pass without much consequence. As one scholar reports, "Lincoln seemed confused, incredulous, at what was happening to his country. He seemed not to understand how he appeared in southern eyes. . . . He could not accept the possibility that his election to the presidency might cause the collapse of the very system which had enabled him to get there."[42] Now here we must demur. Either, as Douglas professed, Lincoln's "House Divided" speech was so inflammatory as to be the likely spark of civil war and Lincoln knew it, or, if not, we cannot escape the inference that Lincoln had taken leave of reality. We doubt very much that he did not understand how he was seen and what the ramifications were. The facts before him were too overwhelming for that excuse to hold water.

Consider the extraordinary fact that Lincoln, the presidential candidate of a national political party, did not even appear on the ballot in ten of the southern states. How could he have doubted that the southern electorate hated him? Given the hostile rhetoric that surrounded him, the public conviction by the moderate Stephen Douglas that Lincoln was calling for no less than a war against the South, and that Lincoln personally had been present to hear Douglas make that declaration, how could he have sustained the belief that the threat of dissolution and war was not real? If that is true, it flies in the face of claims that he was a brilliant politician. If it was not true, then we cannot escape the conclusion that he had maneuvered the country to the brink of dissolution and he had no intention to pull it back from that brink once his election was secured. He was going to make the country, as he indicated it must be, all free; and doing so peacefully, as he had written five years earlier, was an extinct possibility.

Still, one might object on the grounds that he had good reason to believe dissolution was a bluff. After all, many of the secession votes were close. In Virginia, for instance, the University of Richmond reported: "On April 4 [1861], as Unionist delegate John Baldwin met with Abraham Lincoln in Washington to discuss how war might be averted, the convention voted a second ordinance of secession down by a two-thirds majority. On April 17, after troops in South Carolina fired on Ft. Sumter and Lincoln called for troops to suppress the rebellion, delegates from Virginia voted to secede from the United States, 88 to 55."[43] Three other states seceded following Lincoln's decision to defend Fort Sumter. Until then, many southern states, as Virginia illustrates, were deeply divided but chose—for the time being—against secession.

Just about every southern state was divided on the question of secession. Of course, these divisions could have fueled Lincoln's alleged misconception that the crisis would pass without damaging the Union. But then, the close votes might also reflect the idea that he could have found a compromise to save the Union—but chose not to. Such a compromise had been put forward. The Crittenden Compromise proposed in December 1860, for instance, seemed to meet Lincoln's avowed interest in preventing the spread of slavery while also addressing the slave South's interest in preserving its "peculiar institution." Senator Crittenden's compromise included constitutional amendments that would have secured slavery "forever" where it already existed. His proposal included restoration of the Missouri Compromise of 1820, which had been voided in the Dred Scott ruling. In the end, Crittenden's constitutional amendments and legislative proposals were supported in the South but were rejected by Lincoln and the Republican Party. In all likelihood, the decision to oppose the Crittenden Compromise probably reflected the loss of the last best hope of avoiding war.

Lincoln had advocated what the Republican core constituency wanted when, in 1858, he emphatically argued in the "House Divided" speech, "I believe this government cannot endure, permanently half *slave* and half *free*." And he again supported his core voters in 1860 even though doing so came at the expense of the Union. His actions throughout the lame duck period, and after he was inaugurated, supported and reinforced Stephen Douglas's interpretation in 1858 of Lincoln's intentions: "Lincoln advocates boldly and clearly a war of sections, a war of the North against the South, of the free States against the slave States, a war of extermination to be continued relentlessly until the one or the other shall be subdued, and all the States shall either become free or become slave."[44]

With the introduction of the Crittenden Compromise, it was clear as day that the South was prepared to give up on its Dred Scott gains and live within the federal bargain modified, as it had once been, by the Missouri Compromise. Loyalty to Lincoln's electoral constituency, however, trumped his commitment to preserve the Union and did so in a way that belies the claim that he just did not see dissolution coming. Rather, a nation all free was his goal and that goal was anathema to the South. Just as Washington needed to rid himself of the British and the Indians, Lincoln needed either the unlikely acquiescence of the South or, more likely, to rid himself of the South so that he could go about the business of forging a nation that was all free. That meant, as Douglas had stated, war and, if victorious, that war meant Lincoln could both change the nation and vanquish the South. He stated as much in the "House Divided" speech, clear enough in meaning for anyone who chose to listen: "We shall not fail—if we stand firm, we shall not fail. *Wise councils* may *accelerate* or *mistakes delay* it, but, sooner or later the victory is sure to come."[45] And, with many of his own mistakes delaying it, Lincoln proved right, victory did come.

Okay, so we have seen that the South was divided on the question of secession, and that Lincoln and his Republican Party were emphatic that they would not accept a compromise that meant the preservation of slavery. With that, some may conclude that the Civil War was inevitable. But was it? Secession was a hugely unnecessary step that reflected poor political judgment by southern leaders both about the likely response and the likely consequences of their actions. For starters, let us ask why in the world did the Civil War happen? Certainly there was not a united view in either the South or the North that secession should be allowed or should be prevented. Prominent journalists of the day, such as Horace Greeley and Wendell Phillips, shared the perspective

Lincoln had articulated back in 1848 that it was a revolutionary right "upon the principles of 1776, to decide the question of a separate government for themselves."[46] In that view, the South's secession would have been accepted quietly (with a mix of undoubted regret and relief) and no war would have happened. Still others in the North called for accepting the South's terms, but as we have seen that was completely out of the question. Lincoln understood his election as a mandate to pursue the policies on which he had run, and those did not include giving in to whatever southern politicians wanted.

The answer to why the war happened, it seems, lies more in the personal quest for power by a number of competing politicians than in necessity, a point to which we will return in the "What If?" section of this chapter. To see why this is so, let's do a tiny bit of "what if" reasoning now, starting with Abraham Lincoln. As central a figure as he was, still the bulk of the responsibility for the war lies, we believe, in the bad choices by a handful of ambitious southern politicians, such as Jefferson Davis and John Breckinridge, and even more so because of the ambition of the most extreme proslavery politicians, such as Robert Barnswell Rhett, William Loundes Yancey, Christopher Memminger, and Francis Wilkinson Pickens; and we will, therefore, assess them, too. That assessment will not be kind or forgiving.

As we have noted, such prominent leading lights of the South as Vice President John Breckinridge and Senator Jefferson Davis opposed secession. These were men whose commitment to the South and to slavery was beyond question. Indeed, Breckinridge, who returned to the Senate following the end of President Buchanan's term, remains the only member of that body to be declared a traitor (on December 6, 1861) for his decision to join the Confederate army. For his part, Davis thought secession such an error that his wife reported that upon learning he had been selected as president of the Confederate States of America (CSA), "He looked so grieved that I feared some evil had befallen our family. After a few minutes he told me like a man might speak of a sentence of death."[47] Still, of course, he did not turn down the invitation to lead the Confederacy, nor did he shy away from exploiting the opportunity it gave him to be a powerful and fulfilled politician. Having accepted the august office, and faced with secession as a fait accompli, Davis looked for a way to avoid war by offering to purchase any of the federal government's property in the South, such as Fort Sumter. He also proposed that the CSA would assume the South's share of the existing national debt. Lincoln, however, refused even to meet the delegation that Davis sent to Washington to offer terms.[48] True to his conviction that the nation—including the South—would be all slave or all free, Lincoln would not entertain any compromise that meant preserving slavery in the South, whether outside the Union through secession (as suggested by Davis's commissioners) or inside (as proposed by the Crittenden Compromise).

How could such powerful and highly respected southern political leaders lose the battle to prevent the secession they so deeply opposed? The short answer is that a group of southern newspapermen and politicians collectively known as fire-eaters, many from South Carolina, the first state to secede, maneuvered their compatriots into secession. A few of the key figures included Robert Barnswell Rhett, who long served in the House of Representatives and the Senate (from South Carolina); William Loundes Yancey, who served in the House (from Alabama) but for one term, like Lincoln; and Christopher Memminger who never rose beyond state-level politics in South Carolina (although he did become secretary of the treasury in the Confederate States of America). All adamantly opposed what they saw as northern efforts to destroy southern political influence. They were hostile to northern, Republican tariff policy and, of course, to antislavery policies. Just how extreme their views were is well illustrated by public declarations by William Yancey. He argued, contrary to the original restrictions in the Constitution: "If slavery is right per se, if it is right to raise slaves for sale, does it not appear that it is right to import them? . . . Let us then wipe from our statute book this mark of Cain which our enemies have placed there. . . . We want negroes [sic] cheap, and we want a sufficiency of them, so as to supply the cotton demand of the whole world."[49] These extremists wanted secession and they were willing to risk the dangers of war, rather than succumb to the immovable Lincoln or remain in what they perceived as an antislavery union.

Behind the efforts of Rhett, Memminger, and South Carolina governor Francis Wilkinson Pickens, the South Carolina assembly voted for secession on December 20, 1860, with other southern states following shortly after, especially following the Union defense of Fort Sumter. And so, the extremist fire-eaters in the South and the "extremist" Republicans in the North prevailed, each true to their core constituencies, and they brought the country to dissolution and war. But what if the cooler, antisecession heads of Davis and Breckinridge had succeeded?

Consider what would in all likelihood have happened had the antisecession southern leadership prevailed on their hot-headed extremist factions to bide their time and wait for the next presidential election. They, of course, would have reminded the hotheads that Lincoln had barely squeaked out a victory and that he did so because the southern interests had failed adequately to coordinate their efforts. Divided three ways, between Breckinridge, Bell, and Douglas, the door had been opened for the "extremist" Republicans to win, a mistake they would not make again in 1864. If Breckinridge (who carried the South in the election), together with Senator Davis, had persuaded their fellow proslavery, antitariff, states' rights advocates to band together to block Lincoln's agenda in the House of Representatives and the Senate rather than seceding, what would have happened?

Lincoln would have faced a Senate consisting of 33 states, 11 of which in actuality joined the Confederacy plus 2 others that were recognized by the Confederacy although they did not actually secede. To pass an amendment to the Constitution that would make the country all free—as he did—Lincoln would have needed two thirds of the House and two thirds of the Senate to vote for the amendment. Even when the Thirteenth Amendment passed the Senate (with the Confederate States, of course, not represented and therefore having no vote) on the eighth of April 1864, still 6 senators voted against it. Had the 11 states that made up the Confederate States of America not seceded, Lincoln would have faced a Senate consisting of 66 members. It is a safe bet that all the senators from the secessionist states would have voted against the amendment. Add to that the 6 who voted against in 1864 and Lincoln would have faced a seemingly insurmountable problem: 28 out of 66 members of the Senate would have voted nay; thus, he would only have had about 58 percent on his side. The amendment would have failed.

Let us bend over backward in Lincoln's favor. Imagine by some clever maneuvering, which, after all, we know Lincoln, the smoke-filled-room politician, was good at, he somehow persuaded the six who we know voted against the amendment in 1864 to instead vote for it sometime during his first term without the backdrop of the war. As unlikely as that is, still he would not be home free. The Constitution requires that an amendment approved by two thirds of each house of Congress must then be ratified by three fourths of the states. As part of the terms of readmission to the Union following the Civil War, southern states were compelled to agree to the amendment, but of course, that lever would not have been available to Lincoln had the South not seceded in the first place. With 33 states he would have needed 25 to ratify, but none of the 11 Confederate states can have been expected to do so. Even if every remaining state had voted in favor—itself rather unlikely—Lincoln would have fallen well short of the three fourths needed to amend the constitution. So, at the end of his first term, what would he have had to point to as his successes?

It is likely, as the highly successful railroad lawyer that he was, that Lincoln would have nudged the states into agreeing to build the Transcontinental Railroad. He would have boasted that, contrary to the expectations of so many, he had in fact successfully kept the country together despite the deep divisions of the 1860 election. Besides boosting the economy through railroad construction, he would during his 1864 reelection campaign (if he got the Republican nomination) have pointed to the national banking system he put into place as well as significant protective tariffs. Of course, these policies would have played well with many northern industrial interests and some northwestern interests, but they would have been—as they had been—anathema to the southern states. And then, being a pragmatic "extremist," he probably would have adopted a more moderate approach to the slavery question, thereby alienating many in the Republican Party who felt the urgency of eliminating slavery more keenly than Lincoln might have appeared to.

Remember, while we think of Lincoln as an abolitionist, that is not how many abolitionists viewed him and, more critically, even if he was an abolitionist, that says nothing about his views on the equality of the races. He, like Senator Lyman Trumbull, who helped author the Thirteenth Amendment, opposed the spread of slavery. Neither, however, supported the recognition of black people as equal to whites in daily life (as distinct from the hypothetical view expressed in the Declaration). We need to remember that prior to Dred Scott, Lincoln's personal dislike of slavery notwithstanding, he remained largely silent on the issue. Furthermore, early in his political career Lincoln had attacked then presidential candidate Martin Van Buren for having supported giving the right to vote to free blacks in New York. During his pursuit of the Senate seat in Illinois, he refused to sign H. Ford Douglas's petition to grant free African Americans the right in Illinois to be witnesses at trials. His views may have evolved over time but practical politics appear to have dominated any personal beliefs.

Consider the following from Frederick Douglass's pen in 1860, after Lincoln was elected but before he was inaugurated as president:

"Mr. Lincoln . . . while admitting the right to hold men as slaves in the States already existing, regards such property as peculiar, exceptional, local, generally an evil, and not to be extended beyond the limits of the States where it is established by what is called positive law. Whoever live through the next four years will see Mr. Lincoln and his Administration attacked more bitterly for their pro-slavery truckling, than for doing any anti-slavery work."[50] Douglass's views only became more positive toward Lincoln with the Emancipation Proclamation in 1863, a proclamation that surely would not have happened without the Civil War and which, in fact, freed no slave within a state controlled by the Union.

By the time of the 1864 election, Lincoln's prophecy in the "House Divided" speech would surely have come back to bite him. Without the votes to pass an amendment, and given his cogent legal arguments in that speech, it is likely that if, as he predicted, the country was going all one way or the other, the way in which it would have been going in 1864 was all slave. Without the war and having failed to eliminate slavery, Lincoln would probably have had a tough time winning renomination, and even if he did, he would almost certainly have lost the general election. Without the war he would just be one of a long line of nineteenth-century presidents who did not accomplish much and, most important, failed to get reelected. Then, he would just be one of the many presidents on whose watch few Americans died in combat, greater prosperity probably would have followed, and we would barely remember him.

Reflections on Lincoln

WHAT IN PARTICULAR MAKES US THINK OF LINCOLN AS A GREAT president and how might we have ended up thinking otherwise? One arrow in his historical quiver is the simple fact that he was the first president to be reelected since Andrew Jackson in 1832. His reelection is all the more noteworthy when we recall that before the fall of Atlanta on September 2, 1864, just a few weeks before the election, Lincoln as a wartime sitting president was nevertheless expected to lose to George McClellan. His reelection, of course, is an important part of Lincoln's legacy, but it is more indicative of his political success than being the cause of the reverence in which he is remembered. The same might be said of the fact that he did, of course, give fantastic speeches from which many still quote today. And who could fail to admire his terrific, self-deprecating sense of humor. What is more, his status in our collective memory surely rose following his assassination so shortly after his second inauguration and victory in the Civil War. All these elements have helped make him memorable, but his ultimate standing as the greatest president rests most firmly on the fact that he successfully passed the Thirteenth Amendment, thereby ending slavery. This consummate achievement followed a victorious war that killed more Americans than any war in history. That, of course, is far from laudable in itself. Still, weighing everything together, we ask, was Lincoln great? And we conclude, yes, we think so.

If judged by his noblest acts, he was quite remarkable. He did, after all, stake out what were for the time courageous views on African Americans. He argued vigorously that the ideas in the Declaration of Independence—that all men are created equal—applied to all men, black or white, a view that was exceedingly unpopular in his time. He understood when to be silent on an issue (a campaign strategy he used to great effect) and when to be clear about his intentions. He was slow to find an effective leader for the Union Army, but he persisted and carried the war to victory, even though logic and evidence suggest he should have won the war much more quickly, and he mapped out a noble—and sadly unimplemented—plan for the reunification and reconstruction of the country.

If judged by his less noble acts, then his limitations loom large and draw our attention to the very concerns that James Madison expressed about the dangers of presidents at war. His personal ambition (and the dirty tricks he used to advance it), when combined with shortsighted choices by a handful of southern leaders, ensured war (and with it, the end of slavery). Did the ends justify the means? Certainly for those held in bondage, the answer must be yes. For those who were committed to ending slavery, as much of the Western world was, the answer is probably yes. For those millions of Americans whose families suffered personal, devastating losses during the Civil War the answer may be more questionable. The United States, after all, lost a substantial portion of its future. With 1,087,000 northerners and southerners killed, wounded, or missing, out of a prewar population of 31 million, America suffered indescribable grief and vast economic losses that surely lingered for decades after the war's four years. That was a price Lincoln was prepared to risk to become president; it was a price the fire-eaters and such men as Jefferson Davis were prepared to pay to try to preserve their dying and oppressive way of life.

Whether slavery would have persisted long without the war is a hotly debated subject. Lincoln seemed to fear that it would. Against that, the influx of cheap labor from Ireland and elsewhere might have produced insurmountable pressure against slavery over the following two decades. In addition to economic pressure, we must remember that slavery had already been eliminated in Europe, Latin America, and much of Asia. The United States was not a leader in the movement to eradicate the scourge of slavery; it was Johnny-come-lately. How great a leader Lincoln was must ultimately rest on the benefits gained and the costs endured under his presidency. History has decided on his side.

What If?

A S WE HAVE SEEN, ABRAHAM LINCOLN WAS UNWILLING TO COM-
promise with secessionist leaders. As we have also seen, the secessionists made a grave mistake in leaving the Union, given their interests. Had they remained in the Union, he would not have been able to amend the constitution to outlaw slavery. Now we must ask, given that they did secede, why didn't Lincoln just let them go? Had he simply said good riddance to the Confederate states, he would have had a Congress through which, in time, he could have amended the Constitution. Then, the remaining states would have ratified the amendment, as in fact they did. The difference would have been that there would not have been more than a million killed and wounded. Of course, the other difference would have been that the slave institutions would have persisted in the eleven states that formed the Confederacy, at least for a time. The tragedy—admittedly with hindsight—of Lincoln's decision to fight rather than accept secession, which he earlier had called a "most sacred right," is that by fighting he and his successors failed as a practical matter to reunite the country.

What do we mean when we say that the country was not reunited? The facts seem to contradict that claim. The North won the war and the Confederate states rejoined the nation in short order. That is true, but it is also true that America's electoral picture was fundamentally changed by Lincoln's election. To see that letting the South go might have been the better alternative, let us consider the changed American electoral picture.

We already know that the southern states voted as a bloc against the Republican presidential candidates Frémont and Lincoln in 1856 and 1860. If we look at the presidential elections from 1860—Lincoln's first—through the end of Herbert Hoover's term seventy-three years later, we see that there really were two countries, not one. Of the eighteen presidential elections from Lincoln through Hoover, the Republican candidate won fourteen times. Only Democrats Grover Cleveland (twice) and Woodrow Wilson (twice) won the presidency, and Wilson's first election was largely due to Theodore Roosevelt's third-party candidacy that divided the Republican vote. If there were one united country, then we might reasonably expect that the South would have looked pretty much like the North in its voting pattern. Yet we see that of the fourteen times a Republican won the presidency, the South voted as a bloc for the Democratic Party candidate eleven times, and split three times across the southern states (1868 and 1872—the two Grant elections—being elections in which southern politics was captured by Reconstruction and carpetbaggers, and 1928). The southern states were uniformly on the winning side only when Cleveland or Wilson was the victor. We would see a similar picture if we looked at elections to the House or Senate.

Lincoln's victory did not give America a united nation. Rather, it replaced slavery with the only somewhat lesser evil of Jim Crow segregation in the South and persistent regional tension, largely over civil rights, for more than a century. How long slavery would have persisted in an independent Confederate States of America, no one can say. Surely it would have persisted beyond 1865. Against this, if the United States declined to purchase southern goods, the plantation cotton industry would have been—as it was during the Civil War—under great pressure, as European demand was probably not sufficient to sustain the CSA's economy. Perhaps then, some of the CSA states, especially where the secession vote was deeply divided, would have sought voluntarily to rejoin the United States. That might have led to a less sectionalized nation and would have avoided the devastation of the Civil War at the price of some—possibly not very long—delay in the collapse of slavery.

Chapter 4

Roosevelt's Vanity: Avoiding War for Domestic Gain

Make a beginning by putting some good Negro bands aboard battleships.

—Franklin Roosevelt

FRANKLIN ROOSEVELT'S FOUR ELECTIONS AS PRESIDENT GAVE THE PEOPLE of the United States two remarkably distinct Franklin Roosevelts. One, the Roosevelt of 1933, became president during the most challenging economic times in US history. That Roosevelt was a visionary leader who showed himself willing to lead mainstream American thinking to a new understanding of human nature. He asked people to abandon their materialism in favor of what he deemed deeper moral values. Implicitly comparing himself to Jesus, he proclaimed in his first inaugural address, "The money changers have fled from their high seats in the temple of our civilization. We may now restore that temple to the ancient truths. The measure of the restoration lies in the extent to which we apply social values more noble than mere monetary profit."[1] Memorably, he awakened the depressed American people to the realization that "the only thing we have to fear is fear itself."

The messianic, visionary Roosevelt resurrected these same themes in his second inaugural address, inspirationally assuring the American people that the democratic process had brought them to an era of good feeling, noting, "We are beginning to wipe out the line that divides the practical from the ideal; and in so doing we are fashioning an instrument of unimagined power for the establishment of a morally better world."[2] Wow, who could fail to listen to such a leader! Love him—as most did—or hate him—as some did—there was no doubt that he was a force of nature and that, because the country followed his lead, nothing would ever be the same again.

The second Franklin Roosevelt, seemingly born as the German army marched into Poland in September 1939, was elected to a third (and then a fourth) term as a worldwide crisis challenged the very survival of democracy. It was an even more profound and far-reaching threat than the economic collapse of the Great Depression. By his third inauguration in January 1941, the inspirational first Roosevelt seems to have utterly disappeared. Whereas bold new ideas, captured in unforgettable phrases about fear and good feeling had characterized his first two inaugural messages, his third was a flatter speech, neither inspirational in its message nor memorable in its phrasing. In the campaigns of 1932 and 1936 he declared that he would lead the way to a morally better country, a country of people dedicated to doing good rather than merely enriching themselves. In 1940, however, his commitment was to follow rather than to lead; there was no promise of bringing the United States to a better place. Rather, he looked back in US history, back to Lincoln, back to Washington, for inspiration, barely looking ahead or envisioning a better future. The core of the speech can be summarized by the president's decision to borrow from George Washington's first inaugural address. As FDR said, "The destiny of America was proclaimed in words of prophecy spoken by our first President in his first inaugural in 1789—words almost directed, it would seem, to this year of 1941: 'The preservation of the sacred fire of liberty and the destiny of the republican model of government are justly considered . . . deeply, . . . finally, staked on the experiment intrusted to the hands of the American people.'"[3]

The second Roosevelt proved true to his words, entrusting America's destiny to American public opinion. This new Roosevelt was a cautious disciple of the polls; a follower of the mainstream voter; a dangerously slow, reluctant foreign policy plodder rather than the innovator of his first incarnation. At a time when the nation—and the world—needed, as it had in 1932, a leader with courage to shape opinion, it got, instead, a president shaped by opinion. Both Franklin Roosevelts, like so many political leaders, were vain men. The difference was that the first believed deeply in his ability to make others see the world as he saw it. The second apparently believed that the nation needed him at the helm in times of crisis even if he no longer had a clear vision and message about what needed to be done. Geoffrey C. Ward's explanation for the origins of Roosevelt's vanity traced his self-image back to his childhood: "FDR was supremely confident. . . . His mother taught him that he was the center of the universe and that he was the sun around which everything revolved. He never lost that attitude."[4] Maybe that is right; maybe not. Whatever the source, the strength of his vain self-confidence seems beyond question. The crucial difference between the Roosevelt of 1932 and of 1940 was that the vanity of the first was bolstered by illuminating ideas; the vanity of the second failed to define the nation's destiny in the maelstrom of war in Europe and Asia, leaving the world and America the worse for it.

The second FDR was so devoted to his own electoral ambition that he sacrificed his great opportunity to persuade the American people of the importance of a swift and decisive war against tyranny. He seems to have held back solely in the interest of his reelection. An early, decisive war was not the war that the third-term candidate Roosevelt was prepared to fight. He may have wished to do so, appears to have believed it was the "right" thing to do, and certainly seems to have understood the global importance of standing up against tyranny. However, whatever his personal sentiments may have been, they were trumped by the simple fact that the American voter was not persuaded of any of these beliefs. The first Franklin Roosevelt would have convinced the American people of his vision; the second Roosevelt was content to win election even at the risk of losing democracy and freedom. Our concern here is squarely focused on this second Roosevelt, a man utterly unlike his earlier self—a wartime president who feared the voter more than he feared the enemy and hesitated to promote the efficient advancement of US and global security. His caution, we believe, came at a heavy price: millions of human lives.

The First Roosevelt: 1932-1940

BEFORE CONSIDERING OUR MAIN THEME—FDR's VANITY AND URGE FOR power at the expense of decisive leadership—we pause to set the stage by recalling the Roosevelt who led from 1933 until the 1940 election. That Roosevelt came to office with the Depression in full swing. His hands were certainly full. He was confronted with no less than having to find a way to utterly reconstruct the American economy, the national standard of living, and the American way of life. He faced an uphill battle and he knew it. One of the great strengths he brought to his new job was his indomitable commitment to find a way through the morass and rescue the American people. Roosevelt certainly understood that he was not an economist; he was not a successful entrepreneur; he was not the common working man—the forgotten man—or a home-maker wondering where the children's next meal would come from; he was not a philosopher; and he was not a magician. He was a politician with the practical bent of a success-oriented competitor for high office. He had no illusion that he knew the solution to the country's economic woes. Nor did he have any illusion that economists or anyone else had squarely worked out the logic of macroeconomics and, therefore, knew how to fix the terribly broken economy.

What he knew or, at least, what he believed he knew, was that a solution waited to be discovered and, further, that he knew the means to discover it. As he said in his speech at Oglethorpe University in May 1932, "The country needs and, unless I mistake its temper, the country demands bold, persistent experimentation. It is common sense to take a method and try it: If it fails, admit it frankly and try another. But above all, try something."[5] And try something, and then something else, is just what he did. He had no roadmap to lead the way to economic recovery, but neither did he fear to go down untrodden paths, bringing the people along with him. He knew no fear. He did not retreat from his vision when others accused him of socialism or dictatorship. Rather, he pressed forward boldly, looking for a way to make true his declaration that "the only thing we have to fear is fear itself."

Roosevelt inspirationally argued that it was prudent to roll the dice, run social experiments, and see what might salvage the people of the United States. He earned enormous popularity—and not a little hostility—for his frank willingness to gamble on new solutions. His New Deal inspired many by the boldness of its vision and its contents.

Departing from the laissez-faire economics that had been the engine of investment, entrepreneurship, and enormous economic growth in America's first century and a half, Roosevelt recast the country's predominant economic philosophy as a philosophy that had produced great inequalities in opportunity and in outcomes. In redirecting economic thought and redefining social goals, Roosevelt made himself into the beloved champion of the ordinary, forgotten American rather than the extraordinary American. He gave the United States a social safety net, a much bigger government than it had ever had, higher taxes, entitlements, and a sense of a more equitable distribution of chances to realize the American dream. Although it took a world war to rescue the US economy, it was Roosevelt's bold experimental approach that persuaded people to get to work making the recovery last. He led with ideas, correctly confident that the average American would follow him where he wanted to go.

How important the Second World War was to the reestablishment of economic growth and hope has been the subject of vast amounts of debate over the causes and solutions to the Great Depression. These accounts, regardless of their perspective on whether Roosevelt deserves great credit for alleviating the effects of the Depression or whether he is to be faulted for slowing progress to recovery, are not our concern. In this chapter we want to understand how Franklin Roosevelt, the mythological, heroic leader through the long, dark years of World War II, made the war longer, more dangerous, and costlier than it needed to be. We contend that he did so to advance his personal vanity, presenting himself to the American people as their *indispensable* leader in times of crisis. Our critique of Roosevelt, despite being backed by substantial evidence, is in an important regard surprising even to us. His prewar procrastination, dithering, and dissimulation all served his electoral ambitions but, we believe (with the benefit of hindsight), not nearly as well as they might have been served had he made bolder decisions to enter the war in Europe along with Britain, France, and numerous Commonwealth nations, joining before Germany was given the time to create a massive calamity. The inventive Franklin Roosevelt of 1933 was much better suited to the challenges faced in 1939–1945 than the Johnny-Come-Lately Roosevelt who refused to lead.

Consider Figure 4.1, which compares the US and British gross domestic products (GDP) to each other from 1929 (that is, the beginning of the Depression) through 1945, marking the end of the Second World

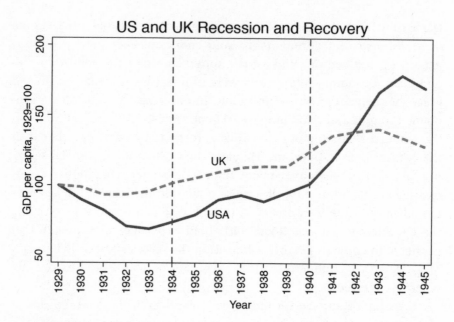

Figure 4.1. Economic Recovery and the War
Source: https://www.ushmm.org/wlc/en/media_nm.php?ModuleId=10005453&MediaId=2063

War.[6] Here we can begin to see a bit about the difference between the Roosevelt elected in 1932 and 1936 and the Roosevelt reelected again in 1940 (and 1944).

The two economies are "normalized" in the graph so that each begins with a base value of 100 in 1929. Britain, without the New Deal programs but with a continuing ability to engage in international trade, declines economically only slightly in the first few years of the worldwide Depression, returning to its 1929 baseline gross domestic product by about 1933, coincidentally the year Roosevelt became president. Herbert Hoover's approach to the severe economic contraction, in contrast, seems utterly to have failed. With trade snuffed out by the Smoot-Hawley tariffs, the US economy, unlike Britain's, had lost its global reach. As the graph shows, the US GDP was only a little better than half of what it had been in 1929 by the time Roosevelt took the oath of office (denoted by the left-hand vertical dotted line).

Having hit its bottom, the economy began to recover slowly following Roosevelt's inauguration. For those who thought Roosevelt's policies were wrong-headed, the New Deal ideas were the road to disaster, slowing rather than hastening economic recovery. Wendell Willkie, the Republican nominee for president in 1940—and himself a former backer of FDR's—decried the New Deal in the speech in which he accepted his party's presidential nomination in August 1940. His critique encapsulates the general critique of the minority who opposed Roosevelt at the time. As Willkie said,

> For the first time in our history, American industry has remained stationary for a decade. It offers no more jobs today than it did ten years ago—and there are 6,000,000 more persons seeking jobs. As a nation of producers we have become stagnant. Much of our industrial machinery is obsolete. And the national standard of living has declined. It is a statement of fact, and no longer a political accusation, that the New Deal has failed in its program of economic rehabilitation. . . . To accomplish these results, the present administration has spent sixty billion dollars. And I say there must be something wrong with a theory of government or a theory of economics, by which, after the expenditure of such a fantastic sum, we have less opportunity than we had before.[7]

The same data that Willkie saw as all negative can, of course, also be interpreted as showing the success of the New Deal. Returning to Figure 4.1, we see that the GDP was rising after FDR took office, lending support to those who point to Roosevelt's vision as having revived the economy. Growth had resumed under the New Deal, but despite his many economic and social experiments, the US economy did not grow enough to return to its pre-Depression baseline level until the end of 1940 or the beginning of 1941. That was when, after most of continental Europe had fallen to the Nazis, Roosevelt finally initiated the wartime economic stimulus of the Lend-Lease Act (in March 1941) that opened American factories to massive arms production. We will, of course, have more to say about that. For now, it is useful to consider what might have happened had he geared up to defend Europe earlier. Had he launched the arsenal for democracy in, say, 1939, after the German invasion of Poland, or even earlier, say, after Germany's remilitarization of the Rhineland in 1936 overthrew key principles of the Versailles Treaty, instead of in late December 1940, war production might have proven the great job creator that it later became. With this surge in US ordnance, Hitler's threat to the world might have been nipped in the bud, to the benefit of millions who suffered under Nazi occupation and rule. Once Roosevelt finally got around to arming what was left of those fighting Nazi Germany in Europe, the US economy really took off. We see this quite clearly by looking at the graph to the right of the second vertical dotted line. Thus, Figure 4.1 suggests, with hindsight, what the right economic, as well as military, strategy was, given the situation in the world.

What Figure 4.1 does not show is whether the right economic strategy would have been the right reelection strategy for the Franklin Roosevelt who pursued—and won—a third term. That, we contend, was Roosevelt's dominant consideration and it was one that did not encourage a bold experiment in the defense of freedom. Had he defanged Hitler in late 1939, he might have had good reason to worry that he wouldn't be reelected (as we will show). Could he have used his success against Hitler to reshape public opinion in his favor? We cannot know the answer, but the persuasive record of the first FDR and the great popularity he took into 1940 suggest his caution on these points was misplaced and most unfortunate. True, public opinion was set against entering the war in Europe, but equally true, the president was doing almost nothing to alter that perspective. He had led the nation to the promised land of the New Deal; he did no such thing when faced with the destruction of freedom.

Waiting for War

OUR ACCOUNT BEGINS IN 1940 WHEN PRESIDENT ROOSEVELT DECIDED to pursue a third term. Although he was the only US president to succeed in that undertaking, there was plenty of precedent for the effort. Grant had sought his party's nomination for a third term, as had Cleveland and Roosevelt's distant cousin Theodore Roosevelt. What is remarkable about FDR's decision is the extent to which the justification he offered for a third term deviated from his actual course of action. To understand Roosevelt's decision and its significance for our understanding of this American president's approach to war we need to set the global stage.

Today we think of the Second World War as having begun with the German invasion of Poland on September 1, 1939, but many people at the time saw the invasion of Poland as the beginning of a limited German-Polish war. Even Hitler doubted that the British and French were serious about defending Poland, despite their having declared war against Germany. Albert Speer, Hitler's minister of armaments and war production, reports that "Hitler . . . quickly reassured himself . . . that England and France had obviously declared war merely as a sham, in order not to lose face before the whole world. He was convinced of that."[8] Still, the larger danger was not lost on anyone paying attention anywhere. While the *New York Times* headline for the day reported in bold print "German Army Attacks Poland," in a separate, high-profile article it noted that the British navy was being mobilized to its full strength. Hitler may have doubted Britain's sincerity, but the British government undertook serious, costly actions to indicate that it intended to respond to the changed course of European affairs.

The threat that Hitler's Germany represented had already long been the subject of discussion and negotiation starting at least when the German army marched into the Rhineland, essentially throwing away the Versailles Treaty's restrictions on the use of German military force. By 1938 the danger that Hitler represented in Europe was evident to anyone paying the slightest attention. British prime minister Neville Chamberlain, having had a face-to-face summit with Hitler in Munich, received a hero's welcome on his return, announcing,"My good friends, for the second time in our history, a British Prime Minister has returned from Germany bringing peace with honour. I believe it is peace for our time. We thank you from the bottom of our hearts. Go home and get a nice quiet sleep."[9] Sleep might have been quiet on that night, but it was not to be quiet in Britain for many long, painful years to come.

Of course, now we know that it was not peace for our time, but one can forgive the optimistic mood on Chamberlain's return. Allied forces' having concluded "the war to end all wars" less than twenty years earlier, the hope for peace was surely remarkably strong. Back in the United States, geographically remote from the drama in Europe, it is easy to understand that the focus of attention was squarely on rebuilding the economy, with relatively scant attention to or fear of another great war on the horizon. Little had changed since the redesign of the continent at the end of the First World War. The American people certainly might be forgiven for not contemplating the great danger that was to befall Europe and the world a short time later. But Roosevelt did contemplate that danger and he conveyed his concern—and his tragically cautious approach—to the American public in a fireside chat on September 3, 1939, a speech that could have paved the way for restoring world peace but didn't.

The president's radio address to the nation started out in a manner that could easily have been turned toward the importance of American participation against the evil spreading in the world. As FDR said,

> Until four-thirty this morning I had hoped against hope that some miracle would prevent a devastating war in Europe and bring to an end the invasion of Poland by Germany. . . . And it seems to me clear, even at the outbreak of this great war, that the influence of America should be consistent in seeking for humanity a final peace which will eliminate, as far as it is possible to do so, the continued use of force between nations. . . . You must master at the outset a simple but unalterable fact in modern foreign relations between nations. When peace has been broken anywhere, the peace of all countries everywhere is in danger.

With these words, constituting the first half of his fireside chat, the president seemed to be laying the foundation for an active US role to restore world peace and stop German aggression by highlighting to the American people that "when peace has been broken anywhere, the peace of all countries is in danger." But then the conservative, public opinion–minded FDR took command of the microphone. He goes on to the climax of his speech, "Let no man or woman thoughtlessly or falsely talk of America sending its armies to European fields. At this moment there is being prepared a proclamation of American neutrality. *This would have been done even if there had been no neutrality statute on the books, for this proclamation is in accordance with international law* [emphasis added] and in accordance with American policy. . . . As long as it remains within my power to prevent, there will be no blackout of peace in the United States."[10]

If, as is generally taken to be true, FDR personally desired to enter the war in defense of Britain and of other democratic nations, here was the golden opportunity to turn American opinion in that direction. He chose not to do so, electing to echo the public's reticence to become involved instead of building on his introduction of the danger faced by the United States, to convince the nation that there was no way to stop the threat of tyranny while sitting on the sidelines. We will return in particular to the italicized part of this speech when we turn shortly to the president's declaration of neutrality two days later.

In June 1940, one month before Franklin Roosevelt accepted the Democratic Party's nomination for a third term as president and nine months after he reassured the American people that there was no prospect of American soldiers in European fields, all of continental Western Europe, other than neutral Sweden and Switzerland, both continuing to trade with Germany, and profascist Portugal and Spain, was now controlled either by Hitler's Germany or by Mussolini's Italy. This could not have been a more alarming change to anyone who cared to see liberty preserved in the world. Neither Hitler nor Mussolini was shy about their ambitions and neither had a reputation as a man who kept his word.

By now, anyone reflecting on Hitler's claims back in 1938 could not have been more convinced of Hitler's utter falsity. Franklin Roosevelt, even from the safe remove of Washington, DC, could not have misunderstood the stark contrast between what was happening in Europe and what Adolf Hitler had declared in Berlin in 1938: "I extended a hand to England. I renounced voluntarily ever again joining any naval conference so as to give the British Empire a feeling of security, not because I could not build more—and there should be no illusion about that—but exclusively for this reason: to safeguard permanent peace between both nations. . . . I have gone further. Immediately after the Saar had been returned to the Reich by plebiscite, I told France there were no more differences between France and us. I said: Alsace-Lorraine does not exist anymore for us. . . . And we all do not want any more war with France. We want nothing of France, absolutely nothing."[11] By the early morning of May 10, 1940, when Germany began its assault on France, the Netherlands, and Belgium, Hitler's words were obviously revealed as lies. And on that day, as Winston Churchill became the new prime minister of Great Britain, Hitler's close adviser, Hermann Göring, understood "the war is really on."[12]

It was against the backdrop of calamity in Europe that Franklin Roosevelt chose to pursue a third term. Public opinion polls showed that his popularity was sufficient to defeat any of the frontrunners in the Republican Party. Unlike his predecessors who had tried to gain their party's nomination for a third term, little stood in Franklin Roosevelt's way. To be sure, some even in the Democratic Party thought a third-term was going too far, but if Roosevelt was watching the polls—as surely he was—he knew the nomination was virtually a sure thing and he knew that he had a very good chance of winning the general election.

Having quietly pursued the nomination, while giving no public indication that he sought to continue in office, he sent his wife, Eleanor, on July 18, 1940, to address the Democratic Party's nominating convention in Chicago. Her task was to press them to accept Franklin's choice of Henry Wallace for vice president. Mrs. Roosevelt addressed the extraordinary circumstances the country faced, saying, "You must know that this is the time when all good men and women give every bit of service and strength to their country that they have to give. This is the time when it is the United States that we fight for, the domestic policies that we have established as a party that we must believe in, that we must carry forward, and in the world we have a position of great responsibility. We cannot tell from day to day what may come. This is no ordinary time. No time for weighing anything except what we can do best for the country as a whole, and that responsibility rests on each and every one of us as individuals."[13] Although she refers to the great responsibility the United States has in the world, it is noteworthy that her emphasis was on the fight for "the domestic policies that we have established as a party that we must believe in, that we must carry forward." That is, her initial justification for her husband's run for a third term was not primarily the changed map of Europe, or the changes in the Pacific, but "the domestic policies . . . that we must believe in"; that is, the New Deal.

When, just a few hours later, FDR accepted the nomination via a radio address to his party's convention on June 19, the president's emphasis, unlike the First Lady's, was squarely on the threat to world peace and the necessity, for the good of the nation, for him to sacrifice his personal desire for retirement and seek a third term, giving his utmost just as every American was being called upon to do. As he said,

> During the spring of 1939, world events made it clear to all but the blind or the partisan that a great war in Europe had become not merely a possibility but a probability, and that such a war would of necessity deeply affect the future of this nation. . . . As President of the United States, it was my clear duty, with the aid of the Congress, to preserve our neutrality, to shape our program of defense, to meet rapid changes, to keep our domestic affairs adjusted to shifting

world conditions, and to sustain the policy of the Good Neighbor. It was also my obvious duty to maintain to the utmost the influence of this mighty nation in our effort to prevent the spread of war, and to sustain by all legal means those governments threatened by other governments which had rejected the principles of democracy. . . . Plans for national defense had to be expanded and adjusted to meet new forms of warfare. . . . Every day that passed called for the post-ponement of personal plans and partisan debate until the latest possi-ble moment. . . . And so, thinking solely of the national good and of the international scene, I came to the reluctant conclusion that such declaration should not be made before the national Convention. It was accordingly made to you within an hour after the permanent organization of this Convention.[14]

Hearing these words on the radio that night, or reading them in the morning newspaper, the average American voter must have believed—and rightly so—that the world was in dire circumstances, democracy itself was under siege, and that their government had now "to shape our program of defense . . . to maintain to the utmost the influence of this mighty nation . . . to sustain . . . those governments threatened by other governments which had rejected the principles of democracy." This was a stirring message from the president who, however, in the same breath, explained that the United States' defense of democracy was limited to the preservation of US neutrality, which he had formally declared on September 5, 1939—right after Britain, France, India, Aus-tralia, and New Zealand had declared war on Germany. Now, every-thing we know about FDR indicates that he did not want to be neutral, but even less did he want to risk his future reelection. Roosevelt had, for instance, tried to persuade Congress in early 1939 to repeal the Neutrality Act of 1935 and he failed. He wanted the ability to provide armaments in particular to Great Britain but was prohibited from doing so under the embargo provisions of the Neutrality Act.

With the concerns prompted by developments in Europe in mind, FDR went before Congress on September 21, 1939, and in apparent direct contradiction to the italicized portion of his fireside chat on September 3, he said, "Beginning with the foundation of our consti-tutional government in the year 1789, the American policy in respect to belligerent nations, with one notable exception, has been based on international law . . . The single exception was the policy adopted by this Nation during the Napoleonic Wars, when, seeking to avoid involvement, we acted for some years under the so-called Embargo and Non-Intercourse Acts. . . . Our next deviation by statute from sound principles of neutrality and peace through international law did not come for 130 years. It was the so-called Neutrality Act of 1935. . . . I regret that act. I regret equally that I signed that act. On July fourteenth of this year I asked the Congress in the cause of peace and in the interest of real American neutrality to take action to change that act. . . . I seek a greater consistency through the repeal of the embargo provisions and a return to international law."[15] While these remarks before Congress highlight his judgment that it was sound policy to lift the arms embargo in order to help arm Britain, we should not lose sight that in the same speech he reiterated, "The executive branch of the Government did its utmost, within our traditional policy of noninvolvement, to aid in averting the present appalling war. Having thus striven and failed, this Government must lose no time or effort to keep the Nation from being drawn into the war." As with the September 3 fireside chat, when speaking before Congress the president had a remarkable opportunity to advance his vision, to bring the "appalling war" to a rapid end by defending our natural, democratic allies; but instead he chose only to ask for the authority to sell arms and to do everything "to keep the Nation from being drawn into the war." It is hard to imagine the Franklin Roosevelt of the 1932 or 1936 election forgoing such opportunities.

Perhaps his reticence to get involved was warranted in September 1939, when one could argue, as many did, that Germany was fighting no more than a localized war against Poland. When FDR accepted his party's nomination in July, however, Germany had already conquered Norway, Denmark, France, Holland, Belgium, Luxembourg, and the Channel Islands. Democratic, continental western Europe virtually no longer existed: it was almost all under Nazi control. Still, the president did not seize the bully pulpit to launch, for instance, a presidential initiative to stop tyranny from sweeping democracy into the dustbin of history. He did not even speak directly to the enormous threat faced by Great Britain, nor did he name Hitler as the lying, tyrannical scourge he was. Whereas the prenomination Roosevelt had at least named Germany as the aggressor against Poland (as if there were any doubt), in his speech accepting his party's nomination and in his September 3 fireside chat, third-term candidate Roosevelt did not, choosing instead to be vague, referring only to "governments which had rejected the principles of democracy." FDR's subdued words stand in remarkable contrast to Wendell Willkie's nomination acceptance speech one month after FDR's. Willkie, the candidate of a mostly isolationist political party, nevertheless dared to be specific and rightfully alarmist:

> [W]e must honestly face our relation-ship with Great Britain. We must admit that the loss of the British Fleet would greatly weaken our defense. This is because the British Fleet has for years controlled the Atlantic, leaving us free to concentrate in the Pacific. If the British Fleet were lost or captured, the Atlantic might be dominated by Germany, a power hostile to our way of life, controlling in that event most of the ships and shipbuilding facilities of Europe. This would be a calamity for us. We might be exposed to attack on the Atlantic. Our defense would be weakened until we could build a navy and air force strong enough to defend both coasts. Also, our foreign trade would be profoundly affected. That trade is vital to our prosperity. But if we had to trade with a Europe dominated by the present German trade policies, we might have to change our methods to some totalitarian form. This is a prospect that any lover of democracy must view with consternation. The objective of America is in the opposite direction. We must, in the long run, rebuild a world in which we can live and move and do business in the democratic way.[16]

Willkie's fear of calamity reflected the reality of the changed map of Europe as of June 1940. FDR's call for expanding the national defense may well have had the same rhetorical purpose. Unlike Willkie, who could afford campaign hyperbole, Roosevelt was president and commander in chief. In those capacities he had to come to a sober judgment of the right course for America. Popular sentiment was for staying out of Europe's affairs. The president was responding to that sentiment even as he seemed to recognize that this was a dangerous course to follow. When confronted with choosing between the possibility of electoral setbacks if he followed an aggressive foreign policy and the threat of the loss of practically the final surviving democracy in Europe—Great Britain—he elected to gamble on the latter course.

While the president spoke of the need for an expanded national defense—and indeed the country surely did need it—the facts

showed that he had not prepared the nation for the vigorous defense it potentially needed. Expanding national defense meant more
job opportunities, enhancing economic recovery, and more national
security against the growing threat from Germany and Japan. However, he was pursuing a minimalist rearmament strategy in his alleged
commitment to expand national defense and military preparedness.
As late as September 1940, the US army was only eighteenth in the
world in size, smaller than the armies of the nation's potential adversaries Germany and Japan; smaller than its prospective allies England
and France, before the latter's fall; and even smaller than the armies
of Belgium, Holland, Portugal, Spain, and Switzerland. To be sure,
Roosevelt responded to urgings from Charles Lindbergh and William
Bullitt (US ambassador to France) to expand US air power. They had
independently noted that Germany had air superiority relative to everyone in Europe, and that the French and the British needed to rely on
American airplane production to resist the Germans.[17] The expansion
that was undertaken could be seen as proportionately large, but then
it is easy to achieve high growth when the baseline starting position
was near-zero military aircraft. Thus, in 1940, during the presidential
campaign and before his nation's entry into the war, the US military
had 3,807 airplanes compared to 19,433 in 1941 and 47,836 in 1942,
when the United States was in the war.[18]

Despite FDRs declaration on behalf of expanding America's defense
capability, the actual expansion was rather modest, given the world
situation. Consider the facts depicted in Figure 4.2. This figure shows
US military spending as a percentage of gross domestic product for the
years from 1929—the beginning of the Depression—through 1945.
Roosevelt told the Democratic Party faithful in his July 19 speech that
only the blind or the partisan could fail to recognize as of the spring
of 1939 that war was nearly inevitable and that "such a war would of
necessity deeply affect the future of this nation." Yet looking at the figure, we are hard-pressed to see evidence of a serious effort to prepare
for the defense of the nation before the United States entered the war at
the end of 1941. Indeed, defense as a portion of the national economy
slightly declined between 1936 and 1940.

The president's acceptance speech spoke of preserving democratic
governments against the attack by dictatorship; that is, by the un-
named Nazi Germany. Here again he substituted rhetoric for action,
even as the calamity in Europe pulled the noose ever tighter. While he

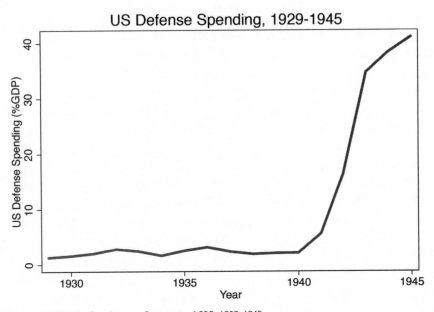

Figure 4.2. US Defense Spending as a Percentage of GDP, 1929–1945
Source: http://www.usgovernmentspending.com/defense_spending

declared that it was America's duty "to sustain by all legal means those governments threatened by other governments which had rejected the principles of democracy," at the time of the speech there was barely any surviving democracy in Europe. Britain was alone in sustaining the fight against Hitler west of the Soviet Union. Where was Roosevelt's decisive action to go with his bold words? It was not to be found.

Roosevelt was certainly not blind to what was happening—to what, in fact, had happened—in Europe. He was, however, a candidate for office and, as such, naturally partisan. Especially in the face of calamitous times, leaders are expected to lead. If their constituents have not yet understood the necessities of the moment, it is the leader's job to educate them to the threat they face. Wendell Willkie, for his own partisan purposes, tried to do just that when he accepted his party's nomination. He did not mince words. He explained why the defeat of Britain would be a calamity for the military and economic security of the United States. President Roosevelt was more reserved. It seems he chose to follow voter opinion rather than to sway that opinion. For example, consider the series of Gallup polls conducted during 1940.[19]

The Gallup survey conducted during the first week of February 1940, asked, "Do you think the United States will go into the war in

Europe, or do you think we will stay out of the war?" Of those responding, 68 percent indicated the United States would stay out, a sentiment
that the president echoed regularly. The same poll also inquired, "If
it appears that Germany is defeating England and France, should the
United States declare war on Germany and send our army and navy to
Europe to fight?" The response: 77 percent said no! The numbers are
all the more depressing when one realizes that when asked which side
they favored (March 8–13, 1940), 84 percent of respondents said they
wanted to see England and France prevail but they were not prepared
to help make that happen. Asked, "Should we declare war on Germany
and send our armed forces abroad to fight?" at the end of March and
beginning of April, 96 percent responded no!

What politician, facing such overwhelming public opinion, would
dare to reeducate the population that its view was "blind" to the facts
on the ground? Well, we know that Franklin Roosevelt was not to be
counted among any such profile in courage. The man who courageously
had led America to embrace the New Deal, which represented a radical
departure from standard economic thinking at the time, was nowhere
to be found in 1940. He was not reeducating the American people; he
was following their lead. He had not taken the opportunity presented
by Germany's invasion of Poland to redirect American thinking. At
that time, the more distant, less headline-grabbing conflict in Asia was
not foremost in American minds. In the Pacific theater, the president
imposed embargoes and took a tougher line, but that was less likely to
harm his reelection than taking bold steps to challenge Hitler.

The polls we have thus far summarized were all conducted before
France, Holland, Belgium, Norway, and Denmark had fallen under Nazi
control, leaving Britain alone to defend democracy in Europe. In a Gallup survey conducted on May 5–10, 1940, on the eve of Germany's
expansion of the war, people were asked who was winning in Europe.
Two thirds said Germany, only 8 percent thought England and France,
with 13 percent thinking the sides were even, and the rest having no
opinion. Here we can see that the overwhelming majority of respondents understood the reality on the ground in Europe, although 55
percent in the same survey still thought the Allies would ultimately
win the war, an unlikely outcome without US involvement. In the
week of May 18–23, 1940, respondents were asked, "Do you think the
United States should declare war on Germany and send our army and
navy abroad to fight?" France, Holland, and Belgium had been attacked

on May 10, one to two weeks earlier, and democracy was nearly nonexistent on continental Europe. Still, 93 percent of respondents answered no! The president was not leading opinion to the recognition of reality, although he almost certainly favored stopping Germany and backing Britain. He was, after all, actively engaged with Winston Churchill even while assiduously assuring the American public that he would keep the United States out of the war.

It seems that prior to the election, seeking to minimize his political risks, Roosevelt chose to blindly follow the blind, failing to prepare adequately for the defense of the United States or, indeed, for the preservation of freedom and democracy. Even after Adolf Hitler implicitly threatened the United States, following a pact signed among the Axis powers in September 1940, stating, "There are two worlds that stand opposed to each other. . . . Others are correct when they say: With this world we cannot ever reconcile ourselves. . . . I can beat any other power in the world," still FDR failed to use his powers of persuasion to bring American public opinion around to the inevitability and necessity of defeating the Axis.[20] Indeed, Roosevelt reported these and other statements by Hitler in his "Arsenal for Democracy" speech on December 29, 1940, two months *after* Hitler made them and nearly two months *after* the US election, marking the first time the American people heard them![21]

The hostility to participation in the war among the public was truly remarkable. In an April 1940 Gallup survey, 65 percent of Americans thought Germany would attack the United States if it succeeded in defeating France (which happened two months later) and Britain. Yet, with the country unprepared to defend itself against such an eventuality, still 79 percent reported that the president was doing a good job in dealing with the war crisis. That opinion must have been heartening to Roosevelt as he contemplated pursuit of a third term. The continuing blindness to the threat the country faced persisted even after France, Holland, and Belgium were all defeated. A poll conducted during the last few days of June and the first two days of July 1940 showed that 86 percent of Americans responded, "Stay out," when asked, "If the question of the United States going to war against Germany and Italy came up for a national vote within the next two weeks, would you vote to go into the war or to stay out of the war?" So reluctant were Americans to get involved that 62 percent opposed sending food on US ships to alleviate starvation in France, Holland, and Belgium during the winter. This response must be understood against the backdrop of Germany's intensive U-boat campaign in the Atlantic against merchant shipping. Americans were unwilling to gamble on being drawn into the merchant marine struggles even to help starving people. By September a minority believed that England would win the war. Despite that change in view and despite Willkie's explanation of how calamitous a British defeat would be, still survey respondents split almost equally between advocating fighting to save Britain or remaining on the sidelines. A month before the presidential election, 83 percent of Americans responding to the Gallup survey still said, "Stay out," when asked whether the United States should enter the war. Thus, the president, the great shaper of public opinion from 1932 to 1939, now followed public opinion, campaigning on the principle that he would keep the United States out of the war.

Finally, once the election was over, Franklin Roosevelt began to use the power of his office to educate public opinion, leading rather than following. Echoing Willkie's recognition of the disaster that would follow if Britain fell to Nazi Germany, Roosevelt finally, on December 29, 1940, in his famous "Arsenal for Democracy" speech, said,

> If Great Britain goes down, the Axis powers will control the continents of Europe, Asia, Africa, Australasia, and the high seas—and they will be in a position to bring enormous military and naval resources against this hemisphere. It is no exaggeration to say that all of us, in all the Americas, would be living at the point of a gun—a gun loaded with explosive bullets, economic as well as military. We should enter upon a new and terrible era in which the whole world, our hemisphere included, would be run by threats of brute force. To survive in such a world, we would have to convert ourselves permanently into a militaristic power on the basis of war economy. Some of us like to believe that even if Great Britain falls, we are still safe, because of the broad expanse of the Atlantic and of the Pacific. But the width of those oceans is not what it was in the days of clipper ships. At one point between Africa and Brazil the distance is less than from Washington to Denver, Colorado five hours for the latest type of bomber. And at the North end of the Pacific Ocean America and Asia almost touch each other.[22]

Yet, even after acknowledging both the evil intentions of Germany, Italy, and Japan, and the real danger they posed to the United States, still Roosevelt was unwilling to commit to defend Britain. He went on in this same speech to say, "There is no demand for sending an American Expeditionary Force outside our own borders. There is no intention by any member of your Government to send such a force. *You can, therefore, nail any talk about sending armies to Europe as deliberate untruth* [emphasis added]."[23]

Roosevelt's foray into turning public opinion around was, as we have seen, exceedingly cautious. Having finally echoed the concerns raised explicitly by Willkie during the campaign, the president also echoed the First Lady's efforts to tie the grave danger in Europe to the reconstruction of the American economy. As he said, "I would ask no one to defend a democracy which in turn would not defend everyone in the nation against want and privation. The strength of this nation shall not be diluted by the failure of the Government to protect the economic well-being of its citizens."[24] That well-being was to be promoted by building and sending arms to Britain, but there was to be no commitment of soldiers even as Roosevelt endorsed and signed the Selective Service Act, creating a "peacetime" draft. Indeed, when it came to making the strongest possible case for a war in defense of liberty, he dissembled, becoming downright disingenuous. He claimed, "The people of Europe who are defending themselves do not ask us to do their fighting. They ask us for the implements of war, the planes, the tanks, the guns, the freighters which will enable them to fight for their liberty and for our security. Emphatically we must get these weapons to them in sufficient volume and quickly enough, so that we and our children will be saved the agony and suffering of war which others have had to endure."[25]

The minimalist, cautious Roosevelt continued to insist that American children could be spared the pain of war if all the nation did was rearm Britain and, outrageously, he claimed that the British government asked no more of the United States than this. Yet, juxtaposed to this statement by the president in late December 1940, we cannot help but consider Winston Churchill's profoundly moving statement of June 1940—six months earlier. Faced with the fall of Europe and standing alone against Germany, Churchill said, "We shall fight on the beaches, we shall fight on the landing grounds, we shall fight in the fields and in the streets, we shall fight in the hills; we shall never surrender, and if, which I do not for a moment believe, this island or a large part of it were subjugated and starving, then our Empire beyond the seas, armed and guarded by the British Fleet, would carry on the struggle, until, *in*

God's good time, the New World, with all its power and might, steps forth
to the rescue and the liberation of the old [emphasis added]."²⁶ Surely
the power and might of the New World to which he referred was not
the power and might of Canada—already in the war—or of Mexico or
Brazil or Argentina; he was asking for the help from the United States
that President Roosevelt denied was being sought.

Maximalist at Home, Minimalist at War

"GOD'S GOOD TIME" CAME FINALLY TO THE UNITED STATES ON
December 7, 1941. The attack against the naval base at Pearl
Harbor did what Nazi Germany's conquest of Europe could not: it
turned American public opinion and brought the United States into the
war. Now, with the United States finally committed to the liberation
of Europe and the defeat of all of the Axis powers, one might have
thought that FDR would have fully committed the nation with "all its
power and might" to the swift and efficient defeat of the adversary. If
we are to judge by the proportion of US wealth dedicated to the war
effort, then we must judge Roosevelt a maximalist in defense of American freedom. While the German upper middle class continued to enjoy
ready access to consumer goods until late in the war, Americans more
widely faced rationing starting in 1942. As we can see in Figure 4.3,
which extends Figure 4.2 through the end of the war and to just before
the start of the cold war, once the United States was in the war, the
president devoted a huge percentage of gross domestic product to the
military: by 1944–1945 about forty cents of every dollar produced in
America was spent on national defense. Never before, and, thank goodness, never since have Americans been called upon to dedicate so much
of their labors to a war effort.

Yet, we should be careful not to overstate the financial and material
sacrifices that were demanded of US citizens in World War II. Between
1941 and 1945, the arming of America and its allies nearly doubled the
size of the US economy (Figure 4.1). The enormous growth of the economy and huge proportion of the nation's wealth dedicated to the war
effort largely offset each other. Not until the war ended and spending
declined could Americans enjoy the fruits of their labors.

The story of war spending portrays a Franklin Roosevelt who was
true to Churchill's expectation that finally, in God's good time, the

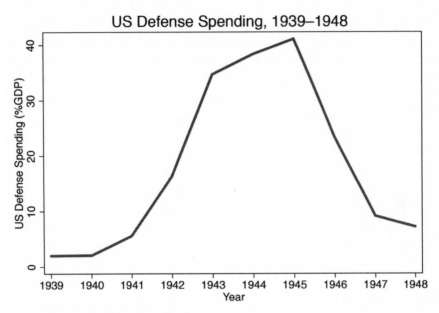

Figure 4.3. The Burden of Defense in World War II

United States would enter the war "with all its power and might." In reckoning all that power and all that might, however, Churchill surely did not count on Roosevelt's unwillingness to commit those portions of the nation's power and might that might prove politically unpopular. Yet, the cautious, minimalist, electorally hungry president showed just such an unwillingness.

Political expediency dictated FDR's slow-as-molasses approach to entering the war and, once in, it dictated his reluctance to fight with all of the nation's power and might. The first Roosevelt came to office with new ideas on how to resuscitate the American economy. He was bold in the pursuit of those ideas, perhaps because that is exactly why he had been elected in 1932 and again in 1936. To borrow a term from economics, his "comparative advantage" as a politician was in promoting new domestic policies. In doing so, he reset public opinion by creating popular programs like social security. But he seems to have lacked bold ideas about how to be a wartime president.

Foreign affairs was not his policy passion and perhaps he lacked the courage to implement the policy experimentation indicative of his first two terms. Perhaps he simply lacked the energy to do so. By this time his health was in serious decline and he would survive only four months into his fourth term.[27] In the absence of big ideas, lacking the

will to experiment and perhaps being thoroughly exhausted, he re-
verted to a more hesitating, cautious approach. Like most successful
politicians, Roosevelt was willing to risk long-term disaster (with the
long-term defined as after his watch) for America to avoid short-term
political defeat. His policies before and after entry into the war reflected
his sensitivity to what the electorate favored and what they opposed.
FDR just does not seem by 1940 and beyond to have had the big ideas
that he had in addressing the Great Depression.

In May 1939, for instance, Roosevelt turned away hundreds of Jews
who had escaped Nazi Germany on board the ship *St. Louis*. After being denied entry into Cuba in May 1939, the Jewish passengers sought
refuge in the United States. To their request, the State Department
responded that the passengers must "await their turns on the waiting
list and qualify for and obtain immigration visas before they may be
admissible into the United States."[28] As the *Holocaust Encyclopedia*
notes in explaining the decision not to admit these refugees, "President
Roosevelt could have issued an executive order to admit the *St. Louis*
refugees, but this general hostility to immigrants, the gains of isolationist Republicans in the Congressional elections of 1938, and Roosevelt's
consideration of running for an unprecedented third term as president
were among the political considerations that militated against taking
this extraordinary step in an unpopular cause."[29]

Hitler's morally despicable policies against Jews and others were
well known to Roosevelt and anyone else who was reading the daily
newspaper. Indeed, he may well have been personally sympathetic
with those oppressed by Hitler's regime. What we do know is that anti-
Semitism was an electoral reality at the time in the United States and
Roosevelt had no interest in risking his political fortunes on behalf of
oppressed foreign Jews. A public opinion poll a year after the German
anti-Jewish laws were passed still indicated that 82 percent of Americans were against the admission of large numbers of Jewish refugees.[30]
The US immigration quota for German Jews was not increased. The
Roosevelt administration followed the policy that was popular rather
than the policy that was humane.

Before the United States became a combatant in the war, Roosevelt,
the social reformer, had won over some new constituents as African
American voters (of whom there were some in the North and virtually none in the Jim Crow South, where only 3 percent of African-
Americans were registered to vote).[31] Blacks began to defect from the

Republican Party in 1936 and give their support to FDR's New Deal policies, especially after his 1935 executive order that prohibited (more in theory than in practice) racial discrimination in employment on New Deal projects. Still, after his election in 1936 and until the middle of 1941, Roosevelt had been long on sympathetic words but short on action. As William Doyle observed, Roosevelt "was torn between his sense of decency and fair play . . . and his pragmatic, political side, which feared those powerful Southern Democrats who prevented him even from supporting a federal anti-lynching campaign. By the mid-1930s, his juggling act was succeeding, as the party held together in the South while his wife spoke out for civil rights and convinced blacks moving onto voter rolls of northern cities that they had friends in the White House."[32] The conviction that African Americans had a friend in the White House began to wear thin as the 1940 campaign—in which Willkie, not Roosevelt, was the more actively pro–civil rights candidate—unfolded and as the imminence of war became more apparent.

Following pressure from civil rights leaders and the threat of a march on Washington, the president issued Executive Order 8802 on June 25, 1941. By this order, Roosevelt prohibited discrimination on account of race in the defense industry, creating real opportunities for the African American labor force to benefit from his lend-lease program. One might have looked at this action, taken after the election, and concluded that now, unfettered by electoral competition, FDR might have done everything he could to improve the efficient use of manpower as the likelihood of the US entry into the war grew. Such an expectation, however, would have been dashed by the reality of the second Roosevelt's keen sensitivity to following, rather than leading, public opinion. Yes, his third presidential election campaign was over, but there was always a congressional election looming on the near-term horizon and then, too, there was the possibility of a fourth term in a few years.

The civil rights movement had been invigorated by the hardships of the Depression. Its most prominent leaders, such as the NAACP's Walter White, the Urban League's T. Arnold Hill, and the forceful trade unionist A. Philip Randolph, founder and leader of the Brotherhood of Sleeping Car Porters, threatened the president with a march on Washington against racial discrimination. To avoid the march, Roosevelt agreed to meet with these leaders in the Oval Office and he issued the executive order we have already discussed. During that meeting (which Roosevelt secretly recorded) on September 27, 1940, the question of an integrated military was brought up by Randolph and White. Here is the transcript of that portion of the discussion:

> VOICE: The Negro is trying to get *in* the army!
>
> FDR: Of course, the main point to get across in building up this draft army, the selective draft, is that we are not as we did before so much in the World War, confining the Negro in to the non-combat services. We're putting him *right in*, proportionately, into the *combat services*.
>
> RANDOLPH: We feel that's something.
>
> FDR: Which is, something. It's a step ahead. It's a step ahead.
>
> WHITE: Mr. President, may I suggest another step ahead?
>
> This has been commented on by many Negro Americans, and that is that we realize the practical reality that in Georgia and Mississippi [FDR: Yeah.] it would be impossible to have units where people's standard of admission would be ability. . . . I'd like to suggest this idea, even though it may sound fantastic at this time, that in the states where there isn't a tradition of segregation, that we might start to experiment with organizing a division or a regiment and let them be all Americans and not black Americans or white Americans—working together.
>
> Now, there are a number of reasons why I think that would be sound, among them that I think it would be a practical work for democracy and I think it would be less expensive and less troublesome in the long run.
>
> FDR: Well, you see now Walter, my general report on it is this. The thing is, we've got to *work into* this. . . . [33]

Despite FDR's statement that Negroes would be represented proportionately in combat units, this proved not to be the case throughout his presidency. Even when there were eventual efforts to have a proportionate number of African Americans in the armed forces, they were overwhelmingly placed in noncombat positions, mostly serving either as unskilled laborers or as cooks and servants. Following the meeting in the Oval Office, the White House issued a press release implying that the civil rights leaders had agreed to the president's proposed program, which called for a segregated military rather than the integrated military the recording showed had been asked for. As army historian Morris MacGregor reports, "To have their names associated with any endorsement of segregation was particularly infuriating to these civil rights leaders, who immediately protested to the President. The White House later publicly absolved the leaders of any such endorsement, and Press Secretary Early was forced to retract the 'damaging impression' that the leaders had in any way endorsed segregation."[34]

The president's cautious, politically fearful approach to desegregation in the armed forces was very much in keeping with the second Roosevelt. As commander in chief he could have integrated the military by fiat, but he dared do no such thing. Instead, he took a minimalist approach, despite the fact that there had been integrated combat units during the American Revolution and throughout the Union's army and naval efforts in the Civil War. The idea was not new and it was not untested, although it had been abandoned in favor of segregated units following the Civil War. The great experimenter, the man who had declared, "It is common sense to take a method and try it: If it fails, admit it frankly and try another. But above all, try something," was unwilling to try this experiment.[35] FDR's hypocrisy was not lost on the civil rights leadership. He had declared the four freedoms (freedom of speech, freedom of religion, freedom from want, and freedom from fear) in his 1941 State of the Union address. The African American leadership in turn pushed their Double V campaign: freedom from fascism abroad and freedom from Jim Crow at home.

Segregation ran the gamut of military practice. There were segregated selective service call-ups; blacks were relegated to labor rather than combat in the army, and to unskilled shore duty or to serve— literally to serve—as stewards on board ships in the navy. Even the steward role came in for complaints. Blacks were generally kept off navy ships because the navy did not have sufficient resources to maintain all-black ships and its leadership was hostile to the idea of integrated vessels. Secretary of the Navy Frank Knox told the president that "men live in such intimacy aboard ship that we simply can't enlist Negroes above the rank of messman."[36] Roosevelt reluctantly accepted this judgment even as he looked for a way, as he had said in the Oval Office meeting, "to *work into* this." That way, according to his politically supercautious approach, was to "make a beginning by putting some good Negro bands aboard battleships."[37] What exactly "good Negro bands" would do on battleships was not obvious, but that was the president's idea of how to "work into this." His idea seemed to gain traction as he continued to press for an additional role beyond just messmen for African American members of the navy. "[T]he Inspector General of the Navy, Rear Adm. Charles P. Snyder, . . . suggested that the board consider employing Negroes in some areas outside the servant class: in the Musician's Branch, for example, because 'the colored race is very musical and they are versed in all forms of rhythm.'"[38]

The opportunity for combat roles or other duties that gave black soldiers or sailors an equal opportunity to contribute to the war effort were few and far between. The chance for promotion to the rank of officer was almost nonexistent, and where it did exist, black officers were clearly treated as beneath even lower-ranked white officers. Pressure for change was tied to the election cycle and not to the war effort per se. Indeed, so electorally motivated was Franklin Roosevelt that he allowed the segregation of the armed forces to become a financial and administrative burden that impeded the war effort. Training facilities were separate by race and, most assuredly, they were not equal. The same was true of mess halls, recreational facilities, officers clubs, and every other aspect of the black military experience. The inefficiencies produced by across-the-board segregation and its associated duplication of effort were not lost on the military, although their solutions were as risk averse as Roosevelt's.

Colonel Edwin Chamberlain headed an army group in 1942 that created what became known as the Chamberlain Plan. As his group observed,

It was a waste of manpower, funds, and equipment, therefore, to organize the increasingly large numbers of black recruits into segregated units. . . . To avoid both the waste and the strife, Chamberlain recommended that the Army halt the activation of additional black units and integrate black recruits in the low-score categories, IV and V [allegedly measuring ability but actually measuring education], in to white units in the ratio of one black to nine whites. The black recruits would be used as cooks, orderlies, and drivers, and in other jobs which required only the minimum basic training and which made up 10 to 20 percent of those in the average unit. Negroes in the higher categories, I through III, would be assigned to existing black units where they could be expected to improve the performance of those units. . . . To those who objected on the grounds that the proposal meant racial integration, Chamberlain replied that there was no more integration involved than in "the employment of Negroes as servants in a white household."[39]

The oddity of all of this discrimination and willingness to import Jim Crow into the military was twofold. First, when late in the war the military finally began to experiment with volunteer integrated units, they enjoyed success and found no unusual difficulties in white and black soldiers working together. So, from a military perspective, once the experiment was run, the evidence was that integration was an enhancement and not a detriment to the military. Second, FDR's fear of losing southern electoral support may have been correct but it was irrelevant.

Roosevelt won the 1940 election with 449 Electoral College votes to Wendell Willkie's 82. Even had Willkie taken the approximately 100 southern Electoral College votes, Roosevelt would still have won handily. And then, too, we should not forget that Willkie was a civil rights advocate, so it was not as if Roosevelt was in grave danger of losing support from segregationists who were exceedingly unlikely to view Willkie as the lesser of two evils. No, lacking the vision that he had in 1932, Roosevelt was just a cautious candidate and a cautious politician committed, as so many politicians naturally are, to personal victory over doing what he surely believed was right. The integration of the United States military was forced to wait until after he died and Harry Truman believed he was unelectable. He desegregated the military in 1948 as the polls declared his presidential candidacy—incorrectly—as dead in the water. With nothing to lose politically, finally the right thing got done!

FDR's electoral caution and personal vanity for victory combined in 1944 to further demonstrate how the second Roosevelt, the post-1939 Roosevelt, followed rather than led. Recall that the president had ordered the internment of Japanese Americans, fearing that they were spies or otherwise likely to engage in sabotage of the American war effort against Japan. By 1944, his close adviser and secretary of the interior, Harold Ickes, was urging Roosevelt to release the internees. Doing so was politically unpopular in California, which was where most of the internees were from. Roosevelt put off Ickes, not having been willing to risk losing California in the 1944 presidential election. He lifted his executive order in December 1944, after he had been reelected.

What If?

ROOSEVELT PLAYED IT SAFE IN TERMS OF REELECTION. HE CONTINUED to press the popular New Deal policies and he continued to insist, commensurate with the indications in the Gallup polls, that he would keep the United States out of the war. By these means he won an unprecedented third term. No one who thinks of him primarily as a politician can fault his cautious approach to the war, but that does not mean that he did not have an alternative strategy that could have won him a third term and possibly saved vast numbers of lives in the process. Consider the facts on the ground as he and Wendell Willkie competed against each other for the support of the American voter.

Willkie's campaign against Roosevelt was three-pronged. He argued that the social safety net aspects of the New Deal were good policies and should be preserved, but that the New Deal had also made the government into an unfair competitor against private business. Willkie, a corporate executive with no prior political experience, had become an opponent of Roosevelt in large measure because of such New Deal projects as the Tennessee Valley Authority, which produced energy without having to turn a profit and so drove its private sector competitors out of business. This prong of Willkie's campaign against Roosevelt was popular with many businessmen who were, by and large, already inclined to vote Republican. It was not likely to win over many working-class or middle-class voters who saw the New Deal as a great benefit to them.

The second prong of Willkie's campaign focused on the threat of war. Willkie had risen in the ranks of prospective nominees in the Republican Party as Nazi Germany swept across Europe. Still, the Republican Party was, broadly speaking, an isolationist party. Consequently, Willkie felt political pressure to run toward the party's core voters by emphasizing that he, more so than Roosevelt, was likely to keep the country out of the war. Earlier we quoted a section of his nomination acceptance speech in which he highlighted the danger for the United States if Britain fell and Germany controlled the Atlantic. The speech then went on to assure the Republican nominating convention and the American people that Willkie was the man to keep the United States at peace. As he said,

> I cannot follow the President in his conduct of foreign affairs in this critical time. There have been occasions when many of us have wondered if he is deliberately inciting us to war. I trust that I have made it plain that in the defense of America, and of our liberties, I should not hesitate to stand for war. But like a great many other Americans I saw what war was like at first hand in 1917. I know what war can do to demoralize civil liberties at home. And I believe it to be the first duty of a President to try to maintain peace. But Mr. Roosevelt has not done this. He has dabbled in inflammatory statements and manufactured panics. . . . The President's attacks on foreign powers have been useless and dangerous. He has courted a war for which the country is hopelessly unprepared—and which it emphatically does not want.

So, while Willkie accused FDR of plotting war, both he and Roosevelt assured the American voter that the other candidate was more likely to take the country into the war. The facts provided the voter with little basis to believe that Willkie or Roosevelt was more likely to keep America out of the war.

The third prong of Willkie's campaign emphasized the danger to democracy represented by Roosevelt's pursuit of a third term. This was on the surface a sound campaign strategy, as polls, such as the Gallup survey in December 1939, showed the electorate was more opposed to a third term for FDR than in favor ("If President Roosevelt is a candidate for a third term, will you vote for him?" the poll asked; 47 percent said yes and 53 percent said no). But that was long before the campaign was under way. By May 1940, in response to the question, "Do you think Roosevelt has done a good job or a poor job in dealing with the war crisis in Europe?" 79 percent responded that he was doing a good job.

Apparently, Willkie's three prongs were not working. He was largely undifferentiated from FDR on the war; his views of the New Deal were less popular than the president's; and the fear of a third term did not resonate with that many voters. Given these facts—that Willkie's campaign was essentially doomed to failure—Roosevelt could have afforded to take a bit more risk. Every indication was that he believed the right thing to do was to come to the defense of Britain and of democracy in Europe. Although the opposition to going to war was strong, everyone knew that Willkie won his party's nomination because he was the more hawkish Republican on the question of war. Thus, Roosevelt might readily have entered the war earlier without sacrificing any precious votes to his rival. Early entry into the war probably would have quickly crushed Germany in Europe and Japan in Asia, especially if the president had decided to expand US defense spending seriously in 1936 after Germany remilitarized the Rhineland. Then, he could have produced increased employment, as he did later, through arms production, and achieved full employment by seriously expanding the manpower of the armed forces to protect democracy. Then, he would have been in a position to argue that the New Deal and economic recovery were fully compatible with the advance of freedom and democracy and won election on that basis. His caution in not doing so was, in our view, a mistake if one is to place doing what is right in first place, and electoral politics—which he still would almost certainly have succeeded at—in second.

Reflections on FDR and on When to Fight

NO ONE WOULD ACCUSE FRANKLIN ROOSEVELT OF HAVING BEEN trigger happy. His 1940 campaign, like Woodrow Wilson's in 1916, assured the American people that he was the candidate to keep the nation out of war. Under many circumstances this is indeed a commendable policy. War is an inefficient way to solve problems. If one could just accurately estimate the outcome and costs of war, then there generally is a compromise that could be struck beforehand that would leave all sides—winners and losers—better off than they were after fighting.[40] But compromise is not always a better path forward. When an opponent cannot be trusted to carry out whatever compromise he or she has agreed to, then there is no point to compromise.[41] Adolf Hitler certainly proved to anyone paying attention that he was just such an adversary. He made promises to Chamberlain in England, to the government in France, to Stalin in Russia, and to a great many others, and he broke them all. When facing an opponent whose demonstrated intention is to take lots of little bites of the apple until there isn't any apple left, the wise policy is to knock out his teeth quickly. Roosevelt understood that Hitler was such a foe.

The US electorate seemingly was blind to the facts, either out of ignorance or out of wishful thinking. The job of a democratic *leader* is to try to convert public opinion to his or her point of view. The job of a democratic *politician* is to follow the voter and not risk losing reelection. Maybe it is asking too much to expect a politician to be a leader, too. Roosevelt had demonstrated that he could be both in his 1932 and 1936 elections. Perhaps that is because he had a genuine vision regarding the Depression and a bold preparedness to experiment with alternative approaches to achieve his vision. Apparently he had no such vision in 1940, when it came to the looming world war. The Roosevelt of the 1930s was a leader first and a politician second. The Roosevelt from 1940 onward was a politician whose failure to lead made the war longer and costlier than it needed to be.

Chapter 5

LBJ's Defeat by Debit Card, W's Victory by Credit Card

It's damned easy to get in a war but it's gonna be awful hard ever to extricate yourself if you get in.

—Lyndon Baines Johnson, May 27, 1964

L YNDON JOHNSON AND GEORGE W. BUSH WERE ACCIDENTAL presidents. President Johnson, having been relegated to the vice presidency after John Kennedy defeated him for the Democratic Party's nomination in 1960, achieved his ultimate ambition to be president but only as the consequence of Kennedy's tragic assassination on November 22, 1963. Having taken the presidential oath of office, Johnson had no intention of forgoing the opportunity that tragedy placed within his grasp. He was hell-bent on achieving greater equality in America. Having never hesitated to fight hard political battles throughout his career, he was prepared as president to sacrifice himself—and his Democratic Party, too—in pursuit of that greater equality to which he was dedicated. The Vietnam War and his policy of equal risk for all draft-age Americans contributed mightily to the fulfillment of the philosophy behind his Great Society agenda, as well as to his own political demise.

George W. Bush won the presidency in 2000 amid perhaps the largest constitutional election crisis in American history. Bush[1] was far from unique in winning the Electoral College vote without securing a plurality of the popular vote, but he does stand alone in being the only president whose election was ultimately determined not by the voters, not really by the Electoral College, not by the House of Representatives, but by the Supreme Court. With hanging chads, butterfly ballots, and miscast votes, a few hundred Florida voters—with real uncertainty about their intended voting choices—elected Bush over then-Vice President Al Gore, according to a 5–4 Supreme Court judgment. True, the presidency would have been seen by a great many Americans as only slightly less accidental had the outcome gone Gore's way, but nevertheless George W. Bush took the oath of office amidst controversy, national disunity, resentment, and real doubts about who was actually elected.

When he later sought an unambiguous public mandate for a second term, Bush brandished his Iraq War as an exemplar of the president's battle against terrorism, containment of weapons of mass destruction, and the promotion of democracy in the Middle East. His sales pitch was a great success. Indeed, shortly before the 2004 presidential election, a majority of Americans had a favorable view of the US decision to invade Iraq and a favorable assessment of the job done by President Bush. Not surprisingly, Bush rode the wave of public enthusiasm to victory in 2004, sealing his ambition to be a two-term president and freeing himself to carry out the policies he believed in when, as a lame duck, he had no need to be concerned with future personal political gains or losses.

It is ironic that of these two presidents, Bush, not Johnson, is the one who pursued reelection. LBJ, the youngest-ever majority leader in the Senate, is sometimes described as the most skillful politician ever to occupy the White House. George W. Bush, colloquially known as "W" or as 43, in contrast, is often thought of as a bumbling, even inept leader. The standard judgments, paradoxically, may be completely consistent with the policy outcomes achieved by each but certainly are inconsistent with the way their respective political careers ended. Johnson surely wanted another term as president, but even more he wanted to do great things. Bush may have wanted to do great things, too, but he assuredly chose a political course in the way he waged war that was designed to ensure his reelection, his uncontested claim on the presidency, whether he did great things or not.

The electoral outcomes for the incumbent presidents in 1968 and in 2004 were as different as can be, but they may be understood as the consequence of each president's personal ambition. Each may be adjudged a victor despite Johnson's being driven from the political stage and Bush's having remained firmly ensconced on it, front and center. We can see a clue to the differences in their personal ambitions and how they used their time in office by probing the latter-day assessment of historians regarding each of them. Reflecting back on LBJ's prodigious achievements, including the Civil Rights Act of 1964, the Voting Rights Act of 1965, and, in that same year, the passage of Medicare, historians have resurrected LBJ's reputation despite the public's dislike of the Vietnam War. In August 1968, a few months after Johnson announced he would not seek reelection, his approval rating was only 35 percent. With the benefit of the passage of time, however, historians today rank Johnson fourteenth among the forty-three presidents from George Washington through George W. Bush. Among those who rank ahead of LBJ, only John Adams unsuccessfully sought to win a second term. It seems that Johnson's reputation has outgrown the quagmire of Vietnam, giving greater weight to his transformative legislative record.

George W. Bush, in contrast, ranks thirty-fouth among presidents, and only one president who ranks below him—Ulysses S. Grant—succeeded in winning a second term. We are still much closer in time to Bush's presidency than to Johnson's. Thus far—and it may only be thus far—the war that helped get W reelected now serves to crush his reputation. Of course, Johnson, no less than Bush, pursued his own interests as president, but it seems that Johnson's interests made him great in hindsight even as they contemporaneously destroyed him politically. Bush's interests made him a two-term president with the hope—and for now it is only a hope—that history will resurrect him. War played fundamentally different parts in their two presidencies. While their two wars have much in common, they produced radically different political consequences for Johnson and Bush. Here we want to understand how two unpopular wars led to such radically different political outcomes for their protagonists, Lyndon Johnson and George W. Bush.

Two Wars: Superficial Similarities, Fundamental Differences

THE BATTLEFIELD EXPERIENCE AND THE POLITICAL FALLOUT FROM BOTH the Vietnam War and the Iraq War are similar. In each instance, things mostly went well in combat and yet turned sour when it came to politics, though in the case of Iraq, the sourness did not set in until after Bush was reelected, whereas Vietnam deprived Johnson of a second term. The United States was militarily dominant in classic battle terms between regular army units in both Vietnam—mostly a war of set-piece battles, despite its reputation—and in Iraq. Despite military success against regular army units, in both cases US forces proved vulnerable to unconventional warfare and US military commanders struggled against enemies who could not be readily brought to the negotiating table and who could not be effectively controlled following settlement of each conflict.

Eventually, the American public tired of both conflicts, producing disastrous political results for Johnson but, curiously, not for Bush. Explaining why that was so is the central theme in this chapter. In resolving why Vietnam destroyed Johnson while Iraq did not destroy Bush, we will hear an echo of James Madison's War of 1812. Making partisan adversaries bear the cost of war, as the Democrat-Republicans did in 1812 and as Bush did in 2003, is great for reelection prospects and awful for the unity and well-being of the country. Conversely, a pay-as-you-go, debit-card plan to cover the costs of war while it is being fought helps secure the country's economic and social future, but at a heavy personal price for presidents who choose that course of action. Johnson was ruined by his war payment scheme. This ruination was caused by his use of taxation to cover the financial burden of war and of an equal-risk scheme to populate the military. Bush, in contrast, was made by his war payment scheme!

We begin with a review of public opinion polls for each war. Figure 5.1 shows the percentage of Americans who thought that US intervention in Vietnam was a mistake (solid line), according to Gallup polls from the summer of 1964 through the election of Richard Nixon.[2] We quite intentionally start in the summer of 1964. On August 2, 1964, the USS *Maddox* reported being attacked by three North Vietnamese torpedo boats in the Tonkin Gulf. A second alleged incident occurred two days later. We say "alleged" because serious doubts have been raised over whether the reported events actually happened, at least as publicly described. In any event, Congress believed the attacks occurred as reported and responded with the Tonkin Gulf Resolution. The resolution authorized the "President, as Commander in Chief, to take all necessary measures to repel any armed attack against the forces of the United States and to prevent further aggression." It went on to note that "the United States is, therefore, prepared, as the President determines, to take all necessary steps, including the use of armed force, to assist any member or protocol state of the Southeast Asia Collective Defense."[3] This resolution passed against only two nay votes, by Democratic senators Wayne Morse of Oregon and Ernest Gruening of Alaska. Thus, the summer of 1964 may be seen as marking the start of Lyndon Johnson's phase of the Vietnam War and hence as a sensible place for us to begin to evaluate how public views of the war unfolded and what that unfolding meant for him.

Figure 5.1's right vertical axis and the dotted line show the cumulative number of US casualties during the Vietnam War. The solid line, linked to the left vertical axis, displays the percentage of the American public that assessed the war as a mistake between July 1964 and the fall of 1972.[4] We can see clearly that the American public initially was

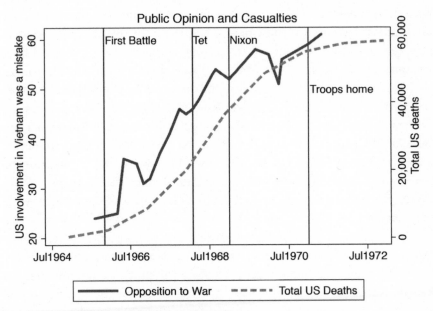

Figure 5.1. US Public Opinion and Casualties in the Vietnam War
Sources: http://www.gallup.com/poll/2299/americans-look-back-vietnam-war.aspx,
https://www.dmdc.osd.mil/dcas/pages/report_oif_month.xhtml

firmly behind Johnson's decision to intervene following the Gulf of Tonkin incident and subsequent congressional resolution. Less than a quarter of the population opposed Johnson's first serious Vietnam engagement in 1965. However, as US casualties mounted, opposition to the war increased. Declining public support and rising casualties track each other closely throughout the war.

Looking at the vertical line in Figure 5.1 that denotes the North Vietnamese's Tet Offensive, it is interesting to recall that Tet resulted both in a decisive US military victory and in just as decisive a US political defeat. Although initially the US military was shocked and stunned, perhaps having believed its own propaganda about the weakened condition of the North Vietnamese and Viet Cong (VC), US forces quickly organized and counterattacked. They killed around 37,000 Viet Cong soldiers compared to 2,500 US losses. The Tet Offensive seriously depleted North Vietnam's military capacity but it produced a stunning North Vietnamese political victory as American public opinion turned more sharply against the war. CBS's news anchor, Walter Cronkite, often described as "the most trusted man in America," reported, "To say that we are closer to victory today is to believe, in the face of the evidence, the optimists who have been wrong in the past. To suggest we are on the edge of defeat is to yield to unreasonable pessimism. To say that we are mired in stalemate seems the only realistic, yet unsatisfactory, conclusion." Johnson understood the significance of Cronkite's assessment. He retorted, "If I've lost Cronkite, I've lost Middle America."[5] That is, he lost a big chunk of his personal base of political power.

Johnson had indeed lost Cronkite and America. US government declarations by the president, his foreign policy team, and senior generals had led the public to believe that the North Vietnamese no longer were capable of mounting an offensive. Following Tet, opposition to the war rose sharply, surpassing 50 percent for the first time, as a credibility gap expanded between what the president was saying and what the American people believed.

From early on in his presidency, Johnson's official pronouncements came increasingly to be seen as inconsistent with the media's reports out of Vietnam. He had chosen to follow the modus operandi that he had perfected in the Senate, maneuvering to create the impression of a happier vision of reality than the facts on the ground warranted. As Johnson's special assistant, Joseph Califano, stated, "At his worst, Lyndon Johnson destroyed his own credibility. He hid the true cost of the military buildup in Vietnam as he first unfolded it. He heard what he wanted and hoped to hear from the military about the war and passed their optimistic reports on to the American people as his own. . . . He learned too late that the manipulative and devious behavior commonplace in the back alleys of legislative politics appalled the American people when exposed in their President. He paid a fearful price as first the press corps in Washington and Saigon and then millions of Americans came to doubt his word. He never seemed able to accept what the war did to the American spirit."[6]

As the war effort escalated with ever growing numbers of American troops in Vietnam, Johnson recognized that optimistic reporting combined with a prolonged war had the potential to create devastating political consequences. Even a year before the Tet Offensive, in his 1967 State of the Union Address, he admitted that the end was not yet in sight:

> I wish I could report to you that the conflict is almost over. This I cannot do. We face more cost, more loss, and more agony. For the end is not yet. I cannot promise you that it will come this year—or come next year. Our adversary still believes, I think, tonight, that he can go on fighting longer than we can, and longer than we and our allies will be prepared to stand up and resist. . . .
>
> So I must say to you that our pressure must be sustained—and will be sustained—until he realizes that the war he started is costing him more than he can ever gain.[7]

Johnson's surmise that the North Vietnamese leadership believed they could outwait the United States government was well justified. After all, if the North Vietnamese followed American public opinion polls, as they surely did, then they knew, as we saw in Figure 5.1, that American support for the war was collapsing. At the time of his 1967 State of the Union Address, just shy of 50 percent of Americans judged the war to have been a mistake. By the summer of 1968, eighteen months after his 1967 State of the Union Address, a majority of Americans considered the Vietnam War a mistake. Seeing the handwriting on the wall, on March 31, 1968, Johnson, still unable to see the path to a US victory in Vietnam, announced, "I shall not seek, and I will not accept, the nomination of my party for another term as your President."[8] The North Vietnamese may well have interpreted this statement as meaning, with justification, that the war was costing Johnson "more than he can ever gain."

Figure 5.2 shows public opinion of the war in Iraq in 2003. It is largely a reprisal of the story of Vietnam, with one huge difference. It shows, as Figure 5.1 does regarding Vietnam, that American public opinion about the Iraq War of 2003 and its aftermath strongly tracked the US casualty rate. That rate, of course, was an order of magnitude lower than in Vietnam, yet that difference does not seem to be the explanation for Bush's political success and Johnson's failure. As Johnson failed to defeat the Vietnamese, Bush failed to secure the peace in Iraq. Overrunning the Iraqi military proved easy enough as these things go, but the Bush administration seemed unprepared to turn military success into effective postcombat governance. Instead, open warfare against Saddam Hussein's regime ended quickly, only to be replaced by insurgency verging on civil war. Whereas it took three years for a majority of the American public to turn against Johnson's war, it took barely a year, albeit with many rises and declines in support, for Bush to experience for the first time—and not the last—the same loss of support. Johnson was unable to reverse the trend against his war; Bush managed to engineer a saw-toothed pattern of rises and declines

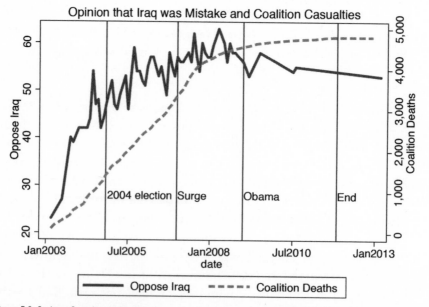

Figure 5.2. Coalition Casualties in Iraq

Sources: http://icasualties.org/IRAQ/index.aspx, http://www.gallup.com/poll/1633/iraq.aspx

in support, and got himself reelected during a period of relative popularity, even though the war was later seen as a failure. That, of course,
leaves us with big questions: What did Bush do right politically; what
did Johnson do wrong; and how can lessons from their experiences be
used to reduce the danger of needlessly engaging in costly wars? The
answers are not hard to find, although they may be hard to digest.

LBJ: A Reluctant Warrior

THE LINES IN THE SAND HAD LONG BEEN DRAWN IN SOUTHEAST ASIA
when LBJ became president. To be sure, it was he, not Eisenhower
and not Kennedy, who sought and secured the Gulf of Tonkin Resolution and, likewise, it was he, not Eisenhower or Kennedy, who first
openly committed American combat troops to the mission of defeating
South Vietnam's North Vietnamese and Viet Cong adversaries. But that
was against a backdrop of long-established views that relentlessly
pushed President Johnson toward intervention and toward incremental
but massive escalation in Vietnam.

Intervention not only followed the consensus opinion regarding
Vietnam at the time; it was also consistent with the principal goal
of US policy since the end of World War II: to contain communism.
Involvement in Vietnam was a gradual process in which Johnson
sought and listened to differing opinions. In hindsight, many judge
US involvement in Vietnam to have been a tragic mistake. The United
States spilled much American and Vietnamese blood and treasure and
still, in the end, South Vietnam was lost. But it is unfair to judge decision making from the perspective of a Monday morning quarterback.
The appropriate standard for evaluating decisions is whether the right
choice—that is, a reasonable, well-considered, justifiable choice—was
made given the information available at the time. This is precisely the
analysis that Leslie Gelb and Richard Betts undertook in a 1979 book for
the Brookings Institution, the title of which conveys their central argument: *The Irony of Vietnam: The System Worked*. They argued that "the
paradox is that the *foreign policy* failed, but the *domestic decision-making
system* worked."[9] In particular, the system worked because "(1) the core
consensual goal of postwar foreign policy (containment of communism)
was pursued consistently; (2) differences of both elite and mass opinion
were accommodated by compromise and policy never strayed very far

from the center of opinion both within and outside the government; and (3) virtually all views and recommendations were considered and virtually all important decisions were made without illusion about the odds for success."[10]

So, putting hindsight aside, what were the competing arguments that Johnson heard and weighed at the time he had to choose his course of action? Advice from senior members of his foreign policy team ranged across the entire spectrum from those in favor of escalation to those in favor of withdrawal. To stress the openness of the internal discussion at the time, consider the account Johnson's special assistant, Jack Valenti, provided of Cabinet Room debates that started on July 21, 1965, and continued until LBJ's announcement of substantial escalation on July 28. Secretary of Defense Robert McNamara had just returned from Vietnam. His memorandum proposed a massive increase in US forces, without which he predicted South Vietnam would be overrun by the communists. Johnson, as Valenti tells it, was far from gung-ho for war. He pushed George Ball, undersecretary of state, to express his reservations. Ball answered, "Mr. President, I have grave misgivings about our ability to win under these conditions. . . . But let me be clear. If the decision is to go ahead, I will support it. . . . There is no course that will allow us to avoid losses. But if we get bogged down, our cost might be substantially greater. The pressures to create a larger war would be irresistible. . . . We can take our losses and let their government fall apart, Mr. President, knowing full well there will be a probable takeover by the Communists. This is an unpleasant alternative, I know." LBJ responded, "I don't think we have made any full commitment yet, George . . . I want another meeting, more meetings, before we take any definitive action. We must look at all other courses of action carefully. Right now I feel it would be more dangerous to lose the war than it would be to risk a greater number of troops down the road. But I want this fully aired."[11]

Later in the discussion, Ball prophetically reveals his reservations: "We cannot win, Mr. President. This war will be long and protracted. The most we can hope for is a messy conclusion. . . . I think a long, protracted war will expose our weakness, not our strength. The least harmful way to cut losses in South Vietnam is to let the government decide it doesn't want us to stay there. Therefore we should put proposals to them that they can't accept, although I have no illusions that after we are asked to leave South Vietnam, that country will soon fall under Hanoi's control."[12]

While Ball feared that the United States would be bogged down without winning, others expressed support for expansion. For instance, General McConnell said, "If you put in these requested forces and increase air and sea effort, we can at least turn the tide to where we are not losing anymore. We need to be sure we get the best we can out of the South Vietnamese. We need to bomb all military targets available to us in North Vietnam. As to whether we can come to a satisfactory solution with these forces, I don't know. With these forces properly employed, and cutting off the VC supplies, we can surely do better than we are doing now."[13]

Clearly LBJ heard all sides of the debate and everyone recognized the limitations of each choice. In the end, the need to maintain credibility against future communist incursions was deemed to trump the risk of becoming bogged down. The president announced his decision to the nation in a July 28, 1965, press conference:

> We have learned at a terrible and a brutal cost that retreat does not bring safety and weakness does not bring peace. It is this lesson that has brought us to Viet-Nam. . . . Our power, therefore, is a very vital shield. If we are driven from the field in Viet-Nam, then no nation can ever again have the same confidence in American promise, or in American protection. . . . I plan, as long as I am President, to see that our forces are strong enough to protect our national interest, our right hand constantly protecting that interest with our military, and that our diplomatic and political negotiations are constantly attempting to find some solution that would substitute words for bombs.[14]

In hindsight, as in the foresight of Undersecretary George Ball, as we have noted, many judge US involvement in Vietnam to have been a mistake. As clear as hindsight is, we should remember that Johnson was following a well-trodden path to promote what was understood to be the US's national security interest. While his interests were elsewhere—in his proposals for the Great Society—he also understood the need for continuity and predictability in policy following Kennedy's assassination. Indeed Johnson's Vietnam policy is best understood as a perpetuation of Kennedy's policy and of the post–World War

II US commitment to prevent the spread of communism. That effort had already failed in China and in Cuba; Johnson was not keen to be the one to oversee its failure in Southeast Asia.

With the urgency of both the appearance and the reality of policy and programmatic continuity in mind, and despite some personal frays in relations, Johnson retained most of Kennedy's cabinet and perpetuated the fallen president's policy agenda, including his agenda to contain communism. In a meeting on November 24, 1964, he declared, "I am not going to lose Vietnam. I am not going to be the President who saw Southeast Asia go the way China went."[15] Continuity in foreign policy and stability at home all dictated that he continue to resist the expansion of communism. But most assuredly this was not his primary interest as president. As he said well before his escalation of the American effort in Vietnam, "What the hell is Vietnam worth to me? What is Laos worth to me? What is it worth to this country? No, we've got a treaty but, hell, everybody else's got a treaty out there and they're not doing anything about it. Of course if you start running from the Communists, they may just chase you right into your own kitchen."[16]

Vietnam was very much the chosen battlefield in the fight against communism and LBJ certainly supported the US security objective of containing communism just as JFK, Dwight Eisenhower, and Harry Truman had before him; however, had he not come to the presidency in the awful way that he did, it is quite plausible that his Vietnam choices would have been different. Jack Valenti often posed a fascinating hypothetical to student audiences when he spoke of LBJ and Vietnam: "If the United States had not had any soldiers in Vietnam in 1963, would the new president have sent them in?" His answer never varied: "I believe LBJ would not have sent in troops for the simple reason that his first objective was to build the Great Society. He knew this would be expensive and demand his focused energies. A war in a jungle half a world away would intrude seriously, and perhaps fatally, on his goal of lifting up the quality of life in this nation."[17]

While the situation in Vietnam compelled changes in Johnson's emphasis, his focus, especially early in his first full term, was to embark on his monumental domestic agenda to build what he called a Great Society. In his memoir, presidential aide Joseph Califano lists 202 legislative bills passed by Congress during Johnson's presidency.[18] Vietnam simply was not high on the agenda in 1964 or early 1965. For instance, Johnson's inaugural address in 1965 made no reference at all to Vietnam.[19]

He mentioned it only once in his 1964 State of the Union Address, and then in connection with the ability of people of different races to work together. His 1965 State of the Union Address contained one reference to Vietnam, this time in direct connection to communist expansion in Asia. Subsequent State of the Union Addresses were dominated by the conflict, with the word "Vietnam" (or its derivatives) appearing 34 times in 1966, 46 times in 1967, 10 times in 1968, and 18 times in 1969.[20]

To Johnson, Vietnam was an unwanted but also an unavoidable distraction from what he in fact wished to do. Despite the growing pressure to escalate in Vietnam after the Gulf of Tonkin incident, he made no secret that he intended to wield the power he had attained to implement his agenda. In his March 15, 1965, message before Congress, the president was explicit about his intention to promote equality in America. Talking about civil rights, he said:

> There is no Negro problem. There is no Southern problem. There is no Northern problem. There is only an American problem. And we are met here tonight as Americans—not as Democrats or Republicans— we are met here as Americans to solve that problem. . . . This is the richest and most powerful country which ever occupied the globe. The might of past empires is little compared to ours. But I do not want to be the President who built empires, or sought grandeur, or extended dominion. I want to be the President who educated young children to the wonders of their world. I want to be the President who helped to feed the hungry and to prepare them to be taxpayers instead of taxeaters. I want to be the President who helped the poor to find their own way and who protected the right of every citizen to vote in every election. I want to be the President who helped to end hatred among his fellow men and who promoted love among the people of all races and all regions and all parties. I want to be the President who helped to end war among the brothers of this earth.[21]

In the same speech Johnson made clear that he was not just articulating a rhetorical wish-list. Rather, he made it evident that now that he had the power to fulfill these goals he intended to act: "But now I do have that chance—and I'll let you in on a secret—I mean to use it. And I hope that you will use it with me."[22]

Johnson is widely recognized as a political master whose abilities to put together support for a bill was unrivaled, even if the way he got things done made him a huge SOB.[23] When he achieved the highest level of power, he used it to implement his vision for equality in America. As a master politician, he surely knew that magnanimity, fairness, and the promotion of equality were political suicide. As we shall see, LBJ knew that in the long run his policies would drastically weaken his party. Perhaps he anticipated that he could achieve reelection for a second (full) term before the consequences of his civil rights legislation would jeopardize his position. The Vietnam War, and particularly how he extended his normative ideals of fairness and equality to the conduct of the war, undermined any such hope. We will return to this theme after reviewing Bush's Iraq War, a war in which, unlike Johnson's war, the president does not seem at all to have been a reluctant warrior.

Bush: A Willing, Optimistic Warrior

BUSH'S DECISION TO INVADE IRAQ IN 2003 FOLLOWED A RADICALLY different course from Johnson's decision to escalate the existing American effort following the Tonkin Gulf Resolution. Despite the failure by President George H. W. Bush to topple Saddam Hussein's regime following military victory in the 1991 Gulf War, when George W. Bush assumed the presidency in 2001, an invasion of Iraq certainly was not a consensus position either in the American public or among leading foreign policy advisers and decision makers. Indeed, it was an option to which very few people gave real consideration even in the immediate aftermath of 9/11.

President Bush decided that he wanted to depose Saddam Hussein's regime. The heightened fear of plots against the United States that followed 9/11 gave him an opportunity to engineer a war. Unlike the reluctant Johnson, Bush actively sought a conflict with Iraq. For him the problem was gaining sufficient support to enact a policy that he wanted and that the majority at the time did not. There are strong parallels between Bush and James Madison and the War Hawks of 1812. They, too, sought war, in their case with Britain to achieve territorial expansion, and, like Bush, they needed to find "legitimate" issues on which to mobilize support for the war they desired.

In Chapter 2, we explained that the 1812 War Hawks pointed to impressment of US seamen and British interference with America's Atlantic trade as the top two grievances against the United Kingdom even as these issues were already being resolved. Their actual reasons for wanting war resided in the War Hawks' urge to absorb Canada and to take lands from the Indians. In the case of the Iraq War the legitimate motivations for fighting so far from home became both an obscure and a moving target. We cannot be sure what the "real" justification for the war against Iraq was. We tend to think that President Bush, like President Madison, believed that war would help him with his reelection prospects. We certainly know that Bush floated numerous justifications until he found reasons that people would rally behind. In arguing for the need to depose Saddam Hussein, who had managed to survive in power despite the utter defeat of Iraq's army at the hands of 43's father, Bush the son pointed to (1) Iraq's development of weapons of mass destruction (WMD), (2) Iraq's support for global terrorism, and (3) Saddam Hussein's generally oppressive regime.

The WMD Gambit

To gain both domestic and international support, Bush pushed the case that Iraq was developing weapons of mass destruction. Although his administration accused Saddam Hussein of many foul things—from creating regional instability to violating human rights through the use of oppression within Iraq (certainly an accurate charge), from supporting terrorists to simply being a madman—the claim that the Iraqi government was developing WMD and was intent on using them gained the most traction both with the American public and the international community. Indeed, although Bush offered many casus belli, he focused on the alleged WMD threat in making his primary case for war. In his 2002 State of the Union Address, the president identified Iraq as a member of an "axis of evil":

> The Iraqi regime has plotted to develop anthrax, and nerve gas, and nuclear weapons for over a decade. This is a regime that has already used poison gas to murder thousands of its own citizens—leaving the bodies of mothers huddled over their dead children. This is a regime that agreed to international inspections—then kicked out the inspectors. This is a regime that has something to hide from the civilized world.
>
> States like these, and their terrorist allies, constitute an axis of evil, arming to threaten the peace of the world. By seeking weapons of mass destruction, these regimes pose a grave and growing danger.

They could provide these arms to terrorists, giving them the means to match their hatred. They could attack our allies or attempt to black-mail the United States. In any of these cases, the price of indifference would be catastrophic.[24]

Bush's arguments were strongly couched, designed to raise fear of Saddam Hussein's threat to the American people and the nation's friends in the world. Although many today scoff at his contention that Iraq possessed weapons of mass destruction—none were found during or after the 2003 war—still on the face of it at the time, the claim, at least for nonnuclear WMD, was entirely plausible. During the Gulf War of 1991, the victors discovered large quantities of chemical and biolog-ical weapons in Iraq's arsenal, including anthrax, botulin toxin, mus-tard gas, and nerve gas. Furthermore, Iraq's written records showed more such warheads than were actually discovered, meaning that some such weapons apparently were still lurking around somewhere. Still, by 2003 the evidence for the idea that these weapons still existed had become thin. Naturally, there were many demands for more evidence. Against these demands, Bush assured congressional legislators that there was definitive evidence of WMD and in October Congress voted to authorize the use of force in Iraq with a yea vote of 297 to a nay vote of 133 in the House and 77 to 23 votes in the Senate. These vote totals suggest far less appetite for war than the votes in favor of the Gulf of Tonkin Resolution in the run-up to Vietnam, but still it was a strongly bipartisan vote in support of action against Saddam Hussein's govern-ment. Nearly all Republicans in both the House and the Senate voted in favor of the war, as did a majority of Senate Democrats and a large minority—40 percent or so—of House Democrats. All this represented a vastly more bipartisan vote than the decision to declare war on Brit-ain in 1812, when virtually all Democrat-Republicans voted in favor and the Federalists lined up against.

The dearth of hard evidence notwithstanding, still Bush pressed the case for military intervention based on the threat of Saddam Hussein's alleged arsenal of weapons of mass destruction. In the interest of slow-ing progress toward war, the international community wanted the issue referred to the United Nations. Although the president initially resisted, he eventually agreed. On November 8, 2002, the UN Security Council unanimously passed Resolution 1441 that offered Hussein's government a final opportunity to comply with its disarmament obli-gations issued under previous UNSC resolutions. Iraq agreed to admit weapons inspectors from the United Nations Monitoring, Verification and Inspection Commission (UNMOVIC) and the International Atomic Energy Agency. Although there were great inconsistencies between Iraqi declarations and what the inspectors found, still the inspectors found little conclusive evidence of WMD.

This presented a problem for the Bush administration. When pushed on the issue of WMD, the head of the CIA, George Tenet, assured Bush, "Don't worry, it's a slam dunk."[25] However, in reality the administration's evidence was shaky and circumstantial. Sometimes it resorted to devious methods to maximize the impact of the evidence it had. For instance, it would leak stories to newspapers and then reference these stories as evidence to support its case.[26] No significant cache of WMD was found after the invasion. In March 2005 a presidential commission filled with people sympathetic to the Bush administration produced a damning report on intelligence failures:

> We conclude that the Intelligence Community was dead wrong in almost all of its prewar judgments about Iraq's weapons of mass destruction. This was a major intelligence failure. Its principal causes were the Intelligence Community's inability to collect good information about Iraq's WMD programs, serious errors in analyzing what information it could gather, and a failure to make clear just how much of its analysis was based on assumptions, rather than good evidence. On a matter of this importance, we simply cannot afford failures of this magnitude.
>
> After a thorough review, the Commission found no indication that the Intelligence Community distorted the evidence regarding Iraq's weapons of mass destruction. What the intelligence professionals told you about Saddam Hussein's programs was what they believed. They were simply wrong. . . .
>
> Through attention-grabbing headlines and repetition of questionable data, these briefings overstated the case that Iraq was rebuilding its WMD programs.[27]

The inconclusive reports of the weapons inspections failed to provide the smoking gun Bush sought. The delays created by the process also imposed difficulties as US forces amassed in neighboring countries. Many nations—the French were particularly vociferous advocates—thought the issue should again be referred to the United Nations. But President Bush was not keen for further delay. He did not need wide ranging domestic and international support for the war he proposed to fight; he just sought enough support at home and abroad to justify his actions at the time the US forces would be in place. Congress had granted its approval. Now all he required was sufficient international backing to support his plans. To get that international backing, he sent his secretary of state, Colin Powell, to make the administration's case before the UN General Assembly on February 6, 2003:

> I asked for this session today for two purposes: First, to support the core assessments made by [weapon inspectors] Dr. Blix and Dr. El-Baradei. As Dr. Blix reported to this council on January 27th, "Iraq appears not to have come to a genuine acceptance, not even today, of the disarmament which was demanded of it."
>
> My second purpose today is to provide you with additional information. . . .
>
> I cannot tell you everything that we know. But what I can share with you, when combined with what all of us have learned over the years, is deeply troubling.[28]

Powell was highly respected within diplomatic circles and his testimony enhanced the administration's credibility, especially as he was believed to be reluctant to invade Iraq. With international support tilting in his favor, Bush met with key allies in the Azores. After returning to the United States, he gave a televised address to the nation in which he gave Saddam Hussein and his sons forty-eight hours to leave Iraq.[29]

Bush clearly believed that Iraq possessed WMD, but it is evident that he exaggerated the extent and conclusiveness of the evidence the United States possessed. Once he had secured sufficient support for his position, he proceeded with the invasion. In hindsight, many commentators and politicians who initially supported that invasion now see it as a mistake. What we know today, while critically relevant to our assessment of the war, is, however, not pertinent to evaluating what people believed at the time or the choices they made without the benefit of hindsight. On that front—identifying what the casus belli was—the Bush administration left itself lots of maneuvering room. The alleged threat of WMD was but one basis for justifying a war that seems, in any event, to have been much more about deposing Saddam Hussein than it was about the danger he represented to the United States—which was virtually nil.

The Terrorism Claim

EIGHT MONTHS INTO PRESIDENT BUSH'S TERM, ON SEPTEMBER 11, 2001, al-Qaeda terrorists hijacked commercial passenger aircraft and crashed them into the World Trade Center in New York City and the Pentagon in Washington, DC. Thanks to the bravery of the passengers on board, an additional commercial airliner was crashed into a field near Stonycreek Township in Pennsylvania rather than into the White House or some other high-profile target in the Washington, DC, area. Nearly three thousand people died in these attacks. Intelligence linked the terrorist groups responsible for 9/11 to the Taliban government of Afghanistan. President Bush demanded that Afghanistan hand over al-Qaeda leader Osama bin Laden and that it expel the terror group. When Afghanistan was not forthcoming, Bush launched Operation Enduring Freedom, in which US and UK forces and insurgent groups known as the Northern Alliance invaded Afghanistan and deposed the Taliban.

More than a year later, on March 20, 2003, the president ordered the invasion of Iraq. As we have noted, one justification for the war was to destroy Iraq's WMD. Another justification, following on his 2002 State of the Union Address, was to end Iraq's support for terrorist groups. To date, as at the time, however, there is virtually no evidence that Saddam Hussein's regime supported terrorist organizations. Indeed, despite President Bush's effort to link Saddam Hussein's government to the 9/11 attacks, neither logic nor evidence supported the notion. The case against the effort to tie Hussein to terrorism was made forcefully by a most convincing source, a person who was expected to be sympathetic to Bush's cause, or at least to remain silent on the subject out of loyalty to Bush: Brent Scowcroft. In an August 2002 article in the *Wall Street Journal*, Scowcroft, who had been President George H. W. Bush's national security adviser, argued against the linkage that W drew between Saddam Hussein and the threat of terrorism:

> [W]e need to think through this issue very carefully. We need to analyze the relationship between Iraq and our other pressing priorities—notably the war on terrorism—as well as the best strategy and tactics available were we to move to change the regime in Baghdad. [T]here is scant evidence to tie Saddam to terrorist organizations, and even less to the Sept. 11 attacks. Indeed Saddam's goals have little in common with the terrorists who threaten us, and there is little incentive for him to make common cause with them. . . . He is unlikely to risk his

investment in weapons of mass destruction, much less his country, by handing such weapons to terrorists who would use them for their own purposes and leave Baghdad as the return address. . . . Saddam's problem with the U.S. appears to be that we stand in the way of his ambitions. He seeks weapons of mass destruction not to arm terrorists, but to deter us from intervening to block his aggressive designs. . . . Our pre-eminent security priority—underscored repeatedly by the president—is the war on terrorism. An attack on Iraq at this time would seriously jeopardize, if not destroy, the global counterterrorist campaign we have undertaken. The United States could certainly defeat the Iraqi military and destroy Saddam's regime. But it would not be a cakewalk. On the contrary, it undoubtedly would be very expensive—with serious consequences for the U.S. and global economy—and could as well be bloody. In fact, Saddam would be likely to conclude he had nothing left to lose, leading him to unleash whatever weapons of mass destruction he possesses.

But the central point is that any campaign against Iraq, whatever the strategy, cost and risks, is certain to divert us for some indefinite period from our war on terrorism. Worse, there is a virtual consensus in the world against an attack on Iraq at this time. . . . Possibly the most dire consequences would be the effect in the region.[30]

Scowcroft had made a powerful and, as it turns out, prescient argument against war in Iraq and against the notion that Saddam Hussein was backing terrorism. The case for the latter was too thin to be taken seriously as a justification for war. Rather, the terrorism claim seemed to point to a president who wanted, or needed, a war and simply sought to find a reason, whatever it might be, to garner the political support he needed. Whether WMD, the danger Saddam posed, terrorism, the promotion of democracy, or something else was the justification for war did not seem critical. What mattered for President George W. Bush was getting the support he needed for the policy he chose to pursue.

The Iraq Foreplay and Aftermath

BAGHDAD FELL ON APRIL 9, 2003. ON MAY 1, PRESIDENT BUSH declared victory from the deck of the aircraft carrier USS *Abraham Lincoln* under a giant banner declaring "Mission Accomplished." The invasion killed 9,200 Iraqi troops and 3,750 civilians plus 139 US troops. Saddam Hussein fled but was eventually captured in December 2003. A military court sentenced him to death and he was hanged in 2006.

We are still left with the puzzle of why this war was fought, as well as why it did not lead to Bush's defeat in the 2004 election. We come to the latter issue shortly, but now we want to review in a bit more detail the evidence that George W. Bush wanted the Iraq War, was uninterested in settling matters with Saddam Hussein peacefully, and that he planned the war almost from the beginning of his presidency. Then we will be in a position to understand how he used what seems almost to have been a personal vendetta against Saddam Hussein to his own political advantage, while Lyndon Johnson failed to see how to use his war for his own electoral benefit.

In what follows regarding the decision to go to war, we rely extensively on Bob Woodward's 2004 account since he had unprecedented access to the principal administration personnel. Accord to Woodward, in November 2001 President Bush asked Secretary of Defense Donald Rumsfeld to start making plans for the invasion of Iraq, but to keep it secret.[31] At an executive meeting at Camp David on September 15, 2001, none of the president's advisers recommended an attack against Iraq as a first response to the terrorist attacks of 9/11. However, the following day Bush told his national security adviser, and future secretary of state, Condoleezza Rice, "We won't do Iraq now. We're putting Iraq off. But eventually we'll have to return to that question."[32] It seems that 9/11 forced Bush to postpone, but not cancel, plans to take down Saddam Hussein's regime. By charging Rumsfeld to prepare war plans in November, Bush indicated that Iraq's turn had come.

By March 29, 2003, speaking at a National Security Counsil meeting, the president, on the brink of military victory, reiterated the political objectives. "Only one thing matters: winning. There's a lot of second-guessing regarding the post-Saddam world. Our job is to speak to the American people, tell them how proud we are of the soldiers; to the world, to tell them that we will accomplish this mission; to our European allies, thanks for your help; the Iraqi people, we will be coming to liberate the entire country. Don't worry about the carping and second-guessing. Rise above it, *be confident, remember your constituencies.*"[33]

"Remember your constituencies"! Bush was himself focused, and asked others to focus, on the political reception of his actions. And in fact, he gained a political advantage by taking them. He achieved reelection in 2004, despite a worsening security situation in both Afghanistan and Iraq.

In Pursuit of Equality or Inequality: Why LBJ Failed and Bush Succeeded

FROM A POLITICAL STANDPOINT, PRESIDENT BUSH'S PROSECUTION OF the war was expertly conducted. He declared victory even as the situation on the ground suggested otherwise. He ensured, as we will now demonstrate, that the war imposed few if any costs on the majority of his supporters. Instead, his opponents disproportionately paid the costs of fighting, in both financial and human terms. Further, when opponents protested, he chastised them for their lack of patriotism and accused them of being anti-American. Bush managed the politics of the war skillfully. He achieved reelection by keeping those upon whom he depended happy and by imposing the bulk of the costs on others. Bravo, George—James Madison could not have done it better.

Lyndon Johnson, like Franklin Roosevelt before him, was reluctant to fight but did so nevertheless. He came to the presidency unexpectedly, but once there he was determined, as had been FDR, to achieve a bold agenda. In pursuing greater equality in America, LBJ pursued the war with fairness to all Americans in mind, meaning he alienated his core base of support by making them pay for the war in every sense every bit as much as he made his political opponents pay for the war. Bush capitalized on favoritism and Johnson sacrificed himself on the altar of equal treatment.

To understand why one disastrous war ended a political career while another disastrous war ended in the ultimate in political success—reelection—we need to understand the agenda that each president sought to achieve and the strategy each adopted to advance those agendas.

Johnson's Agenda: Equal Treatment

FOR JOHNSON, THE PRESIDENCY AFFORDED AN OPPORTUNITY TO FULFILL A well-formulated policy agenda, the so-called Great Society. Jack Valenti describes Johnson's first night in the White House, on the day of

JFK's assassination, as intense and as reflective a time as the new president was ever likely to have. Johnson invited three advisers to his bedroom:

> LBJ began to ruminate. . . . He was simply giving voice to the torrent of thoughts pouring through his mind. "I'm going to pass that civil rights bill that's been tied up too damn long in the Senate. I'm going to get that bill passed by Congress, and I'm gonna do it before next year is done. And then I'm going to get a bill through that's gonna make sure that everybody has a right to vote. You give people a vote, and they damn sure have power to change their life for the better. . . . By God, I intend to pass Harry Truman's medical insurance bill. He didn't do it, but we'll make it into law. Never again will a little old lady who's sick as a dog be turned away from a hospital because she doesn't have any money to pay for her treatment. It's a damn disgrace. . . . We are going to do something about education. We're going to pass a bill that will give every young boy and girl in this country, no matter who they are, the right to get all the education they can take. And the government is going to pay for it."
>
> Before he was president for a full day, LBJ had laid out for the three of us in his bedroom what later became the design for the Great Society! It was a stunning display of LBJ's gifts as a visionary, as well as the political instincts without which no leader ever achieves greatness.[34]

Johnson saw his presidency as an opportunity to advance his Great Society programs and help people at every station of American society. Earlier in his career he had accumulated power and gained personal advancement, often by opposing civil rights legislation as was a political necessity for his Texas constituents. Once in the office of president, however, he personally was no longer beholden to a local constituency. With the power of the presidency in his hands, he was ready to pursue the policy ends he sought, even if those ends harmed the prospects of his party. Johnson wanted to make amends: "Very few people have a chance to correct the mistakes of their youth, and when you do, do it, and I have that chance and I'm going to do it now."[35]

Lyndon Johnson has been described as a political genius.[36] It is inconceivable that he was ignorant of how his pursuit of fairness jeopardized his presidency. He clearly wanted to retain office and regretted it when political realities forced him to step aside. But he is rare in the extent to which he suppressed the desire to retain office in favor of accomplishing his policy goals. His choice to desegregate the South is telling in this regard, as was his decision to make the burden of the Vietnam War as fair as he could. As Valenti tells it,

> Under terrible time pressure, Lyndon Johnson had to make a choice, one whose implications he understood with clear-eyed certainty. Should he push forward with his revolutionary agenda of civil rights and human justice, or should he deploy his considerable energies to fortify the Democratic Party for the next election and possibly for a generation of elections? He didn't hesitate. No president in the twentieth century had ever mounted such an all-out attack not just on one or two barriers, but on every obstacle to social and political equality. He took on racism, discrimination, and bigotry, with an eye to writing freedom into law and revising civic conduct. LBJ recognized the political hazards of unleashing the agents of such radical change, no matter that his central goal was to set right what was so cruelly wrong. He knew that if he waged war on segregation in the only way he knew how—without fatigue, hesitancy, or doubt—it would tear the South apart. And it would drive a spear into the heart of the Democratic Party.[37]

Johnson's civil rights legislation did indeed surrender the South to the Republican Party, a situation that persists until today. LBJ desegregated knowing that this would happen, as an account of a private meeting at the White House with Senator Richard B. Russell of Georgia, who had been instrumental in Johnson's career, makes clear:

> "Dick, I owe you, and I love you. If you hadn't made me leader, I would never have been vice president, and if I hadn't been vice president, I wouldn't be sitting here today. So, I owe you, Dick. I wanted to see you today to ask you not to get in my way on my civil rights bill. If you do, I will have to run you down." His voice was gentle and warm. There was no rancor and no hostility, only one old friend discussing a difficult matter with another. Russell hunched his shoulders. He said in those rolling accents of his beloved Georgia countryside: "Well, Mr. President, you may well do that, but if you do, you'll not only lose this election, you will lose the South forever." In all the years that followed, I was never prouder of Lyndon Johnson

than I was that morning. He put his hand on Russell's in a gesture of respectful affection and in a quiet voice said, "Dick, if that's the price I have to pay, I will gladly pay it."

Later LBJ [speaking to Valenti about this conversation]: "I'll win this election, but he's right about one thing. If I pass my civil rights bills, which I intend to do, the Democratic Party will have lost the South." LBJ's estimate of Senator Russell's forecasts was eerily prescient. LBJ did win the election, but he was the last Democratic candidate for president to win a majority of white male voters in the South. From that election on, the South has moved steadily toward the Republican Party. . . . [In the South] the color of the political map is Republican red.[38]

Just as Johnson wanted to reform the system at home to make it fair, his policies in conducting the Vietnam War were based on the same equality norms. He raised taxes to pay for the war so that its costs would less endanger his social programs. Likewise, he sought equality in terms of who did the fighting. Posing the question "Who serves when not all serve?,"[39] he argued that the existing draft system meant the disadvantaged in society disproportionately fought America's wars. With social justice in mind, he reformed the selective service system—the draft—so that the burden of fighting fell more evenly across society. Laudable as his interest in promoting equal treatment was, whether in voting rights or in serving the nation in wartime, Johnson's policies proved politically disastrous, as he readily could foresee. His draft reforms, especially the lottery system, imposed the costs of Vietnam squarely on the backs of his political supporters. These supporters objected and turned against the war. Ultimately, they deserted him, resulting in his decision not to engage in a futile pursuit of reelection in 1968.

Bush's Agenda: Reelection

BUSH DID NOT MAKE JOHNSON'S MISTAKE. HE, LIKE LBJ, EXPRESSED A willingness to sacrifice his presidency in order to fulfill his policy goals. Woodward reports on a conversation between Bush and senior members of his team in which the president declared, "I am prepared to risk my presidency to do what I think is right." And "it could cost the presidency, I fully realized that. But I felt so strongly that it was the right thing to do that I was prepared to do so." Bush also stated, "I would like to be a two-term president, but if I am a one-term president, so be it." Yet, although he also said that he would be "fully prepared to live with it [losing the presidency],'" unlike Johnson, he fought his war in a way designed to minimize such an eventuality.[40]

Despite the enormous economic cost and loss of life, the war in Iraq imposed relatively few costs on Republican backers. His supporters, typically drawn from the wealthier elements of the US population, were relatively unlikely to serve in Iraq and, if they did so, then they did so by choice. Further, rather than having to pay for the war, on average Bush supporters saw their taxes fall and their prosperity rise. Certainly, cuts in benefits and social programs hurt the poor under this administration. But the political reality is that the poor didn't vote for Bush anyway. Many would argue that the rise in the nation's indebtedness, decline in infrastructure, and growth in economic inequality left the United States weaker at the end of Bush's rule than at its beginning. But again, those who make these arguments were not, by and large, Bush supporters. His backers would remain loyal, reelecting him in 2004. Near financial collapse and recession in 2008 undermined W's popularity with his core constituencies, putting his reputation at risk, but by 2008, late in his second term, it didn't matter. He was, after all, term limited anyway. Just how differently Presidents Bush and Johnson distributed the costs of war is central to resolving why Bush managed reelection following an unpopular war and Johnson felt compelled to step aside during an equally unpopular war. We turn now to the detailed evidence of how differently these two presidents distributed the burden of war.

The Costs of War

POLITICIANS HAVE A COMPELLING INTEREST IN UNDERESTIMATING THE cost of any war they intend to fight. Equally, they have a compelling interest in misleading the public—especially in a democracy—about the true costs of war as it unfolds. Lyndon Johnson and George W. Bush were alike in this regard, although, as the next section makes clear, they were radically different in how they chose to pay the costs of war. Just what do wars like those in Vietnam and Iraq actually cost? A recent report by the Congressional Research Service provides the answer.

Both Vietnam and Iraq were hugely expensive. In 2011 US dollars, the Vietnam War cost $738 billion. In its peak year, 1968, the cost of the war was equivalent to 2.3 percent of GDP (gross domestic product), with total defense spending reaching 9.5 percent of GDP.[41] By the Congressional Research Service's accounting, the overall cost of the US intervention into Iraq is remarkably similar to the cost of Vietnam, $784 billion, with spending in Iraq having peaked at about 1 percent of GDP in 2008. Others argue that the real cost of Iraq is far higher: in an April 2008 *Vanity Fair* article, for instance, Economics Nobel Laureate Joseph Stiglitz, together with Linda Bilmes, argues, taking into account additional military spending, veterans' benefits, and economic losses, that Iraq is "The $3 Trillion War."[42]

To put the costs of Vietnam and Iraq in perspective, Figure 5.3 shows us defense spending in the United States since the end of World War II. We have shaded blocks of years during which the nation was involved in war, including Korea, Vietnam, the Gulf, and Iraq, as well as the period of Ronald Reagan's cold war armaments buildup in the 1980s. Obviously there are difficulties in directly assigning all the military spending to a particular war. As the numbers we just mentioned

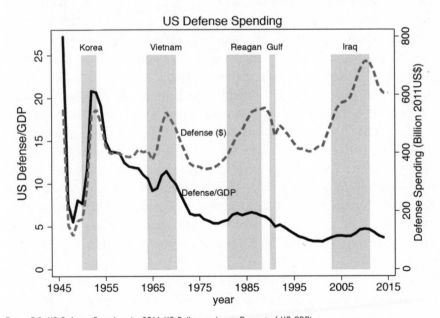

Figure 5.3. US Defense Spending (in 2011 US Dollars and as a Percent of US GDP)
Sources: http://comptroller.defense.gov/Portals/45/Documents/defbudget/fy2015/FY15_Green_Book.pdf and http://www.bea.gov/national/. The area shaded as Vietnam is 1964–1970, the term of major US troop deployment.

show, in 1968 Vietnam War spending accounted for only a quarter of US defense spending. Likewise, Iraq cannot account for all US defense spending as the war on terrorism and the US occupation of Afghanistan started in 2001 and overlapped with the Iraq War. Yet, the patterns are unmistakable. US involvement in Vietnam and Iraq created steep spikes in US defense spending. In the long run, guns can only be purchased at the expense of butter.

LBJ was sensitive to the "guns vs. butter" tradeoff. He realized that spending on the Vietnam War jeopardized his ability to get Congress to pass and fund his Great Society legislation. He used many dubious accounting practices to keep estimates of the war's true cost as low as possible. These cooked estimates undoubtedly contributed to the credibility gap that Johnson accumulated as his term unfolded. For instance, Califano reports, "As early as August 20, 1965, the President had written himself a note: 'McNamara's got to find ways to drag his feet on defense expenditures.' Pressed by LBJ, McNamara got the defense budget down to $60.5 billion, by arbitrarily assuming that the war would end on June 30, 1967, the final day of the fiscal year."[43] All politicians seeking authorization for war want to downplay the potential cost. Remember, for instance, how quickly the Democrat-Republicans in Congress turned on their ally, Treasury Secretary Albert Gallatin, for his estimates of the cost of the War of 1812, estimates that with hindsight turned out to be extremely conservative. Comparison to that war is perhaps more pertinent than one might think. In terms of a percentage of GDP, the peak of the 1812 conflict cost about the same as Vietnam; 2.2 percent in 1813 and 2.3 percent in 1968.[44]

Like LBJ, the Bush administration also sought to hide the costs of their wars in Afghanistan and then Iraq. In September 2002, White House economic adviser Lawrence Lindsey estimated the cost of the Iraq War would be $100–$200 billion.[45] For his pains he was pushed out of his job. Secretary of Defense Rumsfeld estimated the cost at $50–$60 billion.[46] In an evaluation of the Bush administration's assessment of war costs, an article in *The Guardian* newspaper contended that:

> George Bush sold the war as quick and cheap. . . . The most striking fact about the cost of the war in Iraq has been the extent to which it has been kept "off the books" of the government's ledgers and hidden from the American people. This was done by design. A fundamental assumption of the Bush administration's approach to the

war was that it was only politically sustainable if it was portrayed as near-costless to the American public and to key constituencies in Washington. The dirty little secret of the Iraq war—one that both Bush and the war hawks in the Democratic Party knew, but would never admit—was that the American people would only support a war to get rid of Saddam Hussein if they could be assured that they would pay almost nothing for it.[47]

Who Paid the Price of War?

LYNDON JOHNSON'S APPROACH TO FINANCING WAR ON A PAY-AS-you-go, debit card basis was eminently sensible economically, though certainly not politically. So was his approach to taxing the populace for the war effort and distributing the burden of fighting equitably. These were probably good for the nation, but politically ruinous. Bush had a less normatively laudable but vastly more successful strategy: foist the cost of fighting onto political opponents and declare victory.

At the end of the day, LBJ wanted his social programs and he could not have them without putting the defense budget on a sound financial footing. That meant raising taxes to pay for both. While increasing taxes is almost always thought to be a poison pill for politicians, Johnson's 1968 State of the Union Address was frank and urged Congress to pass a tax surcharge:

> I warn the Congress and the Nation tonight that this failure to act on the tax bill will sweep us into an accelerating spiral of price increases, a slump in homebuilding, and a continuing erosion of the American dollar.
>
> This would be a tragedy for every American family. And I predict that if this happens, they will all let us know about it.
>
> Under the new budget, the expenditures for 1969 will increase by $10.4 billion. Receipts will increase by $22.3 billion including the added tax revenues. Virtually all of this expenditure increase represents the mandatory cost of our defense efforts, $3 billion; increased interest, almost $1 billion; or mandatory payments under laws. . . .
>
> The fiscal 1969 budget has expenditures of approximately $186 billion, with total estimated revenues, including the tax bill, of about $178 billion.

If the Congress enacts the tax increase, we will reduce the budget
deficit by some $12 billion. The war in Vietnam is costing us about
$25 billion and we are asking for about $12 billion in taxes—and if
we get that $12 billion tax bill we will reduce the deficit from about
$20 billion in 1968 to about $8 billion in 1969.[48]

In fact, Johnson's tax surcharge created a budget surplus of about
$3 billion in 1969. His overriding desire, his Great Society program,
could not be fulfilled without tax revenue, especially at a time when
the costs of war imposed a heavy financial burden on the government
and the society. Of course, the political anathema associated with tax
increases might be escaped if the increased tax burden was targeted
primarily against the president's political foes rather than his constituents. That, however, was not the path followed by Johnson; it was
Bush's approach.

In his 2002 State of the Union Address, Bush examined the cost
of fighting and the need to pay it. Speaking about Afghanistan at this
point, he declared,

It costs a lot to fight this war. We have spent more than a billion
dollars a month—over $30 million a day—and we must be prepared
for future operations. Afghanistan proved that expensive precision
weapons defeat the enemy and spare innocent lives, and we need
more of them. . . .

My budget includes the largest increase in defense spending
in two decades—because while the price of freedom and security is
high, it is never too high. *Whatever it costs to defend our country, we
will pay* [emphasis added].[49]

However, in the same speech Bush negated the "we will pay"
declaration as he announced plans to reduce taxation:

Congress listened to the people and responded by reducing tax rates,
doubling the child credit, and ending the death tax. For the sake of
long-term growth and to help Americans plan for the future, let's
make these tax cuts permanent. . . . [S]peeding up tax relief so people
have more money to spend. For the sake of American workers, let's
pass a stimulus package. . . .

As we reauthorize these important reforms, we must always remember the goal is to reduce dependency on government and offer
every American the dignity of a job.

War has to be paid for at some point, but Bush ensured that his war
in Iraq—and shortly after this speech, his other war in Afghanistan—
would not be paid for until later, and he also ensured that the wars
would not be paid for by the relatively well-off, many of whom were
his supporters. Figure 5.4 shows that Johnson did not make the politically expedient choice to postpone paying for war, but Bush did.

In the two panels of Figure 5.4, we see the change in the average
federal income tax rates paid by families at different income levels over
the years of Lyndon Johnson's presidency and also during George W.
Bush's presidency. The graph divides the taxpayers into five equally
sized groups (quintiles). The solid black line shows the shifting average

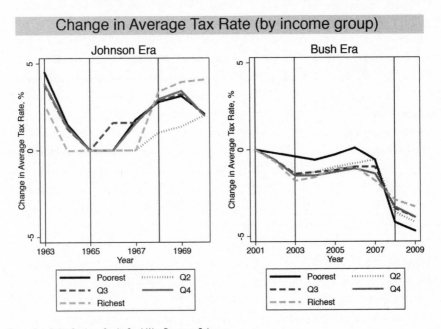

Figure 5.4. Debit Card vs. Credit Card War Payment Schemes
The data reported in the figure are calculated from marginal tax rates and the income of the first four quintiles of the
income distribution and the fifth percentile of the income distribution.
Sources: Tax rate data: http://taxfoundation.org/article/us-federal-individual-income-tax-rates-history-1913–2013
-nominal-and-inflation-adjusted-brackets. Income distribution data: https://www.census.gov/hhes/www/income
/data/historical/families/

level of tax paid by families in the lowest 20 percent of the income distribution. The dashed lines show the average change in tax rate for families 40 percent from the bottom of the income distribution, and so on.

The side-by-side panels tell a powerful story of two radically different approaches to paying for war. The left panel shows that between late 1963, when Johnson first assumed the presidency, and 1965, when he took office following the 1964 election, taxes were cut for everyone. As we have noted, after the Gulf of Tonkin Resolution, the United States greatly increased its war effort in Vietnam. Starting in 1965, the base year—his first as the elected president—against which we have measured changes in tax rates (noting, of course, that shifts in income would have moved people into or out of higher/lower tax brackets), Johnson raised rates on everyone. He was paying for the war and for the Great Society. The rich, likely to be Republican supporters, paid more taxes but so, too, did people with lower incomes, those likely to be Democratic supporters. Johnson's tax hikes affected friend and foe alike.

In comparison, as we can see in the right-hand panel, tax rates by quintile fell for everyone during Bush's presidency. They fell the least for the poorest quintile, those least likely to have been Bush voters. The taxes of the two wealthiest income quintiles fell slightly faster than everyone else's most of the time during Bush's eight years in office. Their advantage is small but notable: the evidence shows that in a progressive tax system, we should expect tax reductions to benefit the poorest quintile the most and the wealthiest the least, the opposite of what we observed during Bush's term.[50] The tax changes further exacerbated the growing disparity between rich and poor. Between 2001 and 2007—before the financial crash—the richest quintile saw their average post-tax income rise from $165,000 to $214,000 (30 percent). In contrast, the comparable changes for the poorest and medium income quintile groups were $26,000 to $30,000 (15 percent) and $55,000 to $60,000 (9 percent), respectively.[51] Since the wealthy tended to be disproportionately Republican during W's 2004 election, those most likely to be Bush voters probably enjoyed greater tax abatement and saw their income soar.[52] Those likely to have voted Democrat fared less well.

Furthermore, whereas Johnson was trying to pay for the war as it was fought by raising taxes, Bush put off paying for the war, thereby avoiding the alienation of his voters. The financial burden of the war was only to come crashing down on the economy with the start of the recession, in the twilight of Bush's time in office.

Figure 5.5 gives us another view of the differences in how the Vietnam and Iraq Wars were paid for. On the left we see the US debt during Johnson's years in office. The debt shrank persistently throughout the years he was in office with only a slight upward burp in 1968, immediately replaced by a resumed downward trend. Not only was he taxing everyone to pay for the war, but between his tax policy and national economic performance, the vast cost of the war was not accumulating as a debt for future generations. Johnson's Vietnam War was paid for as it happened. Conversely, Bush's Iraq War was not only accompanied by tax cuts, especially for the wealthier (read Republican) voters, but it was also funded through deficit spending. Bush's policy pushed the costs of the war off, necessitating that they be dealt with during his successor's term in office. Too bad he did not take seriously President Johnson's admonishment to the Congress that we quoted earlier: "I warn the Congress and the Nation tonight that this failure to act on the tax bill will sweep us into an accelerating spiral of price increases, a slump in homebuilding, and a continuing erosion of the American dollar."[53] Sounds an awful lot like what happened in 2008, as the country faced the economic consequences of a war it had not paid for!

George W. Bush's approach to war financing—buy now, pay later—helped him win reelection; Lyndon Johnson's debit card

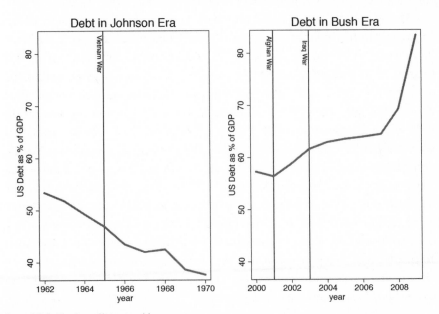

Figure 5.5. Indebtedness, Vietnam and Iraq

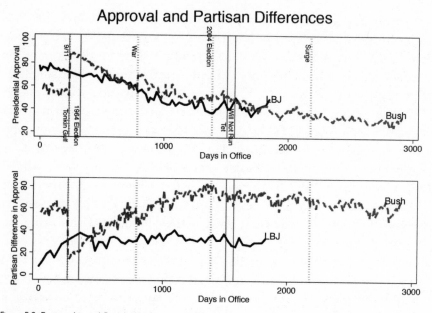

Figure 5.6. Partisanship and Presidential Approval: LBJ and W

approach—pay as you go—contributed to his inability to pursue re-election in 1968. The difference was not that one president was hugely popular and the other hugely unpopular. Rather, the difference was in the partisan spread in popularity. Figure 5.6 shows this clearly.

We see in the upper panel that both LBJ's and W's approval ratings followed almost in lockstep. Approval declined over time, as is the common pattern for most presidents.[54] Evaluations of Johnson's approval rating, of course, end sooner than Bush's, since Bush was president for nearly three thousand days and Johnson for less than two thousand. As we can see, Bush got a short-term burst in popularity following 9/11 and a smaller one at the outset of the Iraq War, but his approval trajectory, like LBJ's, was inexorably downward. If we look at Bush's equivalent time in office prior to the 2004 election as the number of days prior to the 1968 election at which Johnson announced he would not seek reelection, we see that Bush's and Johnson's approval ratings were nearly identical. So, differences in presidential approval do not help us understand why Bush succeeded in his reelection effort and Johnson abandoned his. Rather, the difference between the president who believed he could not be reelected and the one who was is evident from the bottom panel of the figure.

The bottom panel reports the difference in presidential approval by his respective partisans—Democrats in Johnson's case and Republicans in Bush's—and his opposition. As we should expect, Democrats were more approving of Johnson than were Republicans. At the outset, for Johnson, there was virtually no partisan difference in his approval ratings. This should not surprise us, as he assumed the presidency in November 1963 following John Kennedy's assassination, an event that deeply shocked the nation. Once ensconced in his own right following the 1964 election, his approval ratings among Democrats were 30 to 40 percent higher than his ratings among Republicans, a figure that remained relatively stable throughout his presidency. The contrast to the partisan differences in voter approval for Bush could hardly be starker. When he took office, the gap between Republican and Democrat approval of the new president was around 60 percent and rising . . . until the terrorist attacks on September 11, 2001. On that horrific day and for a short time afterward, Republicans and Democrats rallied round the flag, giving the president very strong approval. By the time the United States went to war against Saddam Hussein's regime in Iraq, however, the partisan split in presidential approval was greater than it ever had been for Johnson. It was back to the level of partisan divide that had greeted Bush when he first assumed the presidency amid the hanging-chad controversy. From the onset of the Iraq War forward, for the remainder of Bush's first term and his reelection, the partisan spread in approval hovered in the 70–80 percent range, falling below 60 percent briefly at the very end of Bush's second term. That is, Republicans loved Bush; Democrats hated him.

Here in the difference in partisan divides we see almost the entire story of why two unpopular wars led to such radically different political outcomes. Johnson made Democrats and Republicans alike pay for his war. Bush pushed off paying for his wars, cutting taxes and cutting them least for likely Democrat voters while increasing the deficit, leaving the war to be paid for by his successor(s). Republican voters, having enjoyed a hefty reduction in their tax burden under Bush, looked the other way at the massive deficit he built up—a policy that they adamantly oppose when it is not accompanied by or caused by tax benefits for them—and gave him overwhelming support in his reelection campaign. Voters either loved him or hated him and which they did was strongly driven by their partisanship and, presumably, by their associated tax relief. As Vice President Joseph Biden observed of the massive debt the Obama administration inherited: "And, by the way, they [Republicans] talk about this Great Recession [as] if it fell out of the sky, like, 'Oh, my goodness, where did it come from?' It came from this man [Bush] voting to put two wars on a credit card, to at the same time put a prescription drug benefit on the credit card, a trillion-dollar tax cut for the very wealthy. I was there. I voted against them. I said, no, we can't afford that. And now, all of a sudden, these guys are so seized with the concern about the debt that they created."[55] Of course, from the perspective of the Bush administration, what could be more perfect than getting a second term and then having someone else pick up the credit card bill? And from Johnson's perspective, at least in hindsight, what could have been worse than paying for the Vietnam War as it was fought, thereby losing the chance of a second term?

We have seen who paid the financial costs of Vietnam and Iraq. But war entails other, deeper, more painful immediate costs beyond the out-of-pocket payment with dollars. War's greatest cost is in the loss of life and life's opportunities. We turn now to an assessment of who paid these costs in the cases of Vietnam and Iraq.

The Human Cost of War

Casualties reduce support for war. We saw this in figures 5.1 and 5.2. As US casualties climbed, more and more people thought that Vietnam and Iraq were mistakes. Certainly these broad trends show the correlation between US deaths and Americans' opposition to war. Yet, people are generally very poor at conceptualizing the significance of statistics. They are much more sensitive to how events relate to them personally. The implication of US troop deaths is far more salient when it happens to family, friends, neighbors, or those in the local community. Citizens are more likely to oppose a war when those around them die or when they are personally exposed to danger. In the cases of Vietnam and Iraq, political scientists Scott Gartner and Gary Segura document the impact of casualties at this personal level. They examine local public opinion and voting records and show that voters from localities with disproportionately high casualties oppose wars and vote against incumbents. Voters from locales with few casualties remain more supportive of war. Headlines about national losses are hard for people to process and so they have less impact than the loss of local young adults: "all politics are local."[56]

We have seen throughout that politicians generally adopt positions that serve their interests, even when that means not serving those of the nation's citizens. LBJ's approach to war may be the rare exception and also the telling lesson: a president who did what he thought was right even though it harmed him politically, costing him his chance for reelection. Presidents who put their own interest front and center have been particularly likely to get elected and reelected! Citizens should perhaps not be too harsh on such a politician, they are prone to do the same.

To gain traction on why Bush was reelected and Johnson's prospects were so poor that he did not even run, it is useful to think about who fought in each war. We start by considering who served in Iraq. Since Vietnam, the United States has not drafted soldiers to fight. Instead, the government relies on an all-volunteer army. The socioeconomic and racial composition of the armed forces has undergone substantial changes from the 1970s. For instance, the proportion of nonwhites in the US armed forces has declined markedly from the Vietnam era, although whites are still underrepresented. The educational attainment of soldiers has also increased over this time—in part reflecting the military's increasing reliance on technology and the skills needed to exploit it.

While in the Iraq era US armed forces were drawn from all walks of life, those from the top and the very bottom of the socioeconomic ladder were underrepresented.[57] Members of wealthy families were less likely to serve than those of the middle class. This somewhat reduced the likelihood that supporters and contributors to the Bush campaign would be directly affected by the war. A further consequence of an all-volunteer military is that casualties do not include local young men who were recently drafted, possibly against their will, as was the case in Vietnam. The impact of Iraq War casualties was keenly felt in military towns around the country, but the imagery of coffins of recently drafted young men going back to small towns around the United States was a feature of Vietnam and not of Iraq. Unlike Vietnam, "most Americans were not asked to make any sacrifice for the Iraq war."[58] Outside of military towns, people were unlikely to encounter the human tragedy of war as had been the case in Vietnam; hence casualties were less likely to turn supporters against the administration.

One of the great arguments for democracy is that it is the people who do the fighting, making them reluctant to go to war casually. As philosopher Emmanuel Kant stated:

> [I]f the consent of the citizens is required in order to decide that war should be declared (and in this constitution it cannot but be the case), nothing is more natural than that they would be very cautious in commencing such a poor game, decreeing for themselves all the calamities of war. Among the latter would be: having to fight, having to pay the costs of war from their own resources, having painfully to repair the devastation war leaves behind, and, to fill up the measure of evils, load themselves with a heavy national debt that would embitter peace itself and that can never be liquidated on account of constant wars in the future.[59]

However, as we saw in the case of Iraq, Kant's argument only works if the cost of the war falls on the vast majority of people. If a politician can form a winning coalition of supporters who are immune from the human and financial costs of the war, then these supporters provide little impediment to the leader's conduct of the war. Those groups of people outside of the coalition might suffer greatly as a result of the war and protest the war vigorously, but their suffering is no impediment to a leader kept in office by others.

As we have seen, Bush strongly alienated Democratic (and independent) voters, but he kept Republican voters happy. They turned out to vote for him and he retained office. On aggregate, the war generated protest and disapproval, but such negatives were not evenly spread across everyone. His policies insulated his supporters from the effects of the Iraq War. In contrast, Johnson's drive for equality and fairness ensured that as disapproval for the Vietnam War grew, disapproval grew in all segments of society and, most important, from within his support base. We have already seen that his tax plan harmed middle-class voters who otherwise would have been likely to turn out and vote Democrat. Now we can see a similar pattern in his choice to pursue equality in individual risks during the Vietnam War.

In the Vietnam era, US professional armed forces were supplemented by a selective service draft. In the early 1960s draft boards were organized at the local level. Generally the rich, white, and educated could gain exemptions or deferments. In an earlier time Benjamin

Franklin admonished us as to the fairness of such an arrangement: "The question will then amount to this; whether it be just in a community, that the richer part should compel the poor to fight for them and their properties."[60] Johnson certainly believed that it was wrong that the cost of fighting fell disproportionately on the disadvantaged in society. And as with his social and civil rights programs, he decided to do something about. He organized a board, whose members included blacks and other disadvantaged minorities, to design reforms to the draft procedure.

In a message to Congress regarding selective service, LBJ opened by quoting Franklin Roosevelt to the effect that "America has adopted selective service in time of peace, and, in doing so, has broadened and enriched our basic concepts of citizenship. Beside the clear democratic ideals of equal rights, equal privileges and equal opportunities, we have set forth the underlying other duties, obligations and responsibilities of equal service." However, as we discovered earlier, FDR did not follow through on these lofty ideals. Johnson, for his part, intended to do so. He argued that the extant system was prone to favoritism and corruption. He asked the leading question: "'Who serves when not all serve?' Past procedures have, in effect, reduced the size of the available manpower pool by deferring men out of it. This has resulted in inequities."[61]

Johnson called for a "Fair And Impartial Random (FAIR) system"; that is, a lottery system. The lotteries randomly drew 366 dates and young men born on the first date selected were the first to be drafted. The next set of draftees was selected from those born on the second date selected, and so on. The first of LBJ's selective service lotteries was held on December 1, 1969, at the Selective Service National Headquarters in Washington, DC, and the event was televised. As the president's adviser Joseph Califano observed, "Here was a system more to LBJ's liking, one in which rich and poor, black and white, would face the same odds of military service in young adulthood."[62] Johnson concluded, regarding the revised selective service approach, "We must continue to ask one form of service—military duty—of our young men. We would be an irresponsible Nation if we did not—and perhaps even an extinct one. The Nation's requirement that men must serve, however, imposes this obligation: that in this land of equals, men are selected as equals to serve. A just nation must have the fairest system that can be devised for making that selection."[63]

Johnson may indeed have liked the more equitable treatment induced by his lottery system, but it turned out to work against him politically. In a reflection of local, personal interests at work in politics, regardless of the broader implication for equality and national well-being, it turned out that men with low draft numbers, and hence likely to be sent to Vietnam, were more likely to shift their position to oppose the war as compared to those with high draft numbers.[64]

Johnson's reform of the draft system removed exemptions and greatly increased the chances that everyone had to be called upon to serve. While perhaps normatively desirable and creating a brake against adventurous foreign policies in the manner suggested by Kant, for a leader already at war, shifting the burden of fighting from the poor and minorities (who, despite Johnson's civil rights laws, still voted at lower rates) to middle-class families from whom he drew his support, was political suicide. The president was effectively asking middle-class families to support him as he sent their sons or the sons of their neighbors and friends to fight a very bloody war.

By spreading the burden of service more evenly, Johnson ensured that many US voters had a personal connection to someone forced to serve. This imposition of the human cost on supporters as well as opponents undermined his political support. And indeed, as we have seen, his approval rating, like Bush's later on, was in steep decline. Unlike Bush, however, his equitable treatment of the human and financial costs of war meant that even his own partisans stopped supporting him, a consequence not suffered by Bush, who did not shift the burden of war to everyone. W insulated his backers, and in doing so, he gained the benefit of their continued loyalty. That, we believe, is the essence of what drove Johnson from office and gained Bush the electoral support and legitimacy he desired.

To be sure, both presidents did what they believed was right for America. The big difference was that Bush had the advantage that what he surely and sincerely thought was good for the country—whether it was or was not—happened also to be policies that were good for him politically. Johnson's promoting of equality of treatment in everything the government and society did, made the United States a better place in the long run and did Johnson in politically in the short run. The remarkable aspect of his pursuit of equality is that he understood that it was likely to hurt the Democratic Party and it was likely to hurt his aspirations for a full second term. Indeed, as much as "We, the people" cry out for principled politicians, Americans rejected Lyndon Johnson exactly because he followed a principle that distributed the costs of war—admittedly an unpopular and perhaps mistaken war—not only on to his opponents but to his supporters as well.

What If?

B Y SPREADING THE BURDEN OF SERVICE EVENLY, LYNDON JOHNSON ensured that many US voters had a personal connection to someone forced to serve. As we approach our conclusion and assess how to restrain overly aggressive foreign policies and wanton war making, it is worthwhile to ponder the counterfactual: could Bush have convinced the Congress and the nation to back the invasion of Iraq if Johnson's FAIR draft system had been used? Likewise, if the Bush administration had been legislatively constrained to implement a tax surcharge across all tax brackets to cover the cost of the Wars in Iraq and Afghanistan, would Bush's support have remained as strong?

We know that the Afghan War was viewed by the American public as a well justified response to the al-Qaeda attacks of September 11, 2001. The Iraq War did not share in that widespread support. Had President Bush been compelled to go before the public and address reasonable, external, *nonpartisan* estimates of the human and financial costs of both the Afghan and Iraq Wars before either began, then it seems likely that he would have found the public rallying behind the Afghan War and the public—and their representatives in Congress— becoming more reluctant to initiate a less well-justified war in Iraq. By the simple expedient of exposing his own backers to the human risks and costs of the war through a lottery system for military service, he might have found that prudent political decision making argued in favor of going ahead with the Afghan War and not going ahead with Iraq. That is, had he been made by statute to follow the path that Lyndon Johnson chose to follow—pay the financial costs for each war out-of-pocket, not by building the national debt, and pay the human costs equitably so that all segments of society were equally at risk—then we might not have had an Iraq War. It does not follow, by the way, that this also would have meant putting Bush's reelection at risk. Indeed, it probably would have strengthened his claim for reelection and given him a stronger mandate in 2004. The nation rallied behind the strike against Afghanistan. That war did not suffer from as deep a partisan divide as did the Iraq War. Thus, a war that was justified in the eyes of the public would not have then been as detrimental to his reelection as was a war that was not well justified in the public's estimation, just as Vietnam came to be a war not well justified by the facts in the 1960s.

Against our argument for avoiding the Iraq War by spreading the costs to everyone, some may object that it would have deprived President Bush of his objective to oust Saddam Hussein. But the facts do not seem to support that view. Interestingly, in early February 2003, the son of Hosni Mubarak, who was then Egypt's president, met secretly with Bush with a proposal that the Hussein family would likely go into exile in Egypt if guaranteed safety and $2 billion. Such an arrangement would likely have avoided the need to invade, but Bush refused to assure their safety.[65] Had Bush been looking to avoid war or had he faced the sort of requirements we have set out, this approach would have been well worth exploring rather than dismissing out of hand. Of course, the idea of protecting such an evil person as Saddam Hussein and assuring his vast wealth is exceedingly unpleasant. But in a world of difficult choices, having taken his offer to go into exile, we might then have avoided the death and destruction of the war and the subsequent instability in Iraq that followed from the failure to have a well-worked-out plan for how Iraq was to govern itself in the post–Saddam Hussein period. True as it is that getting rid of Hussein could have been a grand accomplishment, without a sound basis for Iraqi governance after Hussein, it is not evident, contrary to the claims of President Bush and his senior advisers, that the world is better off without him. Certainly it could have been, but then that required a sound and practical vision of governance that was not applied to Iraq either by Bush's administration or the subsequent administration of President Obama. In the end, a few simple expedients and greater openness to compromise could have avoided the Iraq War, husbanded more resources for a better effort in Afghanistan, and protected American society from the deep division that Iraq foisted on it.

Chapter 6

John Kennedy and Barack Obama: Two Paths of "Peace"

I think I would have been impeached.
—**John F. Kennedy**

Dᴇᴄɪᴅɪɴɢ ʜᴏᴡ ᴛᴏ ʀᴇꜱᴏʟᴠᴇ ᴄʀɪꜱᴇꜱ ᴘᴇᴀᴄᴇꜰᴜʟʟʏ ᴡʜᴇɴ ᴛʜᴇʏ ɪɴᴄʟᴜᴅᴇ ᴀ serious risk of leading to war is every bit as important as deciding if, when, and how to wage war. Indeed, the biggest potential wars in history are those that never happened. They were averted out of fear of their consequences or out of recognition that their outsize costs swamped any potential gains. That might have been the story of America's Civil War and the two world wars but for two considerations: uncertainty about the resolve of the other side, and the gap between the interests of everyday people and those of individual leaders.

The avoidance of a potentially huge war is the story of President John F. Kennedy's Cuban missile crisis in 1962. It may or may not be the story that historians will tell about the cautious actions of the

United States government under Barack Obama in dealing with the interlinked tales of Syria's Bashar al-Assad, the Islamic State, renewed Sunni-Shia struggles in Iraq, and the threat of Russian expansion into its neighboring states. In these latter cases a large war may well have been averted. That is to the good as far as it goes. But was war averted in the manner most beneficial to the interests of the average American or, for that matter, the average citizen of the world? Or was war averted without regard to those broad interests, primarily serving instead the short-term electoral interests of the president's political allies? Might the avoidance of war today precipitate a bigger, costlier war tomorrow? We explore how to answer these questions, in the process hopefully improving our ability to think through crisis management in the future.

We have seen that even America's most iconic presidents chose between war and peace based largely on what was good for them rather than whether it was good for "We, the people." In doing so, they always had to face the difficult calculation of the personal and national expected costs and benefits of war and, as is too often overlooked, the costs and benefits of peace. War, after all, is neither inherently always the wrong course to take, nor is it necessarily the right way to solve foreign—or domestic—crises.

Our central concern continues to be an effort to foster an understanding that even as extreme a policy as deciding to wage war—or to live with an uncomfortable peace—is shaped by calculations of personal political interest above any notion of a national grand strategy or national interest. Here we shall further illustrate these ideas with two examples that did not lead to war: the Cuban missile crisis of 1962 and the Ukraine crisis of 2014, each a dispute involving the United States and Russia. Comparing these events will help to nail down the realization that war avoidance—sometimes wisely and sometimes dangerously—follows the same logic that entails all the concerns James Madison so eloquently set forth about the dangers of executive authority over questions of war and peace. Madison, wise man that he was, expressed a clear and compelling judgment of politicians, of which, of course, he was one: "All men having power ought to be distrusted to a certain degree."[1]

Setting the Stage: Cuba and Crimea

Russia's occupation of Crimea in 2014 was followed by a pro-Russian insurrection in East Ukraine that by all appearances was fostered by the Russian government. The 2014 actions by the Russian government of Vladimir Putin had many of the same causes and the same motivations as Soviet premier Nikita Khrushchev's 1962 decision to place nuclear weapons and missile delivery capabilities in Cuba. In each instance the Russian leadership justified its actions in terms of its concerns about US/Western encirclement and expansion against Russian (read: Khrushchev's and Putin's) interests. In Cuba the worry followed from efforts by the US government to depose Fidel Castro's regime, the one government in the Western Hemisphere that was aligned with Russia. In Ukraine Putin was similarly concerned about the deposition of Ukraine's president, Viktor Yanukovych, who, from the Russian perspective, was overthrown in a US-inspired popular uprising and coup. While war was avoided in each case, nevertheless these two crises had radically different results with, we contend, quite different consequences for the prospects of future peace. In that way they offer two quite different tales of how personal political incentives shape efforts to avoid war and how those efforts shape the peace that follows.

The Cuban missile crisis had the potential to become the most destructive war in human history. President Kennedy observed at the time that "the fruits of victory would be ashes in our mouth."[2] Instead of leading to a nuclear holocaust, the Cuban missile crisis became a source of restraint in the dangerous interactions between the United States and the Soviet Union throughout the remaining nearly thirty years of the cold war era. It produced an uncomfortable but sustainable peace. The Crimea crisis and the broader Ukraine crisis hopefully will be an event that fades from memory, a regrettable instance of needless but short-lived border strife, but there is also a chance (small, we hope and believe) that it was an early salvo in an extremely deadly future war in Europe! For now it seems to have led to a fragile, unsettling, un-settled, and uncomfortable peace. Unlike the Cuban crisis, the "peace" in Ukraine today, under the Minsk Protocol of February 2015, which calls for a ceasefire, monitoring, and other conditions, each of which is violated as often as it is respected, seems like the foundation of a peace that "passeth understanding" and that may come back to bite all those who hope for sustained peace *and* justice in the world.[3] We begin our exploration of these two similar and yet also importantly different events with the more recent Crimea crisis and its broader implications for the future of Ukraine and European peace.

The Crimea/Ukraine: Core Voters vs. National Security

To UNDERSTAND RUSSIA'S OCCUPATION OF CRIMEA AND ITS SUBSEQUENT fostering of a broader civil war in Ukraine, we must realize that whenever a national leader makes declarations about matters of war and peace, there are always at least three sets of ears listening on each side of the dispute: rival leaders, domestic backers, and enemy allies. The parties each interpret what the signals mean for them. What were the messages sent by Vladimir Putin when he promoted crisis in Ukraine? What was heard by Barack Obama, by American and European voters, and by Putin's own core backers; that is, the small group of insiders whose loyalty to Putin has been cemented by their fulfilled opportunities to become men—they are just about all men—of power and great wealth? Likewise, we must ask, what are the messages that Barack Obama sent to Vladimir Putin, to Obama's core constituents, and to Putin's key supporters? What did each of these sets of ears hear and what did they try to make heard in return?

To understand the Russian decision to invade and annex Crimea, we must start with the earliest signals that then presidential candidate Barack Obama sent out to the ears of the world regarding the sort of foreign policy he would follow. In interpreting those signals, we rely on analysis done back in 2008, when one of the authors, teaching an undergraduate seminar called "Solving Foreign Crises," worked with students who applied game theory to work out the likely implications of the withdrawal (or nonwithdrawal) of US troops from Iraq, paying particular attention to its consequences for internal Iraqi politics and for Iraq-Iran relations. At the time the study was done the students did not yet know who would be elected president in 2008. Therefore, they did not analyze whether troops would or would not be withdrawn but rather what the consequences of each decision was likely to be. What we report here is a summary of the findings as reported in detail elsewhere and published before any of the important decisions were actually made[4]—which means Vladimir Putin and other world leaders might just as readily have anticipated the subsequent developments as did undergraduate students using a simple political forecasting model. It is important to our argument that this student analysis and the forecasting model that turned their data into projections shows that the subsequent impact of Obama's policies was predictable.

During the 2008 campaign, candidate Obama, appealing to his antiwar electoral base of support, promised that if elected, he would withdraw American troops from Iraq within sixteen months. Later, however, in February 2009, President Obama stretched his preelection withdrawal timetable to August 2010, creating chagrin among the Democratic Party's loyalists who, hearing that there was not a firm commitment to full withdrawal before 2011, complained that he was moving too slowly on what they believed was his firm policy commitment: to pull US forces out of Iraq altogether. Then, too, the possibility remained that the 2011 deadline could be extended indefinitely.

The student assessment indicated that if the United States withdrew its troops, then Iraq's prime minister, Nouri al-Maliki, would be challenged by the leading political representatives of Sunni interests in Iraq and that in response, Maliki would shore up his political position by aligning his government with Iran. The student analysis indicated Maliki would not take this latter action if US troops remained in Iraq. The game theoretic analysis indicated that such a security arrangement between Iraq and Iran would help defend the Iraqi regime against a Sunni-led insurgency or civil war, while bolstering Iran's political position in the region. This is, of course, what we have since seen with the growth of the Islamic State of Iraq and Syria (ISIS) and its seizure of Iraqi territory, followed by the Iranian military presence in Iraq intended to defeat ISIS while keeping other Sunni interests at bay.

Obama's decision to withdraw from Iraq must have begun to instruct Vladimir Putin, then Russia's prime minister and shortly to resume his old place as its president, about his potential future leverage with the US president. In particular, he is likely to have recognized that Obama was constrained by the wishes of his core constituents. In turn, Putin likely believed he could take actions to advance his—and his core backers'—interests, without fear of any countermaneuvers that would contradict the interests of President Obama's core political constituency. To put matters plainly, Obama had promised less fighting, not more, so Putin became aggressive.

By the end of Obama's first term, his constituents saw action—troop withdrawals—that pleased them. Putin and his constituents saw early indications of new opportunities that they might be able to exploit. Now we run the clock forward just a few months from the October 2011 announcement of the complete withdrawal of US troops from Iraq and the beginning of troop withdrawals from Afghanistan. In March 2012 President Obama whispered to the lame-duck Russian president Dimitri Medvedev to pass on to Russia's then president-elect, Vladimir Putin, that this "is my last election. After my election I have more flexibility."[5] Obama was referring to his future flexibility on the big questions that shaped relations between the governments of the United States and Russia, relations he was trying to "reset" after a period of deterioration during the presidency of George W. Bush. Well aware that public statements are heard by everyone, Obama tried to keep his whispered statement to Medvedev for just the ears of Russia's leaders, but surely to his regret, a microphone picked up the message. It became the whisper heard round the world. The message essentially was, "We won't be so tough on you after our election, so give me some space." Fine enough; message sent, delivered, and, alas for Obama, overheard.

Now let's run the clock forward one more year to March 2013. President Obama, having defeated Mitt Romney and being firmly ensconced in his second term, spoke in Jerusalem. He used the occasion to shore up his relationship with Israel's leaders and its people. There were severe tensions, indeed rebellion, in Israel's neighboring state of Syria. The rebellion in Syria was a matter of great concern to both Israel and America. Obama declared that if he discovered that chemical weapons were used in Syria (or really anywhere else) by Bashar al-Assad's government, that would be a "game changer."[6] The implied message was, "American constituents, Israeli friends, Syrian rebels, President Assad, I am speaking publicly, loud and clear: Assad: Don't force me to stop the use of chemical weapons; don't you dare use them! Israeli and US backers: I will not allow Syria's president to use unconventional weapons against our friends in the anti-Assad resistance. Vladimir Putin and any other allies of Assad's regime: There is a line beyond which I will be compelled to act—don't let your friend Assad cross that line."

A tough message? Maybe! Or maybe it was a cheap threat with nothing to back it up. Time would tell. Putin already knew that the first-term President Obama had made decisions regarding Iraq and Afghanistan that ran against the advice of top US military commanders but that were pleasing to American voters, at least those who supported Obama. Now Putin needed to see whether the "game changer" message was really serious or whether it was just intended to mollify the Israelis.

On September 16, 2013, the world learned that "U.N. inspectors said Monday there is 'clear and convincing evidence' that chemical weapons were used on a relatively large scale in an attack last month in Syria that killed hundreds of people."[7] All involved parties were on notice; here was Obama's "game changer." Now the question was, how had the game changed? What were the consequences of Assad's apparent use of chemical weapons—we say "apparent" because the UN did not determine who had used chemical weapons, only that they had been used. Still, only Assad's forces had the capability to deliver such weapons, as they were delivered by rocket. As President Obama stated, "We do not believe that, given the delivery systems, using rockets, that the opposition could have carried out these attacks. We have concluded that the Syrian government in fact carried these out."[8] The ball was now in Obama's court. He now had to reveal to all the ears that were listening whether his earlier statement was sincere or bluff.

In hindsight it seems that Obama thought that his vague message—"game changer"—would be sufficient to deter Assad; now he and the world knew it was not. Apparently uncertain about how to proceed, he asked Congress to decide what course of action they could and would approve. As evidence mounted that Congress would not approve strong action, concern grew at home that to save face Obama would have to act under his authority as commander in chief. At the proverbial last minute, Putin, one of Assad's most critical allies (along with Iran), stepped in with a way out, a strategy that would push Syria to the back burner for Obama and, of course, for Putin as well. Here is where everything gets interesting and begins to tie in to what happened earlier in Iraq and later in Ukraine.

In early September, before the United Nations report, President Putin suggested that the way forward was for Assad to turn over his chemical weapons to be destroyed by the United Nations. Just about everyone grabbed hold of the idea as a way to solve the "game changer" problem while avoiding military intervention in Syria. Here, indeed, was a solution that Obama's key backers could support. What is more, Assad, who had previously denied he had any chemical weapons, proved agreeable to the idea. But he left no doubt about his reasoning:

"Syria is placing its chemical weapons under international control because of Russia. The US threats did not influence the decision," Assad said.[9] Of course, whether anyone believed Assad's message or not was beside the point. A way seemed to have been found to avoid an escalating confrontation that could easily have morphed into military intervention and war.

The solution seemed simple and with all the principal parties on board, it seemed as if the crisis over chemical weapons use had turned a corner. But could Assad be trusted to do as he'd promised?

French president François Hollande suggested a brilliant, straightforward means to hold Assad's feet to the fire. He proposed that the UN Security Council pass a resolution that would establish a timetable for Syrian compliance—everyone was happy with that. He then suggested that the resolution should stipulate that *if* Assad failed to comply with the agreed upon timetable, the Security Council resolution will have authorized the use of force. He went even further, asking the five permanent members of the Security Council (Britain, China, France, Russia, and the United States) to renounce their right to exercise their veto in the Security Council in the case of crimes against humanity, which, of course, includes the use of chemical weapons on civilians.[10] This proposal not only backed up Obama's threats against Assad, it also forced Putin to reveal whether he was sincere about helping enforce the deal.

Because of the contingent nature of the French government's proposed Security Council resolution, the issue of using force would be moot as long as Assad complied with the timetable that, after all, he had already agreed to. So, really all the French proposal was seeking to learn was whether Assad and his Russian ally were truly committed to abiding by the terms to which they said they agreed. This was a clever way to establish whether they, like Adolf Hitler in 1938, were pretending to be compliant when they were not or whether, instead, they were prepared to pay a heavy price if they reneged on the promised elimination of the chemical weapons capability in Syria.

Putin scuttled the French proposal. The Russian government had earlier used its veto in the Security Council to protect the Syrian regime from condemnation in the UN. It certainly was not going to go along with Hollande's much tougher resolution. Instead, a modified resolution was drafted and then passed unanimously in the Security Council. As Russia's foreign minister Sergey Lavrov observed of the resolution that was actually passed, it "does not allow for any automatic use of force or measures of enforcement."[11] Although in theory the resolution allowed the Security Council to invoke Chapter VII of the UN Charter, which is the basis for UN peacekeeping efforts, as the Russians made clear there were no real circumstances in which that would happen. They would veto any such subsequent effort. There were, as Lavrov said, no "measures of enforcement."[12]

The failure to pass a resolution with the real teeth that Hollande had asked for was, in its own way, of great strategic and informational value. That, in fact, is what made the initial proposal so brilliant. Hollande's proposed resolution, and the resolution that actually passed, for sure had implications for Syria, but the bigger implications had to do with finding out just how far Putin and Obama were each willing to go. On the Syrian front, if Putin were committed to making sure that Assad complied with the chemical weapons agreement—an agreement that Assad himself endorsed—then he had no good reason to object to the French idea. After all, if Putin planned to take a strong stance to enforce the timetable Assad had accepted then the contingent condition for using force would never arise: Assad would have no choice and no reason not to comply. If, however, Putin was just interested in shoving the issue out of the headlines so business could continue pretty much as usual then he would, as he did, object to Hollande's proposal.

The moment Putin objected to the French proposal to commit the UN in advance to the use of force under carefully specified conditions, anyone listening should have understood that he was not sincere and, more important, that he was shopping around to find out how tough Obama was. As we now know, while Assad complied, albeit late, by turning over his proscribed chemical weapons, he retained other chemical weapons capabilities that by oversight were left out of the agreement. The evidence indicates that he has since allowed those weapons— especially chlorine gas—to be used against civilians with devastating consequences for Syrians and with no significant repercussions for him or his regime. There is as well, albeit unconfirmed, evidence that he retained mustard gas—a proscribed chemical weapon—which appeared subsequently to have been captured and used by ISIS.

What did the exchange over Hollande's proposal reveal about Obama? The United States government initially backed the French idea of a Security Council resolution with real teeth but then, seeing that it would be vetoed by Russia, went for the much weaker revised resolution drafted by Russia, which carried no real consequences if Assad reneged. Obama, of course, would have had no illusions about Putin's preparedness to veto a tough resolution. After all, as we have noted, he had already done so on three prior occasions. But had the United States backed the tougher resolution, knowing that it would have been vetoed, what everyone would have learned was that its president was willing to suffer a defeat in the UN for what he believed was right. He could then, of course, have voted subsequently for the weaker resolution that ultimately passed.

By failing to bring a tough resolution to a vote, Obama revealed he could be pushed around. By his earlier withdrawal he had indicated that he was not as strongly vested in Iraq as the previous Bush administration, but there was still considerable ambiguity about what his administration would tolerate and when it would intervene. Not forcing a vote allowed Obama to avoid intervention in Syria, an act that would have been unpopular with his supporters; but it also told Putin that he had a free hand there and elsewhere around the world. The Obama administration was unwilling to intervene.

As we can see in Figure 6.1, by not pressing for the French proposal, Obama surely revealed to Putin—and his core constituents, a group of oligarchs interested in expanding their control over actual and potential wealth (especially the oil and natural gas reserves believed to be in the Crimean territorial waters annexed by Russia)—that the US president was not prepared to pay the relatively modest political price of showing resolve regarding his "game changer" declaration. By accepting the weak UN resolution, Obama was signaling a willingness to back down in other situations that were substantially similar. Clearly, he indicated that any action with a greater political cost than taking on Assad wouldn't get a strong reaction.

Why would Obama reveal his weakness and unwillingness to intervene? He presumably understood how it would be heard by Putin and his domestic audience, as well as by US allies. We believe the answer resides in that other set of ears to which every national leader speaks: his or her core backers at home. Table 6.1 shows us what Obama would have known in greater detail about opinion among Democrats, his supporters.

Obama's constituents in the Democratic Party seemed to have become weary of unwanted wars, such as those with Iraq and Afghanistan. They preferred feel-good declarations, such as the "game changer" declaration without teeth, to actual action to enforce policies that their

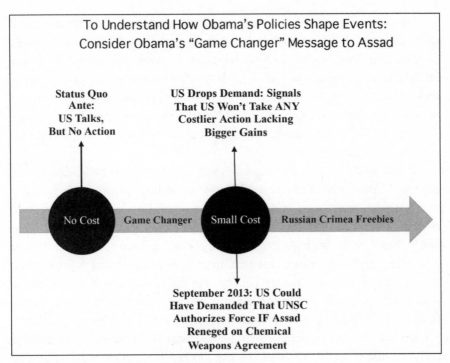

Figure 6.1. Sending the Wrong Message Has Serious Consequences

incumbent leader had suggested were important. Only 29 percent of Democrats, and the same percentage of independents, supported airstrikes in retaliation for Assad's use of chemical weapons. Republicans were somewhat more supportive, though still reluctant. With these numbers in mind and with midterm elections coming up—congressional elections are always coming up in the United States—President Obama focused on what action in Syria might mean for his party's short-term electoral fortunes. In that he was no different, as earlier chapters have highlighted, from any other political leader of any political persuasion.

Table 6.1. Partisanship and Support for US Airstrikes Against Syria

U.S. Airstrikes Against Syria	Democrats	Republicans	Independents
Favor	29%	35%	29%
Oppose	48%	40%	50%
Don't Know	23%	24%	20%

Source: http://www.people-press.org/2013/09/03/public-opinion-runs-against-syrian-airstrikes/

Meanwhile the Russian president focused on what action he could take, having been given a free hand to do anything for which Obama's cost-benefit analysis looked worse than in Syria. And, voilà, a few months later Putin found the opportunity to please his backers at home and further secure his political future: the occupation of Crimea and the launch of a separatist movement in East Ukraine, ostensibly to protect Russians from the imagined threat to their security by developments elsewhere in Ukraine.

If we listen to the messages leaders send and to the audiences to which they are directed, we will understand how personal interests—not national interests, whatever those may be—decide the future course of war and peace.[13] In doing so, we can also understand what might have been done differently to produce a better outcome. In the case of Syria and Ukraine, for instance, President Obama has objected to the idea that the two are linked. He has complained about those who seem to push American policy toward the use of force as the preferred method to resolve these crises; he seeks an alternative to the use of force. In that spirit, we suggested peaceful means to address the Ukraine dispute in May 2014. In the "What If?" section at the end of this chapter, we will reprise our arguments, proposing a path through the Ukraine's problems that could have averted the use of force—satisfying the president's core constituents—and advanced productive, beneficial solutions. For now, however, we turn from the Crimean experience to the Cuban missile crisis in 1962.

Comparing "Game Changers": Syria/Crimea and Kennedy's Cuban Missile Crisis

COMPARING THE 2014 CRIMEAN CRISIS TO THE 1962 CUBAN MISSILE crisis is most pertinent in terms of their shared gravity at their respective moments, the short-term domestic political considerations at play in each, and the implications for future confrontations. Like Putin fifty years later, in 1962 the Soviet premier and general secretary of the Communist Party at the time of the Cuban missile crisis, Nikita Khrushchev, had signals from then US president John Kennedy that he was reluctant to enforce his government's declared interests in the global arena. When Kennedy became president, he inherited a plot designed during Dwight Eisenhower's presidency to overthrow Cuba's Fidel Castro.[14] The idea was for Cuban expatriates to invade Cuba with

American air cover in the hope of fomenting a popular uprising and the fall of Castro's two-year-old, increasingly anti-American, government. The Bay of Pigs invasion went forward on April 17–20, 1961, but at the last minute President Kennedy decided against providing air cover. The result was the defeat of the invasion, with the death, execution, or imprisonment of the invading Cuban expatriates. The message heard by Khrushchev and his core supporters was, "Kennedy is a guy we can push around." This message was strongly reinforced when JFK went to a summit meeting with Khrushchev in Vienna on June 4, 1961. Following his inaugural address's declaration that he would never fear to negotiate, he went inadequately prepared and left the Soviet leadership with the impression that he was reluctant to be tough. As Kennedy himself said of Khrushchev after the meeting, "He beat the hell out of me," telling the *New York Times*, "He savaged me."[15]

Run the clock forward to between September and October 14, 1962, at which time the Soviet Union's emplacement of nuclear-armed missiles on Cuba was confirmed by American U-2 spy planes, and we have Kennedy drawing a line in the sand, just as Obama attempted to. JFK had indicated earlier in public that he had no problem with defensive Soviet weapons on Cuba, but that he would not tolerate any offensive (read: nuclear) Soviet weapons on the island. He did this after having been repeatedly assured by the Soviet leadership both publicly and privately that the USSR had no need to place offensive weapons on Cuba. As he reported to the American people from the Oval Office on October 22, 1962:

> The size of this undertaking makes clear that it has been planned for some months. Yet, only last month, after I had made clear the distinction between any introduction of ground-to-ground missiles and the existence of defensive antiaircraft missiles, the Soviet Government publicly stated on September 11 that, and I quote, "the armaments and military equipment sent to Cuba are designed exclusively for defensive purposes," that there is, and I quote the Soviet Government, "there is no need for the Soviet Government to shift its weapons for a retaliatory blow to any other country, for instance Cuba," and that, and I quote their government, "the Soviet Union has so powerful rockets to carry these nuclear warheads that there is no need to search for sites for them beyond the boundaries of the Soviet Union." That statement was false.[16]

It is useful to recognize that the Soviet leadership did not deny that such assurances had been given. In Sergei Khrushchev's 2001 account of his father's life and times as leader of the Soviet Union, for instance, he reports on a meeting on September 5, 1962, between then US attorney general Robert Kennedy and Anatoly Dobrynin, the Soviet ambassador to the United States. "Robert Kennedy voiced his concern with the growing Soviet military activity in Cuba. . . . Dobrynin relayed to Robert Kennedy Father's assurances that no offensive weapons, in particular surface-to-surface missiles, were based in Cuba."[17] Having believed these assurances, President Kennedy seems to have thought it was a freebie to take a tough public stance. He could talk tough, he thought, whether he carried a big stick or not. And then, having taken a firm public stance against Soviet offensive weapons on Cuba, he learned, as we saw, that the promises he received were false; the Soviet Union was placing offensive nuclear weapons in Cuba and also the surface-to-surface missiles needed to deliver them to targets.

Whereas half a century later Obama spoke vaguely of a "game changer," Kennedy spoke explicitly about how the game would change. Speaking to the nation and to the Soviet leadership—the essential set of ears in the dispute—JFK made several bold, undiplomatic statements that conveyed the consequences to follow if the missiles and nuclear weapons were not withdrawn. As we have already seen, he quoted the Soviet assurances he was given and then stated flatly that these assurances were false. He went on to make clear that what happened in Cuba and how his government responded mattered well beyond the confines of any threat posed by missiles on Cuba. President Kennedy stated in the same address on October 22, 1962, that "this secret, swift, and extraordinary build-up of Communist missiles—in an area well known to have a special and historical relationship to the United States and the nations of the Western Hemisphere, in violation of Soviet assurances, and in defiance of American and hemispheric policy—this sudden, clandestine decision to station strategic weapons for the first time outside of Soviet soil—is a deliberately provocative and unjustified change in the status quo which cannot be accepted by this country *if our courage and our commitments are ever to be trusted again by either friend or foe* [emphasis added]."[18]

In that same address he then took Cuba's government out of the picture so that no third-party excuses could be meaningfully invoked by Nikita Khrushchev. Kennedy stated, "It shall be the policy of this nation to regard any nuclear missile launched from Cuba against any nation in the Western Hemisphere as an attack by the Soviet Union on the United States, requiring a full retaliatory response upon the Soviet Union." There is not a shred of ambiguity in this declaration. It might have been a bluff, but the Soviet audience had no way of knowing.

Whereas Obama had signaled an unwillingness to fight, Kennedy's signals—his threat to use nuclear weapons ("We will not prematurely or unnecessarily risk the costs of worldwide nuclear war in which even the fruits of victory would be ashes in our mouth—but neither will we shrink from that risk at any time it must be faced") and, most important, his concrete actions in stopping and boarding ships in international waters showed that he was prepared to risk war. Khrushchev backed down.

Was Kennedy more motivated by some concern for the national interest than Obama was fifty years later? We think not, and given that Kennedy's first exclamation upon being informed of nuclear weapons in Cuba was, "He [Khrushchev] can't do that to me!", it seems JFK also perceived the crisis first in personal terms and only after that in national terms.[19]

John Kennedy, like Barack Obama, and, we submit, like any leader anywhere, anytime (including, of course, Putin and Khrushchev), was focused on what his core constituents at home needed to hear to continue to back their leader and their party. In Obama's case, his essential voters were tired of fights; embarrassed by their perception of bullying behavior by the United States around the world; and keen for a more dovelike, gentler foreign policy. President Kennedy's constituents, in contrast, were not terribly happy with his job performance prior to the Cuban missile crisis.

It might be appealing to think that the differences between Kennedy's actions and Obama's stemmed from the differences in the magnitude of the threats they faced. Rather than appealing to domestic political considerations, Kennedy may have believed that the Cuban missile crisis was an existential threat to the United States, prompting a tough response. Obama, in contrast, may reasonably have thought that the Syrian crisis and the Ukraine crisis, though troubling, did not rise to the same level of imminent threat as did the Cuban crisis. Yet we know that the premise that the Cuban crisis was an existential threat is not really correct and was not thought to be correct at the time. Even in President Kennedy's speech on October 22, he noted, "American citizens have become adjusted to living daily in the bull's-eye of Soviet missiles located inside the USSR or in submarines. In that sense, missiles in Cuba add to an already clear and present danger. . . . "[20] The missiles on Cuba had not fundamentally altered the balance of power. They had shortened the time it would take for nuclear weapons to reach the United States, but given the technology of the day, that change made little defensive difference.

What mattered to Kennedy were the earlier messages he sent to his domestic political audience and to his foreign rivals, and what those messages were likely to mean for the Democratic Party's prospects in the midterm election. As the president saw the situation, his difficulty was, at least in part, that on September 4, before the crisis began to unfold, but after Soviet SAM missiles (defensive weapons) had been detected on Cuba, he had publicly declared:

> There is no evidence of any organized combat force in Cuba from any Soviet Bloc country; of military bases provided to Russia; of a viola-tion of the 1934 treaty relating to Guantanamo [an American military base on Cuba]; of the presence of offensive ground-to-ground mis-siles; or of other significant offensive capability. . . . Were it other-wise the gravest issues would arise.[21]

In this statement, President Kennedy made clear that he would not tolerate offensive (nuclear) weapons on Cuba, but that he viewed a de-fensive Soviet weapons buildup as acceptable (hence the phrase "were it otherwise"). With repeated Soviet assurances, made in public, that they had no intention of putting nuclear weapons on Cuba, Kennedy repeated his message that defensive weapons were okay but nuclear weapons would not be permitted. He probably believed that such strong language about offensive weapons was politically safe, much as Obama may have believed that his "game changer" statement was sufficient to deter Assad from using chemical weapons. Through strong language, Kennedy may have hoped to recoup some of his credibility as a foreign policy leader in the run-up to the midterm election. He certainly made clear that he was deeply concerned that, having talked tough, if he did not act tough, the Democrats would lose more seats in the midterm election and he would be impeached! In a private, recorded meeting with his brother, Attorney General Robert Kennedy, right after JFK's October 22 address to the nation in which he announced that the US Navy would blockade Cuba, here is what the two had to say about the domestic political fallout from the Soviet placement of missiles in Cuba:

JFK: It looks really mean, doesn't it? But on the other hand there wasn't any choice. If he's going to get this mean on this one, in our part of the world [unclear], no choice. I don't think there was a choice

RFK: Well, there isn't any choice. I mean, you would have been, you would have been impeached.

JFK: Well, I think I would have been impeached.

[Unclear exchange]

If there had been a move to impeach, I would have been under [unclear], on the grounds that I said they wouldn't do it, and . . .

RFK: [Unclear] something else. They'd think up some other step that wasn't necessary. You'd be . . . But now, the fact is, you couldn't have done any less.

[Then, discussing a conversation RFK had with Georgi Bolshakov, a Soviet defense attaché] . . .

JFK: What did he say?

RFK: He said they are going to go through [the quarantine].

JFK: The ships are going to go?

RFK: He said this is, this is a defensive base for the Russians. It's got nothing to do with the Cubans.

JFK: Why are . . . They're lying [unclear] that. Khrushchev's horseshit about the election. Anyway, the sickening thing that's so very bad is what this revealed about . . . This horror about embarrassing me in the election.[22]

Critically, this exchange is not about the national security situation, the wisdom of the blockade, the alternative responses that had been considered by the president's Executive Committee appointed to assess what to do, the danger of war, or any such lofty set of ideas. It is about how Khrushchev was using the American midterm electoral setting to his own advantage and how John Kennedy needed to take tough action, not as emphasized in the speech, to protect the United States and the Western Hemisphere, but because otherwise he would have been impeached. He had, after all, assured the public that the Soviet Union would not place offensive weapons on Cuba and now it was doing so, making the president look weak at best and possibly worse—like a liar.

There are a few crucial lessons to be drawn from the cases of Cuba and Syria/Crimea/Ukraine. In each case, as with all choices of war and peace, leaders have to figure out responses that get what they want out of their foreign adversary, but also give them what they need personally and politically at home. It is possible, even likely in some instances, that there is no happy solution to these two problems. Obama, for instance, could have sent convincing signals to Putin and his backers that might have gotten them to be tougher on Assad and kept them out of Ukraine, but those signals would have turned off his backers at home and possibly benefited the Republican opposition at the expense of Democrats. Remember, only 29 percent of Democrats favored airstrikes in response to Assad's use of chemical weapons. Kennedy was in a happier position in this regard, although he took a monumental risk. He himself estimated the odds of nuclear war "as between one out of three and even."[23] Imagine the consequences had he misjudged Khrushchev's ability to control the Soviet response. Kennedy was able to satisfy his supporters at home *and* get Khrushchev to accept an outcome that was positive for JFK as well.

Unfortunately pundits, journalists, and other "experts" are too quick to think that war and peace is high politics that cannot be brought down to the level of personal politics. Yet these two crises, just like FDR's decisions in the run-up to World War II and Madison's in 1812, remind us that even the biggest decisions are shaped by basic domestic political considerations rather than judgments of national well-being. Remember, again, that President Kennedy understood that nuclear missiles in Cuba did not fundamentally alter the balance of power between the United States and the Soviet Union. From the national perspective, allowing Russia to keep missiles in Cuba reduced US security only slightly. But the partisan and personal consequences were likely to be severe. The Democrats could have expected a drubbing in the upcoming midterm elections and Kennedy expected to be impeached. He was willing to risk "between one out of three and even" chances of nuclear war to avoid these eventualities!

What If?

PRESIDENT BARACK OBAMA HAS BEEN ACCUSED OF BEING INDECISIVE and overly reluctant to use force. If we follow the logic of the Roman fourth-century writer Vegetius, who argued that those who desire peace prepare for war, then Obama's hesitations might be understood as a contributor to the cause of war. Figure 6.2 shows us US defense expenditures as a percentage of gross domestic product (GDP) from

1991—the end of the cold war—through 2015. As the figure makes clear, President Bill Clinton capitalized on the so-called peace dividend at the end of the cold war by markedly reducing defense expenditures. President George W. Bush then significantly increased expenditures, presumably to support the post-9/11 wars in Afghanistan and in Iraq. President Obama, although still having the Afghan War to cope with and coming into office with a large contingent of American combat soldiers still in Iraq, significantly reduced defense spending. From the perspective of those who share Vegetius's view, he was not preparing for war and hence, not bolstering the prospects of peace. Against this, Obama and his supporters believed that there was a better way, a more diplomatic way, to solve foreign crises.

We agree that there generally are better ways to solve foreign crises than to go to war. Here we want to offer some ideas that we first proposed in 2014 to address how President Obama might have sent more successful signals to Putin and to the government in Ukraine, to reduce the dangers in Ukraine that unfolded following his weak response to the chemical weapons crisis in Syria, while also advancing the interests of his and the Democratic Party's electoral base.[24]

We have already indicated that Obama could have left Putin with greater uncertainty about his intentions or about the strength of a US

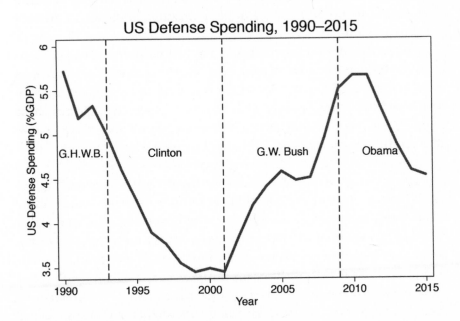

Figure 6.2. US Defense Spending from the End of the Cold War to 2015

response to Russian expansionist undertakings. Obama could have promoted such uncertainty simply by having insisted on pushing the French UN Security Council resolution to a vote. Instead, his failure to act left it clear that he was not prepared to pay the price to militarily oppose Putin's expansion. Given that the military option was off the table—and Putin knew it—we investigate what other policy levers Obama might have used to improve outcomes (from the US perspective).[25]

Once a leader disavows the military option, his or her ability to influence international events is limited, but it is not zero. Presidents still have the choice of sanctions and foreign aid—the sticks and carrots of foreign policy. President Obama used both tools to influence events in the Ukraine, but he could have used foreign aid more efficiently.

In March 2014 he issued a series of executive orders to impose sanctions on Russia in the wake of its involvement in the Ukraine.[26] The usual problem with imposing sanctions, beyond that they rarely work, is that they signal that a leader is not willing to do more. As discussed, Obama's (in)actions over Syria had already revealed his passive approach—so, no harm done there. Further, the sanctions were designed to maximize their political effect. Although his efforts were far from perfect, he targeted sanctions to impose pain on the relatively small group of wealthy oligarchs to whom Putin is beholden, rather than on his domestic political opponents, thus applying additional political pressure.

Obama also used foreign aid to prop up the pro-Western government in Ukraine. Here we believe his policy was misguided. In March 2014, Congress authorized $1 billion of aid to Ukraine. This aid was part of a $40 billion package of aid and financial support from such organizations as the International Monetary Fund and World Bank. The aid did not come without restrictions. For instance, the Ukrainian parliament was required to make legislative changes in the banking and energy sectors so as to receive some of the funds.[27] However, the aid conditionality did not include political reforms. No one in the Obama administration seemed to ask why so many people in East Ukraine preferred to be Russian rather than Ukrainian. Before releasing aid, Obama could have insisted on real democratization that included institutionalized protections for ethnic Russians in Ukraine, but he did not. Instead the aid enabled the pro-Western government of Petro Poroshenko to survive unreformed and to perpetuate Petroshenko's policies, giving Putin the excuse he needed to invade.

Over 8 million Ukrainians, about 17 percent of the total population, identify themselves as ethnically Russian. These citizens were disproportionately concentrated in Crimea and East Ukraine and faced discrimination. By failing to enact legislation and reforms to protect this minority, the Kiev government ensured that ethnic Russians remained alienated.

The United States and European Union nations favored the incumbent pro-Western Ukrainian government that came to power following the deposition of Viktor Yanukovych due to popular protest over his policies to reject agreements with the EU and align instead with Russia. Hence, the West gave aid to prop up the subsequent government of Petro Poroshenko and the pro-Western shift in policies that it enacted. Unfortunately, unconditionally supporting the Kiev government does little to resolve the underlying issues. Instead, we argue that Obama could have substantially weakened Putin's position by making support for Kiev contingent on the Ukrainian government adopting policies and institutional reforms that promoted the interests of ethnic Russians in Ukraine rather than discriminating against them.

If Ukraine implemented institutional reforms that enshrined civil rights, such as freedom of speech and assembly; promoted a free media; and allowed effective political competition, then Russian-speaking Ukrainians would have wanted to be part of the Ukraine rather than part of Russia. Such true democratic reforms, rather than simply the presence of elections, would provide for the welfare of all citizens—those of Russian extraction along with ethnic Ukrainians.

True democracy is the set of governance rules under which winners need the support of many people, not simply a system in which elections occur. Retaining office under such circumstances is extremely difficult—it involves a relentless battle for good policy ideas and frequent political turnover. All leaders, if left to their own devices, prefer to restrict political competition so that their survival depends on a smaller group of backers. But in Ukraine, the exceptional circumstances that make leaders actually willing to really democratize are present: the government is new, broke, and facing mass protests and insurrection. Without financial support the government struggles to pay off supporters and fight Russian separatists. By providing aid unconditionally to the Poroshenko government, the United States allowed him to perpetuate the current form of government that discriminates against ethnic Russians. Such policies might have cost Poroshenko Crimea and parts of East Ukraine, but later they helped him retain power. Ukrainian leaders, like leaders everywhere, think about policy from the perspective of what is good for them and not what is good for the nation. And for a leader it might well be better to be firmly ensconced as head of half a country than to be out of power in a whole country. Hence, Poroshenko took US aid, perpetuated a relatively closed form of government, and accepted the loss of some of the country, while making efforts to limit such losses. A tolerable outcome for him, but one that was highly undesirable from the perspective of the average Ukrainian.

Suppose instead that the United States had withheld all aid to Ukraine until it passed and implemented laws enshrining a free press, the right to free speech, and other rules, including an independent judiciary, that promote genuine political competition. That would have put Poroshenko and his cronies in serious jeopardy of losing power. However, faced with a weakening economy and civil war and without financial support, deposition would have loomed as a real threat. By insisting on such changes before the delivery of assistance, Obama might have promoted genuine democratization in Ukraine, reduced the appeal of separation for ethnic Russians, and weakened the position and legitimacy of Putin to intervene in Ukraine.

Partisan politics more than national needs determine the extent to which presidents are willing to risk war. Kennedy needed to appear tough to avoid large losses in the House of Representative in the 1962 midterm elections and, of course, he acted to avoid the risk of impeachment. He was willing to embark on an aggressive course of action that, by his own estimates, put the United States at a high risk of nuclear war. The gamble paid off for him and the Democrats: Khrushchev backed down. In contrast, Obama's supporters opposed US military engagement. He followed the political incentives, but by dithering over Syria and failing to hold Assad to account, he dealt Putin a free hand. It is impossible to state whether Kennedy's hawkish strategy or Obama's dovish approach is the better. Kennedy won concessions, but in the process risked nuclear annihilation. Obama, by contrast, avoided conflict, but in doing so gave international rivals the opportunity to exploit the United States. Reasonable people can disagree over whether the moral and financial costs of war are justified in a particular circumstance. What we know with confidence is that the personal and political costs are the ones that determine whether wars are fought.

Conclusion

Fixing Flaws

A country may be ruined in making an Administration happy.
—Josiah Quincy III, December 1812

A MERICA'S FOUNDING FATHERS WERE PRESCIENT IN RECOGNIZING THE need to constrain executive power. Their intention was to limit any president's chance to pursue war for personal, rather than national, reasons. We have seen that their efforts notwithstanding, presidents have managed to use war for their own benefit. The fear that James Madison expressed, and that we quoted in the Introduction, was well justified. And in his fear of executive aggrandizement he was not alone, though other founding fathers tended to emphasize this danger among monarchs. John Jay, Madison's cocontributor to *The Federalist Papers*, warned in Federalist No. 4 that

> the safety of the people of America against dangers from foreign force depends not only on their forbearing to give just causes for war to other nations, but also on their placing and continuing themselves in such a situation as not to invite hostility or insult; for it need not be observed, that there are pretended as well as just causes of war.
>
> It is too true, however disgraceful it may be to human nature, that . . . absolute monarchs will often make war when their nations are to get nothing by it, but for purposes and objects merely personal,

such as a thirst for military glory, revenge for personal affronts, ambition, or private compacts to aggrandize or support their particular families or partisans. These, and a variety of motives, which affect only the mind of the Sovereign, often lead him to engage in wars not sanctified by justice, or the voice and interests of his people.[1]

Jay warned of the danger that the United States could be dragged into wars by the urge of foreign monarchs to fight for their own benefit. Real though that danger was and as real as it remains today for nations that are led by dictators, we have endeavored to show that the danger of war motivated by personal gain is prevalent as well even among the presidents of the United States. War, as James Madison noted, and as we have illustrated, too often provides American presidents with the opportunity to put their welfare or partisan politics above the welfare of the rest of us, helping their partisans at the expense of the many, "all in conspiracy against the desire and duty of peace."[2]

War is indeed a dangerous political beast that needs to be tamed. Our plan in this chapter is to state clear, implementable plans that could significantly improve America's war decision making. Only someone wearing the rosiest of colored glasses could believe there is any hope of eliminating presidential eagerness for fame and glory from decisions about war. But there certainly is a hope of tilting the balance of calculations about war and peace more toward the prosecution only of just wars in which the people's interests are truly endangered.

The stories we have told of American presidents at war have been aimed at exposing how important personal interests are in even the gravest choices facing any nation, even a democratic one. The cases we chose to study are not an exhaustive list of presidents who placed their interests above those of the people. We have not, for instance, delved into the Mexican-American War (1846–1848) in detail. However, James Polk's decision to bring Texas into the Union and foment war with Mexico had deep partisan roots that echoed many of the themes of territorial expansion behind Madison's invasion of Canada and the theft of Indian land. Just as readily we might have addressed Woodrow Wilson's World War I, a war he campaigned against vigorously in 1914, promising not to involve the United States in Europe's conflagration. We might have examined William McKinley's Spanish-American War, which was promoted by unabashed imperial expansionists who succeeded in browbeating the president into submission at the threat of his reelection. That was yet another war in which, as James Madison faced in 1812, the urge to remain president outstripped sensible resistance to an unnecessary conflict. But we believe our point has been made and does not need an "exposé" of still more wars. Now we want to use the lessons we have exposed to identify a few practical, feasible steps that the United States as a nation could take to diminish the danger that wars arise out of personal ambition, avarice, or vanity. Of course, we must be realistic. Not every danger to collective welfare can be eradicated, but many can be diminished. We should not let a quest for perfection stand in the way of genuine but incomplete progress.

Improving War Decision Making

WE REITERATE THAT WE CANNOT HOPE TO SOLVE ALL THE DEFIciencies and failures in presidential decision making; indeed, the Economics Nobel Laureate Kenneth Arrow has proven that, given a few assumptions about creating fairness, there is no political system that can assure a match-up between the people's desires and a government's policy choices.[3] In fact, what may look like broad support, even supermajority support, for a war (or a candidate) can be converted to equally large opposition simply by changing the method for counting votes.[4] The same thing can also be achieved by introducing an "irrelevant" presidential option, such as Ralph Nader in 2000, or James Birney in 1844. Ralph Nader's decision to run in the 2000 election cost Al Gore votes—not many votes but enough to prevent his victory in Florida. But for Nader's candidacy, the 2000s might have been spent combating environmental problems rather than insurgents in Iraq. Likewise James Birney had a profound impact on the course of American history. As a third-party candidate in the election primarily between James Polk and Henry Clay, he "made" Polk president, thereby giving us the Mexican-American War.

You see, Polk's call for "Manifest Destiny" and in particular the annexation of Texas was a policy supported by only a minority of US voters. The Whigs opposed such expansion, as did the northern Democrats. So, the only people that really supported Polk's plan were the southern Democrats. Making an extremely crude calculation, we might say that the plan was supported by one quarter and opposed by three quarters. However, the annexation of Texas was not dealt with in isolation. Polk supported America's Manifest Destiny and success-fully tied expansion into Texas with expansion of free territories in the Oregon territories—a position popular in northern states. With such a position, Polk went on to defeat the Whig nominee, Henry Clay, by the narrow margin of about 39,000 votes. During the campaign, Clay, who as you will recall was a southern gentleman from Kentucky and may have supported slavery, vacillated on the extent of his opposition of statehood for Texas. In New York, his failure to commit to the antislav-ery position led to robust support for the third-party candidate, James Birney. By obtaining around 64,000 votes for the Liberal Party, Birney denied Clay New York's 36 Electoral College votes, thereby electing Polk and giving us the Mexican-American War. But for Birney's cam-paign it is likely Clay would have been elected and the country perhaps would have gone in a different direction.

While creating institutions that guarantee the implementation of the people's will is impossible, because what the will of the people is depends upon how the questions are asked and how the answers are assessed, still we can offer straightforward solutions to improve the correspondence between what "We, the people" want and the foreign policies that presidents pursue. Further, in the process of making it harder for presidents to fight wars that are not supported by a broad majority, our proposals will also improve the conduct of war, leading to shorter, cheaper, and less bloody wars.

The Logic of Personal Gain That Supports War

IN THE INTRODUCTION TO THIS BOOK, WE ARGUED THAT DEMOCRACIES DO more than any other form of government to inhibit leaders from going to war for personal gain. This, of course, is because pleasing the few at the expense of the many, as dictators and oligarchs do, is much easier than pleasing the many. The fewer supporters leaders need to come to power and to retain power, the freer is their hand to implement the poli-cies that they want rather than the policies that are good for the masses. Hence, dictators can wage war with relative impunity, at least with re-spect to domestic constraints. This is an issue on which we have written much. Because we believe it is central to the choice between good public policy designed to enrich the polity and one that favors graft and cor-ruption, we risk some redundancy by summarizing our logic here:[5]

As the group of supporters a leader must keep happy grows, it is harder for leaders to retain office. Further, as the group whose support is essential grows larger, the policies that leaders need to enact become the types of policies that enrich the many, what economists refer to as public goods. As a simple metric, the more people a leader is beholden to, the better will be the public policies the leader enacts.

With respect to foreign policy, this principle seems to hold. Absolute monarchs—and the world's autocrats—can act despotically because they are responsible to only a very few and not the many. US presidents are beholden to many and therefore are constrained in their choices. Certainly we would agree that the foreign policies of US presidents are more in line with the wishes of the people than, say, the policies of a Hitler, Stalin, or Mao. However, our argument is one of degrees, not absolutes, and so this comparison does not preclude US policies being brought even closer to the preferences of "We, the people." Here we offer a number of solutions to limit the extent to which the president can deviate from what "We, the people" want through simple procedural reforms that are designed to make the president beholden to more people.

Remedies

WE ARE NOT DOVES AND WE ARE NOT HAWKS. RATHER, WE BELIEVE there are times and places that make the use of force necessary, but that generally disputes are best resolved through negotiation. When circumstances that warrant the use of force arise, leaders should act to win the wars they fight and they should strive to win the peace as quickly as possible with the minimum of financial and human cost. The remedies we discuss are aimed at increasing the number of people to whom leaders are accountable and incentivizing leaders to provide the information necessary to restrain their own desires for personal advantage through war.

To diminish needless war as well as costly reticence to face the occasional necessity of using force, we touch on the following topics: (a) eliminate the Electoral College; (b) establish independent commissions to set electoral boundaries; (c) create independent agencies to estimate the expected financial costs of war and of peace; (d) create an independent panel to estimate the expected human costs of war and peace; and (e) levy war taxes that ensure that all citizens pay at least some of the cost of conflict if the nation goes to war.

Revise the Electoral College

Remember that when a leader depends on few people to stay in office, the leader is likely to pander to the interests of that small group. As the coalition of backers on whom a leader depends expands, so, too, does the president's need to consider the interests of a broader portion of the population, diminishing the very risks that John Jay and James Madison warned us about. We should be wary of any institutions of government that markedly diminish reliance on the will of the many to the advantage of the few. The Electoral College is such an institution. Hence, we believe that it should be abolished in favor of direct presidential elections.

There have been four instances where US presidents have been elected after having lost the popular vote to a rival. That is, just less than 10 percent of American presidents thus far have not been the popular choice of the electorate. Perhaps the incident most of us remember is that of Al Gore versus George W. Bush in 2000. Gore received 543,816 more votes than Bush but lost in the Electoral College, largely because of a misleading ballot design in Florida's Miami–Dade County combined with a Supreme Court ruling. However, there are three other cases of a president's losing the popular vote and winning the presidency (John Quincy Adams in 1824, Rutherford B. Hayes in 1876, and Benjamin Harrison in 1888). Additionally, a total of eighteen elections (and fifteen presidents) were chosen despite having won less than 50 percent of the popular vote. Of these cases, two stand out as particularly egregious. In 1860 Lincoln received only 39.9 percent of the popular vote. At an even greater extreme, in 1824 John Quincy Adams received only 29.8 percent of the vote. More recently, Bill Clinton defeated George H. W. Bush in 1992 while winning only 43 percent of the popular vote. Bush won 38 percent and third-party candidate H. Ross Perot secured the remaining 19 percent. Impolitic as these events might be, they are not the reason that we oppose the Electoral College.

The difficulty that the Electoral College represents is that it violates the widely accepted norm of one person, one vote. Small states, for example, are constitutionally overrepresented in the selection of the president because every state has as many electors to the Electoral

College as it has members of the House and Senate. Thus, a state with so small a population that it has only one House member has three Electoral College votes; whereas a state with, for example, two House members, gets four Electoral College votes. Thus, the state with two House members has roughly twice the population of a state with but one representative in the House and yet only has 1.5 times the number of electors in the Electoral College. The reality is that to be president, a candidate needs to win the marginal states, and so the policies of candidates are distorted to attract half the voters in half a dozen or so states. Of course, the interests of a majority of voters in a small minority of states need not be the same as the interests of the majority in the nation as a whole. The Electoral College reduces political competition, shrinking the number of supporters needed to become president. It is time for a constitutional amendment to rid us of this institution that originally served to promote slavery.

Improve Electoral Competition

The Electoral College is not the only means by which the US political system distorts the relationship between what large numbers of voters indicate they favor and what they get. Gerrymandering, for instance, contributes mightily to the fact that while Congress is an enormously unpopular institution, almost every individual member of Congress seems remarkably popular. The return of incumbents to Congress is nearly a sure thing. This means that presidents can build their core of support around a secure, small group of partisan legislators with limited concern for electoral punishment if they stray into what used to be called wars of choice rather than wars of necessity. We illustrated this phenomenon in Chapter 2's discussion of the War of 1812 and Chapter 5's analysis of George W. Bush's political success in the context of the Iraq War.

Gerrymandering makes a significant contribution to the limited degree of competition for congressional seats. It biases elections to turn power over to the secure few through the simple process of building congressional districts so that they are secure for the party in control of the state assembly. That means that in the end, a small group of politicians choose their voters and hence their representatives in the federal government rather than voters' making the choices themselves. Yet, congressional districts could readily be realigned in a nonpartisan way every ten years while meeting the procedures mandated in the Constitution. Achieving such an end is conceptually easy. State assemblies could delegate the apportionment authority to independent, nonpartisan panels (as some states have done) mandated to ensure that districts not only meet the one-person/one-vote standard, but also meet the standard that the geographic area and contours of the district are as small and compact as possible while being blind to partisan leanings. Indeed, computer programs have existed for years that can draw district boundaries to meet these goals. Adopting such panels and such programs would help introduce real competition into districts, rather than the essentially rigged outcomes currently constructed by partisan reapportionment. That, in turn, would mean that a president's partisan coalition would potentially be in greater flux, forcing them to be accountable to a broader array of interests as they make decisions, including the choice to go to war.

Naturally, the implementation of such institutional reforms is difficult. The key swing states in presidential elections don't want to end the institution that showers them with presidential attention. Similarly, congressmen have no incentive to give up the system that allows them to pick their voters by drawing district lines, rather than have the voters pick them. Hence writing legislation to implement these policies immediately is a fruitless task. Yet while politicians want to afford themselves every electoral advantage, they want others to focus on good politics. The identity of key swing states changes over time—those legislators who benefit from presidential favor today recognize that in twenty years they might not be so lucky. Consequently, their preference today is that in the future their state focuses on national policy rather than on partisan policy that might be contrary to their partisan desires. When the good of the country does not impact their personal aggrandizement, politicians are all in favor of national welfare and so might well pass legislation today to implement the institutional changes we recommend if those changes do not take effect for twenty years.

Independent Estimates of the Expected Financial Costs of War

History teaches us that the costs of conflict are always higher than the estimates provided by the president. Even worse, from time to time, when members of an administration provide higher cost estimates than those offered by the president, they are punished in a manner we refer to as "shoot the messenger." Furthermore, as history has also taught us, successful presidents ensure that when they wage war it benefits their supporters while the costs are borne disproportionately by their domestic political opponents. These pathologies need to be fixed by guaranteeing that estimates of the cost of war are made by independent, nonpartisan bodies.

Wars are highly variable in their cost and duration, but how these factors vary has been successfully and repeatedly estimated by nonpartisan groups, including academic bodies and sometimes by government offices, such as the Congressional Budget Office (CBO). It makes sense to use the strictly nonpartisan CBO and perhaps also its executive branch counterpart, the Office of Management and Budget, to be responsible for estimating the financial costs of war. The CBO already does this for virtually every piece of legislation that comes before Congress. For example, the CBO made an effort to estimate the cost of the Iraq War. Of course, it noted at the time that the information it had about the war's aftermath was highly uncertain. Nevertheless, adopting assumptions made in the media (which could be replaced by detailed military briefings, if our recommendations are followed), the CBO made detailed estimates of the costs of fighting in Iraq and sustaining postwar peace, noting that "CBO has no basis for estimating other costs that might be associated with a conflict with Iraq such as the costs for coalition war fighting, reconstruction or foreign aid that the United States might choose to extend after a conflict ends. . . . "[6]

Given the estimates the CBO made, coupled with a stated war objective that involved regime replacement, what might the cost have been projected to be prior to the war's beginning? Using midlevel values from the CBO estimate and prior US experience, deployment would have cost about $11 billion. Defeat of the Iraqi military and overthrow of the regime might have been projected as a six-month endeavor, costing about $45 billion, and occupation with a nation-building intention maybe required ten years. At the time of the war, Deputy Secretary of Defense Paul Wolfowitz pointed to success in Japan and Germany as the examples of how we could do nation building. In those two cases, it was about ten years after they surrendered that these countries first held competitive elections without US military supervision. Using the same time frame, Iraq's occupation would have cost about $300 billion. Finally, the return of American forces after the occupation would have added $6 billion. Thus, a CBO-based midrange prewar estimate of $362 billion would have been readily supportable, although after the fact we know that would have been very low. Still, that is vastly more than the Bush administration estimated the war would cost. Recall that in Chapter 5 we reported that White House economic adviser Lawrence Lindsey estimated the cost of the Iraq War at $100–$200 billion, a massively conservative estimate. He was fired for his pains. Even the conservative estimate provided above based on the CBO's thinking might have been sufficiently expensive to give rise to greater opposition to the war on the Main Streets of America. The Congressional Research Service eventually put the price of the Iraq War at $784 billion, double our number here.[7] Had that price tag been estimated before the 2002 authorization, the decision to go to war might have been very different.

Obtain Independent Estimates of the Human Costs of War

A problem the CBO or any other panel faces in estimating the costs of war is that it looks at the finances, but it does not look systematically at the other costs in time and lives. In the spirit of our "What If?" sections, let's suppose that Congress passed a law that required every administration that contemplates a war to share confidentially the core of its military plans with a nonpartisan body similar to the CBO. Based on these data, expected casualties and war duration could be estimated. The CBO already has the technical expertise to assess the financial cost of complex legislation. Political scientists know how to estimate the expected length and lethality of wars. Indeed, in Chapter 3 we used just such a study by Scott Bennett and Allan Stam to estimate the expected length of the Civil War and we concluded it should have been five to six months.[8]

Estimates of cost, lethality, and duration could have been readily prepared for every US war and also for the event that the United States chose not to escalate to war. Various nonpartisan academic algorithms for estimating the length of a war generally consider the material and human resource base of each side, the degree of asymmetry in the motivation to fight and win the war (itself a crucial factor in, for instance, the Vietnam War), the geographic distance between combatants, and other estimable factors.[9] It would not be a particularly difficult task to assemble a suitably skilled panel, with retrospective evidence about past wars used to assess their methods.

One potential objection to this plan is that the United States does not always have time for such an assessment. For instance, consider the urgency with which the nation entered World War II in response to the bombing of Pearl Harbor. The need for an immediate response precluded the time to prepare a cost analysis. A similar objection might be raised about Korea, where quick decisive action was needed if South Korea was to be saved. This objection might stand in the case of Korea as there was little prior expectation of an attack, but the question of US involvement in World War II had long been debated prior to Japan's attack, as we discussed in Chapter 4. Thus, it is perfectly reasonable to expect preestablished, standing panels, such as the CBO, to estimate cost, lethality, and duration. Indeed, such information would have been very informative to the political debate between isolationists and interventionists in 1918, 1940, and in every American war since. And, of course, today, thanks to high-speed computing, there need be no material delay arising from running an established algorithm with a suitable data base at the ready.

A third panel of experts ought to be created whose charge is to use the best extant research to estimate the human toll of any given war based on factors identified in advance of the dispute, validated against the record of past wars, and carefully estimated to include the likely range of error and how that range depends on uncertainties re-garding the values on essential variables that make up the human-costs algorithm. Again the panel should be nonpartisan with membership replacement overlapping presidential terms and with qualification for service on this or any of the panels we have discussed based on the individual's prior track record for reliability on producing accurate estimates and not based on the individual's partisan ties or preferences.

Honest, *impartial* estimates of the cost in dollars, lives, and time of conflict would provide Congress, the president, and, most critically, "We, the people" with an objective measure of the likely total cost against which to compare the benefits of fighting.

Clear estimates of the likely costs of war provide many advantages. Most obviously, they provide a basis for Congress to assess whether it wants to declare war or authorize funds for a conflict. Well-publicized estimates also provide performance targets for executives. Leaders who bring a war to a successful conclusion more quickly, at lower cost, and with the loss of fewer American lives than anticipated will be highly regarded as truly competent and deserving of our praise. In contrast, the leader who overshoots predictions on these dimensions is likely to be seen as incompetent. Faced with such prospects, leaders are incentivized to both provide realistic assessments of the costs and to fight wars as efficiently as possible.

Consider how differently Abraham Lincoln might have acted if faced with a public estimate of the loss of lives and the duration of fighting when the Civil War was impending, say, during the four and a half months between his election and his inauguration. Consider that Richmond, Virginia, capital of the Confederacy, is a mere 100 miles from Washington, DC. Yet, despite massively overwhelming strength in terms of economic capacity and manpower, it took four years before the Army of the Potomac could advance that short distance, one that probably should have been traversed in months. Had an impartial estimate of five to six months to victory been widely known, perhaps Lincoln would have interviewed more generals at the outset, asking them what their approach to achieving victory would be, rather than choosing to stay with General McClelland for so long and then accepting Grant's strategy of attrition. Yes, Grant was right, the South would run out of men before the North did, but was this the most cost-effective and quickest way to win? Likewise would FDR have been so reluctant to desegregate the army, if doing so would have helped him come in under budget?

Publicizing estimates of costs, lethality, and duration has another advantage: it can be expected to induce more accurate reporting by presidents. In general, leaders underestimate the cost of wars they want to fight because doing so makes it easier to gain support for their policy. However, this incentive is diminished if cost estimates are used by the voters as a basis for performance measures. Thomas Jefferson advised Madison that "the acquisition of Canada this year as far as the neighbourhood of Quebec will be a mere matter of marching," and Henry Clay thought the Kentucky Militia alone would be sufficient.[10] Of course, their Federalist opponents were far more realistic in their assessment of how much the war would cost, but they had incentives to overestimate the cost as they sought to prevent the war. Perhaps the War Hawks would have been incentivized to provide an impartial CBO-like body with accurate information of their plans and expectations if the estimates generated from such information were advertised as a measure of political performance. Madison declared victory in 1814, and that declaration might have been warranted if the estimates for the war were that it would take two years, cost $90 million (over $1.5 billion in today's terms), and cost the lives of around fifteen thousand Americans. Otherwise, Mr. Madison's War looked like a dismal failure.

Levy War Taxes on All Citizens

War is very costly business. Yet thus far, Americans have not insisted that presidents provide a clear, lucid, well-justified estimate of the costs of war, nor have they insisted that presidents impose a war tax surcharge to pay the carefully estimated cost of any conflict they contemplate involving us in. Failing to take these steps is dangerous, inviting leaders to engage in war for partisan rather than national advantage.

Writing in the *Wealth of Nations*, published in 1776, Adam Smith described the immunity from responsibility that postponing war payments allows:

> The ordinary expence [*sic*] of the greater part of modern governments in time of peace being equal or nearly equal to their ordinary revenue, when war comes they are both unwilling and unable to increase their revenue in proportion to the increase of their expence. They are unwilling, for fear of offending the people, who, by so great and so sudden an increase of taxes, would soon be disgusted with the war; and they are unable, from not well knowing what taxes would be sufficient to produce the revenue wanted. The facility of borrowing delivers them from the embarrassment which this fear and inability would otherwise occasion. By means of borrowing they are enabled, with a very moderate increase of taxes, to raise, from year to year, money sufficient for carrying on the war, and by the practice of perpetual funding they are enabled, with the smallest possible increase of taxes, to raise annually the largest possible sum of money.
>
> In great empires the people who live in the capital, and in the provinces remote from the scene of action, feel, many of them scarce any inconveniency from the war; but enjoy, at their ease, the amusement of reading in the newspapers the exploits of their own fleets and armies. To them this amusement compensates the small difference between the taxes which they pay on account of the war, and those which they had been accustomed to pay in time of peace. They are commonly dissatisfied with the return of peace, which puts an end to

their amusement, and to a thousand visionary hopes of conquest and
national glory, from a longer continuance of the war.[11]

Between 2001 and 2008, wealthy, probably Republican voters saw
their post-tax income increase by many tens of thousands of dollars.
As Adam Smith had said, they could "enjoy, at their ease, the amusement of reading in the newspapers the exploits of their own fleets and
armies."[12] Had instead they been asked to contribute, say, $40,000 to
pay for the occupation of Iraq, they might well have regarded it as
being the same unmitigated failure as Democrats did. However, this was
not what happened. Bush transferred the cost of the war to the poor,
who saw programs that benefited them slashed, and to future generations of taxpayers on the hook for the enormous cost of the war, much
of which was kept off the books for appearance's sake. The $40,000
burden is far from unrealistic. If we take the cost of the Iraq War as $1
trillion, and others estimate the real cost to be as much as three times
higher, then that equates to a little over $3,000 for every person in the
United States. Of course, not everyone pays an equal share of the tax
burden. The top two income quintiles pay close to 90 percent of the
total federal income tax burden, which readily translates into a wealthy
family's paying about $40,000.[13] Of course, these are just back-of-the-
envelope calculations based on relatively conservative estimates of the
Iraq War's total cost. If we believed Joseph Stiglitz and Linda Bilmes's
much larger $3 trillion estimate and factored in the cost of the Afghan
War, too, then the bill would have been an even greater retardant on
the war.

When voting to authorize war, Congress should specify a sched-
ule of taxes to pay for it. Despite the huge cost of the Vietnam War,
Johnson's war taxes left the nation's budget in surplus. When, as with
World War II, the cost cannot realistically be paid on a pay-as-you-go
basis, Congress can outline a repayment scheme for the forthcoming
years. In such a way, people know the financial commitment they are
being asked to make and can moderate their support for war accordingly. If "We, the people" believe that the issue at stake is sufficiently
important that they are willing to pay their share, then congressmen
can safely endorse conflict secure in the knowledge that their reelection
prospects will be unharmed. If a president fails to end the war in the
timely manner predicted, then the new taxes will have to be increased
and "We, the people" will naturally be unhappy. This is bad for a

sitting president, but as a consequence that president will fight to win the war as quickly and cheaply as possible. Further, presidents won't push for war unless they are confident of achieving a rapid victory.

If in 2002 Congress had committed to wartime tax surcharges, that is to say, it actualized the "we will pay" that Bush spoke of in his 2002 State of the Union Address, then it would have sent a powerful message both home and abroad. The American people would have heard that both the president and the Congress perceived the threat that Saddam Hussein posed to vital US interests as serious and grave. This clear, powerful message would also have been heard loud and clear overseas. Allies would be reassured that the United States had real evidence that security was threatened and enemies would know that it meant business. Bush's claim that Hussein was evil and was propagating WMD would have become a costly, and therefore, a harder, message to send. That would have made for greater caution in sending it and greater believability if it were sent. Hussein would have known that Bush was serious. He might have agreed to even more access for weapons inspectors. He might also have contemplated fleeing into exile. And the United States might have saved $1 trillion and thousands of lives.

Once the material and human costs of war, and how they are to be paid for, is well publicized, these costs provide a performance standard against which to measure presidents. Once the people have such estimates they can decide whether they should get behind the president's plan or protest against it. In a recent Internet-based experiment, political scientists Gustavo A. Flores-Macías and Sarah Kreps assessed the impact of taxation on support for a war. They asked voters about their support for a hypothetical war based on how the war is financed. They found that if a tax on war accompanies the proposed conflict, then there is on average 10 percent less support for the conflict than if it is to be financed through existing means and debt.[14] Create that risk for presidents and they will be more thoughtful about the wars we fight. There are, after all, other ways to settle disputes.

When the costs are reasonably well anticipated by the people, the people provide a natural brake on the proclivity of politicians to fight. Instead, leaders must find peaceful means to fulfill their goals. Although paying to acquire land now appears out of fashion, it is worth noting that negotiated purchases followed by settlement expanded US lands to a far greater degree than war. Further, it did so at far lower cost. The Louisiana Purchase increased the United States by 828,000 square miles at a cost of about $15 million (a little more than a quarter-billion dollars today, adjusting for inflation). The incorporation of the enormous Oregon Territory was achieved through treaty negotiations with the British in 1818 and 1846 without a resort to arms. The Treaty of Guadalupe Hidalgo that concluded the Mexican-American War gained 525,000 square miles for the United States in exchange for $18.25 million to Mexico (and to take on Mexican debt liabilities). However, the war cost $71 million to fight. Negotiation and paying for land proved much cheaper than fighting. War should be a last resort, only to be used when vital national interests are at stake. Unfortunately the people provide little retardant to fighting if they bear no costs. If plans such as ours are implemented, the burden of war will be transparently shifted to politicians who will naturally be induced to be more careful in their decisions to resort to force.

A Closing Observation

IMAGINE THAT WE ASSESSED THE QUALITY OF EACH PRESIDENT'S TERM IN office by how much the nation enjoyed peace and prosperity. It seems uncontroversial that periods of peace—when few Americans die in war—and periods of prosperity—when the average American's income grows rapidly from year to year—are the gold standard we all seek in our leaders. Yet if we evaluated presidents based on how the nation did on those two standards during their time in office, we would come up with a radically different view of who the great presidents were from those we currently laud.

Table C.1 has taken the relevant information on growth rates and absence of US war deaths to rank presidents from best to worst.

One might, of course, tweak this assessment to elevate presidents who, though presiding over many American deaths in war, were responding to attack or inherited a war rather than fomenting it. That might, for instance, improve the rankings of Truman, Nixon, Eisenhower, and Franklin Roosevelt. However we might tweak this, the crucial observation is how little regard we seem to have for presidents credited with a time of peace and prosperity. Maybe, just maybe, that is a failing in "We, the people" that we might wish individually and collectively to reflect upon.

Table C.1. Peace and Prosperity Rankings of US Presidents

Rank	President	Inauguration year
1	Harding	1921
2	Ford	1974
3	Kennedy	1961
4	Coolidge	1923
5	Tyler	1842
6	Clinton	1993
7	Reagan	1981
8	T. Roosevelt	1902
9	Hayes	1877
10	Carter	1977
11	Fillmore	1850
12	Arthur	1882
13	Eisenhower	1953
14	Taylor	1849
15.5	Cleveland	1885
15.5	McKinley	1897
17	Jackson	1829
18	FDR	1933
20	Garfield	1881
20	W. H. Harrison	1841
20	Taft	1909
22.5	Buchanan	1857
22.5	LBJ	1964
24	Johnson	1865
25	J. Q. Adams	1825
26.5	Monroe	1817
26.5	B. Harrison	1889
28	Hoover	1929
29.5	Truman	1946
29.5	G. H. W. Bush	1989
31	Nixon	1969
32	Van Buren	1837
33	Grant	1869
34.5	Lincoln	1861
34.5	G. W. Bush	2001
36.5	Jefferson	1801
36.5	Pierce	1853
38	Polk	1845
39	Wilson	1913
40	Madison	1809

*There are insufficient data to assess George Washington, John Adams, or Barack Obama.

Notes

ACKNOWLEDGMENTS

1. As one astute observer noted, "Civil war was not in [Lincoln's] opinion, the worst disaster that could befall the American people." See Don E. Fehrenbacher, "The Origins and Purpose of Lincoln's 'House-Divided' Speech," *Mississippi Valley Historical Review* 46, no. 4 (1960): 615–643.

INTRODUCTION: E PLURIBUS UNUM

1. William Shakespeare, *Julius Caesar*, 3.2.

2. M. Cary and H. H. Scullard, *A History of Rome: Down to the Reign of Constantine*, 3rd edition (Boston: Bedford/St. Martin's, 1976).

3. See http://www.blackpast.org/1860-h-ford-douglas-i-do-not-believe -antislavery-abraham-lincoln and also *Liberator*, July 13, 1860. When we examine President Lincoln in Chapter 3, we will see that the bill Lincoln introduced into the House was more nuanced than Mr. Douglas's account might lead one to infer. The bill was designed to limit the spread of slavery to the District of Columbia and to neutralize opposition by advancing the rights of slaveholders to pursue and recover runaway slaves who made their way to the district.

4. Indeed, the truth is much less flattering for the lives of many Catholic saints, some of whom, such as Pope, later Saint, Damasus I, were power hungry, corrupt, and murderous individuals.

5. We say "mostly honest" in deference to the questions raised about the election of Hayes over Tilden, Kennedy over Nixon, and Bush over Gore. We also note that the United States presents a particularly challenging case because so many believe that American presidents, whatever their personal ambition, accepted a severe limitation on their political power. They allegedly accepted the norm established by George Washington that no president would hold more than two terms. As this is an important challenge to our fundamental assumption, we take it on briefly—and provide evidence that contradicts it.

6. James Madison, no. IV in *The Pacificus-Helvidius Debates of 1793–1794*, by Alexander Hamilton and James Madison (Liberty Fund, 2007).

7. Bruce Bueno de Mesquita and Alastair Smith, *The Dictator's Handbook* (New York: PublicAffairs, 2011); Bruce Bueno de Mesquita et al., *The Logic of Political Survival* (Cambridge, MA: MIT Press, 2003).

8. Speech before a joint session of Congress, April 2, 1917. See http:// todayinclh.com/?event=president-wilson-asks-for-declaration-of-war.

9. Speech delivered at the National Holocaust Museum, April 23, 2012. See https://www.whitehouse.gov/photos-and-video/video/2012/04/23 /president-obama-speaks-preventing-mass-atrocities.

10. State of the Union Address, January 20, 2004. See http://www.cnn .com/2004/ALLPOLITICS/01/20/sotu.transcript.3/.

11. *The Holy Scriptures According to the Masoretic Text: A New Translation* (Philadelphia: Jewish Publication Society of America, 1917), 237.

12. For statistical assessments of these calculations about how war will go for individual leaders, see Bruce Bueno de Mesquita et al., "Political Institutions and Incentives to Govern Effectively," *Journal of Democracy* 12 (January 2001): 58–72; Bruce Bueno de Mesquita and Randolph M. Siverson, "War and the Survival of Political Leaders: A Comparative Study of Regime Types and Political Accountability," *American Political Science Review* 89 (December 1995): 841–855; Hein E. Goemans and Giacomo Chiozza, "International Conflict and the Tenure of Leaders: Is War Still Ex Post Inefficient," *American Journal of Political Science* 48 (July 2004): 604–619.

13. Madison, no. IV in *The Pacificus-Helvidius Debates of 1793–1794*.

14. Alexander Hamilton, James Madison, and John Jay, *The Federalist Papers*, ed. Clinton Rossiter (New York: Signet Classics, 2003). See especially Madison's Federalist #10.

15. Andrew Burstein and Nancy Isenberg, *Madison and Jefferson* (New York: Random House, 2010).

16. John Yoo, *Crisis and Command* (New York: Kaplan Publishing, 2010).

17. Gary Will, *Bomb Power* (New York: Penguin Books, 2011).

18. http://www.cbsnews.com/news/who-says-political-attacks-have-gotten-worse/.

19. http://www.forbes.com/sites/rickungar/2012/08/20/the-dirtiest -presidential-campaign-ever-not-even-close/2/.

20. Marcus Tullius Cicero, *Letters to Quintus, Brutus, Octavian and Commentariolum Petitionis*, attributed to Quintus Tullius Cicero, brother of the Roman orator Marcus Tullius Cicero, trans. W. G. Williams (London: William Heinemann, Ltd., 1972).

21. Kenneth Schultz, "Domestic Opposition and Signaling in International Crises," *American Political Science Review* 92 (December 1998): 829–844; Kenneth Schultz, *Democracy and Coercive Diplomacy* (Cambridge: Cambridge University Press, 2001).

22. Kurt Taylor Gaubatz, *Elections and War* (Stanford, CA: Stanford University Press, 1999).

23. Philip Kurland and Ralph Lerner, eds., *The Founders' Constitution*, http://press-pubs.uchicago.edu/founders/. See Chapter 7, Document 17 for the speech by James Wilson to the Pennsylvania Ratifying Convention on December 11, 1787.

24. See http://warandlaw.homestead.com/files/foundin2.html.

25. President Jefferson fought the Barbary pirates in 1801 to 1805. Congress authorized the defensive use of force in the event, as happened, of a declaration of war by any of the Barbary powers against the United States. Although Jefferson sought and received congressional approval to act, Congress did not vote a formal declaration of war as called for in the Constitution.

26. Don E. Fehrenbacher, ed., *Abraham Lincoln: Speeches & Writings Part 1: 1832–1858* (New York: Library of America, 1989), 168.

27. Against the myth of a two-term norm we note that few presidents who survived two terms failed to pursue a third. Jefferson, Madison, Monroe, and Jackson did not but they were in their late sixties or seventy (in Jackson's case) at the end of their second term, making them very old for their time. The next presidents to survive two terms, Grant, Cleveland, and T. Roosevelt all sought their party's nomination for a third term but failed to get it. T. Roosevelt then ran for a third term as a Bull Moose. Evidence suggests that even Wilson and Coolidge hoped to be renominated by their party, taking us to FDR, who had four terms followed by a term-limiting constitutional amendment.

28. Washington appears genuinely to have believed it was his duty to serve the new country however he could, although he preferred to return to farming and the Potomac Canal Company.

29. We have measured ranking by the average of more than twenty ratings of American presidents. See https://en.wikipedia.org/wiki/Historical_rankings _of_Presidents_of_the_United_States for the aggregate ranking used here. Data on deaths are taken from https://en.wikipedia.org/wiki/United_States _military_casualties_of_war. The Wikipedia article includes detailed source material for the rankings. We have plotted the relationship between deaths per year and US population at the time the president took office, having taken the logarithm of deaths and population to capture order of magnitude changes.

30. Max Eastman, *Enjoyment of Laughter* (New York: Simon and Schuster, 1936), 155.

CHAPTER ONE: GEORGE WASHINGTON'S WARS

1. Per capita income estimates are based on a linear interpolation of Angus Maddison's estimates for 1700 and 1820. The dollar amounts are measured in 1990 international dollars. See J. Bolt and J. L. van Zanden, "The Maddison Project: Collaborative Research on Historical National Accounts," *Economic History Review* 67, no. 3 (2014): 627–651. The data can be downloaded from http:// www.ggdc.net/maddison/maddison-project/home.htm.

2. Unlike the Civil War, which we discuss in Chapter 3, the asymmetry in potential military power in the revolution was somewhat muted in the case of the American War for Independence. The colonists had two things going for

them that were not working on behalf of the Confederacy in its fight with the Union in the Civil War. First, there was, given the technology of the time, a vast distance between England and America, which made the logistics of war challenging for the English. Second, the colonists' had a much greater commitment to victory than was felt by the British government for which the colonies were little more than a sleepy backwater. Both sides in the Civil War were strongly motivated to win. Against the colonists' advantages were the overwhelming potential of the British as well as the fact that the British had been in America for a long time and had invested a great deal in its defense, in hopes of expanding the British Empire. Additionally, there were many British loyalists among the colonists, further diminishing the potential strength of those fighting for independence.

3. See Howard H. Peckham, ed., *The Toll of Independence: Engagements and Battle Casualties of the American Revolution* (Chicago: University of Chicago Press, 1974). British fatalities numbered approximately 5,200. For the British, the difficulties in defeating the colonists revolved around the distance their forces had to travel by sea to get to America, their relatively small army that was spread thin due to Britain's other interests around the world, and the relative lack of enthusiasm for fighting the revolutionaries compared to the latter's enthusiasm for seizing their independence from Britain.

4. Douglas Southall Freeman, *George Washington: A Biography*, vol. 1 (New York: Charles Scribner's Sons, 1948), 325.

5. George Washington, *The Writings of George Washington from the Original Manuscript Sources*, vol. 2, ed. John C. Fitzpatrick, 7. This is available in a Kindle edition.

6. James Thomas Flexner, *George Washington: The Forge of Experience (1732–1775)* (Boston: Little, Brown, 1965), 90.

7. Ibid., 89–92.

8. Ibid., 336.

9. Michael Klepper and Robert Gunther, *The Wealthy 100: From Benjamin Franklin to Bill Gates—A Ranking of the Richest Americans, Past and Present* (New York: Citadel, 1996).

10. Marcus Cunliffe, *George Washington, Man and Monument* (Boston: Little, Brown, 1958), 31.

11. Norman Schofield, *Architects of Political Change: Constitutional Quandaries and Social Choice Theory* (New York: Cambridge University Press, 2006), chap. 3.

12. Flexner, *George Washington*.

13. Willard Rouse Jillson, *The Land Adventures of George Washington* (New York: Standard Printing Company, 1934).

14. The term *dower slaves* refers to slaves she brought to their marriage but who remained her property and passed to her heirs upon her death. Consequently, although George Washington profited from their labor and paid the costs of their maintenance, he had no authority to manumit them on his death or at any other time. They belonged legally to Martha Custis Washington.

15. William Waller Hening, *The Statutes at Large, Being a Collection of All the Laws of Virginia*, vol. 7 (New York: Bartow, 1820), 661–662.

16. Douglas Southall Freeman, *Washington*, abridged edition, ed. Richard Harwell (New York: Charles Scribner's Sons, 1968), 181–182.

17. Ron Chernow, *Washington: A Life* (New York: Penguin Books, 2011), 149.

18. Washington, *The Writings of George Washington*, vol. 33, 407.

19. Bernhard Knollenberg, *George Washington the Virginia Period, 1732–1775* (Durham, NC: Duke University Press, 1964), 185.

20. John E. Ferling, *Setting the World Ablaze: Washington, Adams, Jefferson, and the American Revolution* (New York: Oxford University Press, 2002), 45.

21. Washington, *The Writings of George Washington*, vol. 2, 467–471.

22. See http://www.landofthebrave.info/stamp-act.htm.

23. http://www.constitution.org/bcp/dor_sac.htm.

24. Dunmore is perhaps best remembered for issuing a proclamation offering slaves their freedom if they fought for the British in the Revolutionary War.

25. Stanley Elkins and Eric McKitrick, *The Age of Federalism: The Early American Republic, 1788–1800* (Oxford: Oxford University Press, 1993), 36.

26. Flexner, *George Washington*, 62.

27. Ibid., 62–63.

28. Jefferson wrote the quoted sentence in a letter to the Marquis de Chastellux on June 7, 1785. See Julian P. Boyd et al., eds., *The Papers of Thomas Jefferson*, vol. 8 (Princeton, NJ: Princeton University Press, 1950), 186.

29. See a facsimile of the handwritten manuscript at http://www.masshist .org/thomasjeffersonpapers/notes/nsvviewer.php?page=37.

30. Adam Smith, *The Wealth of Nations*, vol. 4, sect. 7 (London: W. Strahan and T. Cadell, 1776), 163.

31. Ibid., 166.

32. There were a few exceptions, such as the possessions of the East India Company, but these, too, were subject to the ban from 1843 onward.

33. Bruce Bueno de Mesquita et al., *The Logic of Political Survival* (Cambridge, MA: MIT Press, 2003).

34. Akhil Reed Amar, *America's Constitution: A Biography* (New York: Random House, 2010).

35. See Robert M. Calhoon, *The Loyalists in Revolutionary America, 1760–1781* (New York: Harcourt Brace Jovanovich, 1993); Maya Jasanoff, *Liberty's Exiles: American Loyalists in the Revolutionary World* (New York: Random House, 2012).

CHAPTER TWO: CONGRESS'S WAR OF 1812

1. J. C. A. Stagg, *The War of 1812: Conflict for a Continent* (New York: Cambridge University Press, 2012). Chapter 1 provides a discussion of different approaches to historical studies of 1812.

2. The full text of President Madison's letter to Congress can be seen at http://millercenter.org/president/speeches/speech-3614.

3. "A Century of Lawmaking for a New Nation: U.S. Congressional Documents and Debates, 1774–1875," *Annals of Congress*, 12th Cong., 1st sess., H 1547.

4. Hugo Grotius, *On the Law of War and Peace* book 3 (Whitefish, MT: Kessinger Publishing, LLC (1625), 2010), chap. 3, sect. 6.

5. William, Kingsford, *History of Canada*, vol. 8 (Toronto: Rowsell and Hutchison, 1897), 579–80, cited in John Stagg, *The War of 1812*, 12.

6. For basic figures and chronological details we draw on Donald Hickey, *The War of 1812: A Forgotten Conflict* (Champaign-Urbana: University of Illinois Press, 2012), and Stagg, *The War of 1812* (New York: Cambridge University Press, 2012).

7. A. T. (Alfred Thayer) Mahan, *Sea Power in Its Relations to the War of 1812* (Boston: Little, Brown, and Company, 1905), 286.

8. Cited in Hickey, *The War of 1812*, 303.

9. "Report, or Manifesto of the Causes and Reasons War with Great Britain, Presented to the House of Representatives," Committee of Foreign Relations, June 3, 1812 (Washington: A. & G. Way, Printers), 8–9.

10. *Journal of the House of Representatives of the United States, at the First Session of the Twelfth Congress*, November 4, 1811 (Washington, DC: Gales and Seaton), 394.

11. See President Madison's letter to Congress at http://millercenter.org/president/speeches/speech-3614.

12. Mark Zuehlke, *For Honour's Sake: The War of 1812 and the Brokering of an Uneasy Peace* (Toronto: Knopf Canada, 2010), 74–75.

13. The shift in policy followed a change in the prime minister after Spencer Percival's assassination; however, pressure had been building for a reversal of the policy. For a full account, see Henry Adams, *History of the United States 1809–17*, vol. 2 (New York: Viking Press, 1986), chap. 13.

14. "A Century of Lawmaking for a New Nation: U.S. Congressional Documents and Debates, 1774–1875," *Annals of Congress*, 12th Cong., 1st sess., H 1397–1398.

15. See http://millercenter.org/president/speeches/speech-3614.

16. See Zuehlke, *For Honour's Sake*, chap. 6.

17. Ellmore Barce, "Governor Harrison and the Treaty of Fort Wayne, 1809," *Indiana Magazine of History* 11, no. 4 (1915): 352–367.

18. Article 3 of Treaty with the Delawares, Etc., September 30, 1809, in *Indian Affairs: Laws and Treaties*, vol. 2, Treaties, comp. and ed. by Charles J. Kappler (Washington, DC: Government Printing Office, 1904).

19. Zuehlke, *For Honour's Sake*, 57.

20. Augustus John Foster, *Jeffersonian America: Notes on the United States of America* (San Marino, CA: Huntington Library, 1954), 100.

21. Bradford Perkins, *Castlereagh and Adams* (Berkeley and LA: University of California Press, 1964), 11–13.

22. *Annals of Congress*, 12th Cong., 1st sess., H 447.

23. Henry Clay, letter to Caesar Rodney, December 29, 1812, *Papers of Henry Clay*, vol. 1: *The Rising Statesman 1797–1814*, ed. James F. Hopkins, assoc. ed. Mary W. M. Hargreaves (Lexington University of Kentucky Press, 1959), 750.

24. See http://teachingamericanhistory.org/library/document/letter-in-support-of-the-war-of-1812/#doc-tabs-ab.

25. The Republican Party of Jefferson and Madison is distinct from the party of Lincoln and its present-day manifestation. Jefferson's party is often called the Democrat-Republican Party and its lineage relates to the modern Democratic Party.

26. See speech on February 22, 1810, in Hopkins and Hargreaves, *Papers of Henry Clay*, vol. 1, 449.

27. Cited in Adams, *History of the United States*, 438.

28. Kenneth Schultz, *Democracy and Coercive Diplomacy* (Cambridge: Cambridge University Press, 2001).

29. *Annals of Congress*, 12th Cong., 1st sess., H 423–426.

30. Adams, *History of the United States*, 392.

31. Zuehlke, *For Honour's Sake*, 70.

32. Letter to Thomas Bodley, December 18, 1813, in Hopkins and Hargreaves, *Papers of Henry Clay*, vol. 1, 842.

33. Zuehlke, *For Honour's Sake*, 72.

34. Speech on Proposed Repeal of Non-Intercourse Act, February 22, 1810, in Hopkins and Hargreaves, *Papers of Henry Clay*, vol. 1, 450.

35. Adams, *History of the United States*, 440.

36. Ibid.

37. Elizabeth Donnan, ed., *Papers of James A. Bayard, 1796–1815* (Washington: Annual Report of the American Historical Association for the Year 1913, 1915), 190.

38. Adams, *History of the United States*, 400.

39. Zuehlke, *For Honour's Sake*, 72–73; Mahan, *Sea Power*, vol. 1, 259–263.

40. *Annals of Congress*, 12th Cong., 1st sess., H 859–866.

41. To construct this table we obtained congressional roll call votes from https://www.govtrack.us/congress/votes#session=33 and obtained the roll calls for House Vote #214 1812–06–04T00:00:00-TO PASS H.R. 184 (the war declaration) and House Vote #51 1812–01–28T00:00:00-TO AMEND H.R. 24 SO TO PROVIDE FOR COMPLETION OF 74 GUN SHIPS, an amendment to the navy bill.

42. Some congressmen are dropped from the analysis because of data issues, such as changes in congressional membership.

43. Letter dated January 10, 1812, in Albert Gallatin, *The Writings of Albert Gallatin*, vol. 1 (New York: Antiquarian Press, 1960), 501–516.

44. Raymond Walters Jr., *Albert Gallatin: Jeffersonian Financier and Diplomat* (New York: Macmillan, 1957), 247–248.

45. Ibid., 255–256.

46. Speech of Harmanus Bleecker, June 22, 1812, *Annals of Congress*, 12th Cong., 1st sess., H 1523.

47. Earl N. Harbert, ed., *History of the United States During the Administration of Thomas Jefferson and James Madison*, vol. 2 (New York: Library of America, 1986).

48. Hickey, *The War of 1812*, 314.

49. Richard Brookhiser, *James Madison* (New York: Basic Books, 2011), 219.

50. From Foster to Castlereagh, May 3, 1812, MSS, British Archives, cited in Adams, *History of the United* States, 441.

51. Sidney Howard Gay, *James Madison*, American Statesmen series (New York: Houghton, Mifflin and Company, 1898), 297–298.

52. Marion Mills Miller, *Great Debates in American History*, vol. 2: *Foreign Relations* (Current Literature Pub. Co., 1913), 190.

53. Ibid., 194.

54. See http://avalon.law.yale.edu/18th_century/debates_711.asp.

CHAPTER THREE: ABRAHAM LINCOLN AND THE PURSUIT OF AMBITION

1. For a formal and statistical proof of this central claim, see Bruce Bueno de Mesquita et al., *The Logic of Political Survival* (Cambridge, MA: MIT Press, 2003). For a nontechnical explanation of this claim see Bruce Bueno de Mesquita and Alastair Smith, *The Dictator's Handbook* (New York: PublicAffairs, 2010).

2. Letter from Abraham Lincoln to John T. Hale, January 11, 1861, in *The Collected Works of Abraham Lincoln* [hereafter *CWAL*], volume 4, ed. Roy P. Basler, The Abraham Lincoln Association, 1953, 172; see also Ida Tarbell, "Lincoln as President-Elect," *McClure's Magazine* 12 (1899), 163.

3. Article I, Section 2 of the Constitution.

4. Specifically, the Electoral College created two distortions in the election of the president. Small states with only one member in the House of Representatives benefited disproportionately from the fact that every state, no matter how small the population, had two members in the Senate. Hence, states with small populations were overrepresented in terms of electoral votes. Additionally, states with slaves, because of the three-fifths rule, were overrepresented. The latter distortion, of course, no longer exists, but the small-state bias persists, facilitating the opportunity for the popular vote and the electoral vote to be misaligned.

5. Herbert Collins and David Weaver, *Wills of the U.S. Presidents* (New York: Communication Channels, Inc., 1976), 20.

6. His wife owned a great many dower slaves who were beyond the authority of Washington to set free, as they were her property, not his.

7. Henry Wiencek, *An Imperfect God: George Washington, His Slaves, and the Creation of America* (New York: Farrar, Straus and Giroux, 2004).

8. Henry Washington fought on the British side in the revolution, while another Washington slave, Deborah Squash, together with her husband, escaped, supported the British, and were subsequently evacuated under the British policy that promised freedom to slaves who escaped and joined their side.

9. Thomas Jefferson to Jean Nicholas Demeunier, January 24, 1786; see the Library of Congress, The Thomas Jefferson Papers, series 1: General Correspondence 1651–1827; his handwritten document is reproduced at http://hdl.loc.gov/loc.mss/mtj.mtjbib001747.

10. See extract from Thomas Jefferson's Draft of a Constitution for Virginia, available at http://tjrs.monticello.org/letter/1654.

11. On the economic viability of slavery, see both the technical and non-technical volumes of Robert Fogel and Stanley Engerman, *Time on the Cross* (Boston: Little, Brown, 1974) and subsequent debate and responses by Fogel and Engerman.

12. See Anonymous and Henry George Tuke, *The Trials of the Slave Traders, Samuel Samo, Joseph Peters, and William Tufft . . .* (New York: Cambridge University Press, 2014), 44.

13. John Baker, *Collected Papers on English Legal History* (New York: Cambridge University Press, 2013), item 60, *Shanley v Harvey* (1763) 2 Eden 126 at 127.

14. For non-American readers, July 4, 1776, is the day Americans celebrate as the issuance of the Declaration of Independence; April 14, 1865, is the day President Lincoln was assassinated and would have been instantly recognizable as such to anyone who lived through the event; December 7, 1941, was the day of the Japanese attack on Pearl Harbor or, as Franklin Roosevelt described it, "A date which will live in infamy"; November 22, 1963, is the day John Kennedy was assassinated, and all Americans who lived through that can tell you exactly where they were and what they were doing at the time; and 9/11 is the shorthand for the terrorist attack on the World Trade Center on September 11, 2001.

15. Basler, ed., *CWAL*, vol. 2, 492.

16. Robert H. Browne, *Recollected Words of Abraham Lincoln,* ed. Don Fehrenbacher and Virginia Fehrenbacher (Stanford: Stanford University Press, 1996), 61. Browne's recollection of his discussion with Lincoln about slavery is critical to understanding how different his views were before and after Dred Scott. His opposition to slavery was never in doubt but he went from a passive to a proactive approach once the court ruling came down.

Robert H. Browne, *Abraham Lincoln and the Men of His Time* (New York: Katon and Mains, 1901), 285.

17. Jesse W. Weik, *The Real Lincoln: A Portrait* (Champaign: University of Illinois Press, 2009 [1922]), 319.

18. Allen C. Guelzo, *Lincoln's Emancipation Proclamation: The End of Slavery in America* (New York: Simon and Schuster, 2006), 23.

19. David Herbert Donald, *Lincoln* (New York: Simon and Schuster, 1995), 222.

20. Doris Kearns Goodwin, *Team of Rivals: The Political Genius of Abraham Lincoln* (New York: Simon and Schuster, 2005).

21. Randall Calvert, "The Value of Biased Information: A Rational Choice Model of Political Advice," *Journal of Politics* 47, no. 2 (May 1985): 530–555.

22. John Nicolay and John Hay, "Abraham Lincoln: A History: The Formation of the Cabinet," *Century Magazine* 35, no. 3 (January 1888): 420.

23. Edward Conrad Smith, *The Borderland in the Civil War* (New York: AMS Press, 1970), 144.

24. See, for example, William J. Cooper, *Jefferson Davis, American* (New York: Alfred A. Knopf, 2000).

25. D. Scott Bennett and Allan C. Stam III, "The Duration of Interstate Wars," *American Political Science Review* 90 (June 1996): 239–57. Our estimation

requires a proxy for the national capability indicator Bennett and Stam used. Because they looked only at interstate wars, they could use the Correlates of War Project's (COW) national capability index. Those scores are not available for the Confederacy. We used the National Parks Service fact sheet on the Civil War to make proxies for the COW capability index. The table below shows the relevant variables and their values.

COW Concept	Population	Urban Population	Iron and Steel	Military Personnel	Military Expenditure	Energy Consumption
Proxy	Population	Factory workers	Railroad miles	Total military force	Same	Number of factories
North	18.5	1100	20	2,672	3,183	101
South	9	111	9	1,000	1,000	21

Taking the North's percentage of the total for North and South on each variable and then finding the average for these variables, the North's national capability index is equal to approximately 76 percent. Taking the estimated weights for each variable in Bennett and Stam's method and applying those values to the North and South's values, we can predict the expected length of the war given their procedure. That yields a median predicted length for the Civil War of 5.89 months.

26. Stephen W. Sears, *George B. McClellan: The Young Napoleon* (New York: Da Capo Press, 1999).

27. Abraham Lincoln to Joshua Speed, August 24, 1855, in *Lincoln Bicentennial Collection Box Set,* Vol 1 (New York: Library of America, 2008), 360–365.

28. See http://www.abrahamlincolnonline.org/lincoln/speeches/house.htm.

29. William Herndon, "Facts Illustrative of Mr. Lincoln's Patriotism and Statesmanship: A Lecture by William Herndon, delivered on January 24, 1866," reprinted in *Abraham Lincoln Quarterly* 3, no. 4 (December 1944): 183–186.

30. See the letter in its entirety at http://www.abrahamlincolnonline.org /lincoln/speeches/robert.htm.

31. See http://www.ushistory.org/gop/origins.htm.

32. Speech delivered by Stephen Douglas at Freeport, Illinois, on August 27, 1858, during the second Lincoln-Douglas debate. See https://www.nps.gov/liho /learn/historyculture/debate2.htm.

33. For a similar strategic account of Lincoln's political maneuvers against Douglas, see William H. Riker, *The Art of Political Manipulation* (New Haven, CT: Yale University Press, 1986).

34. The full text of Douglas's speech that led Lincoln and Douglas to agree to a series of what became the famous Lincoln-Douglas debates can be found at http://civilwarcauses.org/douglas.htm.

35. Letter by Thomas Jefferson to James Madison, September 6, 1789; see http://press-pubs.uchicago.edu/founders/documents/v1ch2s23.html.

36. See http://teachingamericanhistory.org/library/document /the-war-with-mexico-speech-in-the-united-states-house-of-representatives/.

37. W. Stephen Belko, *The Invincible Duff Green: Whig of the West* (Columbia: University of Missouri Press, 2006), 144.

38. See http://teachingamericanhistory.org/library/document/the-war-with -mexico-speech-in-the-united-states-house-of-representatives/.

39. Letter from Abraham Lincoln to John T. Hale, January 11, 1861, in Basler, ed., *CWAL*, vol. 4, 172.

40. Letter from William H. Herndon to Wendell Phillips, February 1, 1861, in Fehrenbacher and Fehrenbacher, eds., *Recollected Words of Abraham Lincoln*, 253.

41. John Minor Botts, *The Great Rebellion: Its Secret History, Rise, Progress, and Disastrous Failure* (Charleston, SC: Nabu Press, 2010), 196.

42. Stephen B. Oates, *Abraham Lincoln: The Man Behind The Myths* (New York: Harper & Row, 1983), 82–83.

43. See http://collections.richmond.edu/secession/visualizations/vote-maps .html.

44. See http://civilwarcauses.org/douglas.htm.

45. See http://www.abrahamlincolnonline.org/lincoln/speeches/house.htm.

46. Edward Lillie, Pierce, ed., *Memoir and Letters of Charles Sumner* (Ann Arbor: University of Michigan Library, 2009), 5–6.

47. William J. Cooper. *Jefferson Davis, American* (New York: Alfred A. Knopf, 2000), 352.

48. See Jeffrey Rogers Hummel, *Emancipating Slaves, Enslaving Free Men* (Chicago: Open Court, 1996), 138; Jefferson Davis, *The Rise and Fall of the Confederate Government*, vol. 1 (Boston: Da Capo Press, 1990 [1881]), 210–213; on the national debt question see especially Charles Roland, *The Confederacy* (Chicago: University of Chicago Press, 1960), 28; Rembert W. Patrick, *Jefferson Davis and His Cabinet* (Baton Rouge: Louisiana State University Press, 1944), 77; William C. Davis, *Look Away! A History of the Confederate States of America* (New York: The Free Press, 2002), 87.

49. Eric H. Walther, *William Lowndes Yancey: The Coming of the Civil War* (Chapel Hill: University of North Carolina Press, 2006), 214–217.

50. Frederick Douglass, ed., "The Late Election," *Douglass' Monthly*, December 1860, 370.

CHAPTER FOUR: ROOSEVELT'S VANITY

1. See http://www.presidency.ucsb.edu/ws/?pid=14473.

2. See http://historymatters.gmu.edu/d/5105/.

3. See http://www.presidency.ucsb.edu/ws/?pid=16022.

4. Quoted in William Doyle, *Inside the Oval Office* (Montgomery County, OH: London House, 1999), 8.

5. See http://newdeal.feri.org/speeches/1932d.htm.

6. Data from Angus Madison's Historical GDP Data available at http://www.worldeconomics.com/Data/MadisonHistoricalGDP/Madison%20Historical%20GDP%20Data.efp.

7. See http://www.presidency.ucsb.edu/ws/?pid=75629.

8. Albert Speer, *Inside the Third Reich* (New York: Simon and Schuster, 1997), 165.

9. See http://www.wwnorton.com/college/history/ralph/workbook/ralprs36 .htm.

10. Fireside Chat 14. See the full transcript at http://millercenter.org/pres ident/speeches/speech-3315.

11. See http://www.greatspeeches.net/2013/05/adolf-hitler-no-more-territo rial-demands.html.

12. Speer, *Inside the Third Reich*, 165.

13. See http://www.gwu.edu/~erpapers/teachinger/q-and-a/q22-erspeech .cfm.

14. See http://www.austincc.edu/lpatrick/his2341/address1940convention .html.

15. Address by Franklin Roosevelt to Congress, September 21, 1939. See http://www.presidency.ucsb.edu/ws/?pid=15813.

16. See http://www.presidency.ucsb.edu/ws/?pid=75629.

17. David E. Johnson, *Fast Tanks and Heavy Bombers: Innovation in the U.S. Army, 1917–1945* (Ithaca, NY: Cornell University Press, 2003), 167.

18. Ibid., 188.

19. All of the relevant 1940 Gallup survey results, including dates interviews were conducted, specific questions asked, and distribution of responses, can be found at http://www.ibiblio.org/pha/Gallup/Gallup%201940.htm.

20. Extracted from President Roosevelt's radio address on December 29, 1940. See http://www.ibiblio.org/pha/policy/1940/1940–12–29a.html.

21. See http://www.americanrhetoric.com/speeches/fdrarsenalofdemocracy .html.

22. Ibid.

23. Ibid.

24. Ibid.

25. Ibid.

26. See http://www.winstonchurchill.org/resources/speeches/1940-the -finest-hour/we-shall-fight-on-the-beaches.

27. Robert S. Robins and Jerrold M. Post, *When Illness Strikes the Leader: The Dilemma of the Captive King* (New Haven, CT: Yale University Press, 1995).

28. See the US Holocaust Museum documentation at http://www.ushmm .org/wlc/sp/article.php?ModuleId=10005267.

29. See "Voyage of the *St. Louis*," at http://www.ushmm.org/wlc/en/article .php?ModuleId=10005267. The same article reports on the fate of the passengers of the *St. Louis*. Here are the details: "Following the US government's refusal to permit the passengers to disembark, . . . Jewish organizations (particularly the Jewish Joint Distribution Committee) negotiated with four European governments to secure entry visas for the passengers: Great Britain took 288 passengers, the Netherlands admitted 181 passengers, Belgium took in 214 passengers; and 224 passengers found at least temporary refuge in France. Of the 288 passengers admitted by Great Britain, all survived World War II save one, who was killed during an air raid in 1940. Of the 620 passengers who returned to the continent, 87 (14%) managed to emigrate before the German invasion

of Western Europe in May 1940; 532 *St. Louis* passengers were trapped when Germany conquered Western Europe. Just over half, 278, survived the Holocaust; 254 died—84 who had been in Belgium, 84 who had found refuge in Holland, and 86 who had been admitted to France."

30. John Powell, *Encyclopedia of North American Immigration* (New York: Facts on File, 2005), 94.

31. See http://www.crf-usa.org/black-history-month/race-and-voting -in-the-segregated-south.

32. Doyle, *Inside the Oval Office.*

33. A fuller version of the discussion was reported on by the *New York Times*: "President Orders an Even Break for Minorities in Defense Jobs," June 26, 1941.

34. Morris J. MacGregor Jr., *Integration of the Armed Forces, 1940–1965* (Washington, DC: Center of Military History, US Army, 1981), 15.

35. See http://newdeal.feri.org/speeches/1932d.htm.

36. Walter White, *A Man Called White* (New York: Viking Press, 1948), 191.

37. MacGregor, *Integration of the Armed Forces*, 61.

38. Ibid., 63.

39. Ibid., 31–32.

40. James D. Fearon, "Rationalist Explanations for War," *International Organization* 49, 3 (Summer 1995): 379–414.

41. Robert Powell, "War as a Commitment Problem," *International Organization* 60, 1 (Winter 2006): 169–203.

CHAPTER FIVE: LBJ'S DEFEAT BY DEBIT CARD, W'S VICTORY BY CREDIT CARD

1. When we refer to "Bush," we generally mean George W. Bush, the forty-third president. When referring to his father, George H. W. Bush, the forty-first president, we will make clear that we are doing so. Whenever the context makes ambiguous which president is being referenced, we will use the full name.

2. http://www.gallup.com/poll/2299/americans-look-back-vietnam-war .aspx. For additional public opinion data, see W. Lunch and P. Sperlich, *The Western Political Quarterly* 32, no. 1 (1979): 21–44.

3. Pub. L. No. 88–408, 59 Stat. 1031, 6 UST 81 (1964).

4. https://www.dmdc.osd.mil/dcas/pages/report_oif_month.xhtml.

5. Lee Winfrey and Michael D. Schaffer, "Walter Cronkite Dies," *Philadelphia Inquirer*, July 17, 2009.

6. Joseph A. Califano, *The Triumph & Tragedy of Lyndon Johnson: The White House Years* (New York: Touchstone, 2014), Kindle 6902–6907.

7. http://www.pbs.org/wgbh/americanexperience/features/primary-resources /lbj-union67/.

8. Public Papers of the Presidents of the United States: Lyndon B. Johnson, 1968–69, vol. 1 (Washington, DC: Government Printing Office, 1970), entry 170, 469–476.

9. Leslie Gelb and Richard Betts, *The Irony of Vietnam: The System Worked* (Washington DC: Brooking Institution, 1979).

10. Ibid.

11. Jack Valenti, *This Time, This Place* (New York: Three Rivers Press, 2001). Kindle edition. 3761–3764.

12. Ibid., 3793–3807.

13. Ibid., 3913–3920.

14. http://millercenter.org/president/lbjohnson/speeches/speech-5910.

15. Elizabeth N. Saunders, *Leaders at War: How Presidents Shape Military Interventions* (Cornell Studies in Security Affairs) (Ithaca, NY: Cornell University Press, 2011), Kindle 168.

16. Michael R. Beschloss, *Taking Charge: The Johnson White House Tapes 1963–64* (New York: Simon and Schuster, 1997), 370.

17. Valenti, *This Time, This Place*, Kindle 3662–3667.

18. Joseph A. Califano, *The Triumph & Tragedy of Lyndon Johnson: The White House Years* (New York: Touchstone, 2014), Kindle appendix A.

19. Lyndon B. Johnson, "The President's Inaugural Address," January 20, 1965, available at http://www.presidency.ucsb.edu/ws/?pid=26985.

20. All speeches available at http://millercenter.org.

21. Public Papers of the Presidents of the United States: Lyndon B. Johnson, 1965, volume 1, Washington, DC: Government Printing Office, 1966, entry 107, 281–287.

22. Ibid.

23. See, for instance, Robert Caro's three-volume account *Master of the Senate: The Lyndon Johnson Years* (New York: Vintage, 2009).

24. http://georgewbush-whitehouse.archives.gov/news/releases/2002/01/20020129-11.html.

25. Bob Woodward, *Plan of Attack* (New York: Simon and Schuster, 2004), 249.

26. Ibid., 179; Michael Massing, "Now They Tell Us," *New York Review of Books*, February 26, 2004, http://www.nybooks.com/articles/archives/2004/feb/26/now-they-tell-us/.

27. Commission on the Intelligence Capabilities of the United States Regarding Weapons of Mass Destruction, Washington, DC, March 31, 2005. See https://fas.org/irp/offdocs/wmd_report.pdf.

28. http://www.cnn.com/2003/US/02/05/sprj.irq.powell.transcript.09/index.html.

29. http://www.cnn.com/2003/WORLD/meast/03/17/sprj.irq.bush.transcript/.

30. Brent Scowcroft, "Don't Attack Saddam," *Wall Street Journal*, August 14, 2002, http://www.wsj.com/articles/SB1029371773228069195.

31. Woodward, *Plan of Attack*, 1–3.

32. Ibid., 26.

33. Ibid., 405–406.

34. Valenti, *This Time, This Place*, Kindle 548–560.

35. Califano, *The Triumph & Tragedy*, Kindle 386–387.

36. Robert A. Caro, *The Years of Lyndon Johnson: The Passage of Power* (New York: Knopf, 2012).

37. Valenti, *This Time, This Place*, Kindle 680–687.

38. Ibid., 707–726.

39. Lyndon B. Johnson: "Special Message to the Congress on Selective Service," March 6, 1967, available at http://www.presidency.ucsb.edu/ws /?pid=28685.

40. Woodward. *Plan of Attack*, 443.

41. Stephen Daggett, *Costs of Major U.S. Wars*, Congressional Research Service 7–5700, RS22926, June 29, 2010, available at www.crs.gov.

42. *Vanity Fair*, April 2008, http://www.vanityfair.com/news/2008/04 /stiglitz200804.

43. Califano, *The Triumph & Tragedy*, Kindle 2418–2422.

44. Daggett, *Costs of Major U.S. Wars*.

45. Bob Davis, "Bush Economic Aid Saves the Cost of Iraq War May Top $100 Billion," *Wall Street Journal*, September 16, 2002, http://www.wsj.com /articles/SB1032128134218066355.

46. David M. Herszenhorn, "Estimates of Iraq War Costs Were Not Close to Ballpark," *New York Times,* March 19, 2008, http://www.nytimes .com/2008/03/19/washington/19cost.html; Bruce Bartlett, "The Cost of War," *Forbes*, November 26, 2009, http://www.forbes.com/2009/11/25/shared-sacrifice -war-taxes-opinions-columnists-bruce-bartlett.html.

47. Michael Boyle, "How the US Public Was Defrauded by the Hidden Cost of the Iraq War," *The Guardian*, March 11, 2013, http://www.theguardian.com /commentisfree/2013/mar/11/us-public-defrauded-hidden-cost-iraq-war.

48. http://www.pbs.org/wgbh/americanexperience/features/primary -resources/lbj-union68/.

49. http://georgewbush-whitehouse.archives.gov/news/releases/2002/01 /print/20020129–11.html.

50. Bruce Bueno de Mesquita, George W. Downs, and Alastair Smith, "A Political Economy of Income Tax Policies," *Political Science Research and Methods*, forthcoming.

51. Data from CBO report, "The Distribution of Household Income and Federal Taxes, 2011," November 2014, www.cbo.gov/publication/49440.

52. PEW studies of income and party identification, especially for 2004; see http://www.people-press.org/2009/05/21/section-1-party-affiliation -and-composition/.

53. http://www.pbs.org/wgbh/americanexperience/features/primary -resources/lbj-union68/.

54. John Mueller, "Presidential Popularity from Truman to Johnson," *American Political Science Review* 64, no. 1 (March 1970): 18–34; and John Mueller, *War, Presidents, and Public Opinion* (Lanham, MD: University Press of America, 1973).

55. http://www.slate.com/blogs/moneybox/2012/10/15/joe_biden_wars _on_a_credit_card_bush_was_right_to_borrow_the_money.html.

56. Scott Sigmund Gartner, Gary M. Segura, and Michael Wilkening, "All Politics Are Local Local: Losses and Individual Attitudes Toward the Vietnam

War," *Journal of Conflict Resolution* 41, no. 5 (1997): 669–694; Scott Sigmund Gartner and Gary M. Segura, "All Politics Are Still Local: The Iraq War and the 2006 Midterm Elections," *PS: Political Science & Politics* 41, no. 1 (2008): 95–100.

57. Andrea Asoni and Tino Sanandaji, "Rich Man's War, Poor Man's Fight?: Socioeconomic Representativeness in the Modern Military," IFN Working Paper No. 965, 2013, http://www.ifn.se/wfiles/wp/wp965.pdf; Congressional Budget Office, "The All-Volunteer Military: Issues and Performance," Pub. No. 2960, 2007, https://www.cbo.gov/sites/default/files/cbofiles/ftpdocs/83xx/doc8313/07–19-militaryvol.pdf.

58. Boyle, "How the US Public Was Defrauded."

59. Immanuel Kant, "Perpetual Peace: A Philosophical Essay," Section 2, trans. M. Campbell Smith (London: George Allen and Unwin, 1917).

60. Benjamin Franklin, *The Life and Miscellaneous Writings of Benjamin Franklin* (Whitefish, MT: Kessinger Publishing, 2010 [1839]), 69.

61. Lyndon B. Johnson, "Special Message to the Congress on Selective Service," March 6, 1967, available at http://www.presidency.ucsb.edu/ws/?pid=28685.

62. Califano, *The Triumph & Tragedy*, Kindle 4118–4119.

63. Lyndon Johnson. *Public Papers of the Presidents of the United States: Lyndon B. Johnson, 1967,* 92, available at https//books.google.com.

64. Daniel E. Bergan, "The Draft Lottery and Attitudes Towards the Vietnam War," *Public Opinion Quarterly* 73, no. 2 (2009): 379–384.

65. Woodward, *Plan of Attack*, 314.

CHAPTER SIX: JOHN KENNEDY AND BARACK OBAMA

1. James Madison, speech to the Constitutional Convention, July 11, 1787, *The Writings of James Madison, Comprising his Public Papers and his Private Correspondence, including his numerous letters and documents now for the first time printed*, vol. 3, ed. Gaillard Hunt (New York: G. P. Putnam's Sons, 1900).

2. See https://www.youtube.com/watch?v=PEJSCM29ggo for President Kennedy's speech on October 22, 1962.

3. Bible, Philippians 4:7, King James Version.

4. Bruce Bueno de Mesquita, *The Predictioneer's Game: Using the Logic of Brazen Self-Interest to See and Shape the Future* (New York: Random House, 2009), 186–202.

5. See http://www.reuters.com/article/2012/03/26/us-nuclear-summit-obama-medvedev-idUSBRE82P0JI20120326.

6. Mark Landler and Rick Gladstone, "Chemicals Would Be 'Game Changer' in Syria, Obama Says," *New York Times*, March 20, 2013.

7. See the AP news report at http://news.yahoo.com/un-convincing-evidence-syria-chemical-attack-131653691.html.

8. The statement was made by President Obama to the *PBS NewsHour* as reported at 10:43 a.m. by CNN; see http://politicalticker.blogs.cnn.com/2013/08/29/chemical-weapons-a-game-changer-on-u-s-public-opinion-on-syria/.

9. Shiv Malik, Dan Roberts, and Julian Borger, "Bashar al-Assad: Syria Will Give Up Control of Chemical Weapons," *The Guardian*, September 12, 2013, http://www.theguardian.com/world/2013/sep/12/bashar-al-assad-syria-chemical -weapons.

10. "France Calls for Strong UN Resolution to Enforce Syria's Surrender of Chemical Weapons," UN News Centre, September 24, 2013, http://www.un.org /apps/news/story.asp?NewsID=45967#.VYnBwkbYDCo.

11. Sangwon Yoon and Nicole Gaouette, "Syria Chemical-Arms Resolution Passes UN Security Council," *Bloomberg Business News*, September 28, 2013, http://www.bloomberg.com/news/articles/2013–09–28/un-security-council -approves-syria-chemical-arms-measure.

12. Ibid.

13. There is a substantial, but technical, political science literature on what are known as audience costs. To better understand this concept and its implications, see James Fearon, "Domestic Political Audiences and the Escalation of International Disputes," *American Political Science Review* 88 (September 1994): 577–592; Alastair Smith, "International Crises and Domestic Politics," *American Political Science Review* 92 (September 1998): 623–638; Scott Ashworth and Kris Ramsay, "When Are Audience Costs Socially Optimal?" MSS; Kenneth Schultz, "Looking for Audience Costs," *Journal of Conflict Resolution* 45 (February 2001): 32–60.

14. Portions of the analysis and text that follows, especially regarding the role of audience costs in the unfolding of the Cuban missile crisis, are taken from Bruce Bueno de Mesquita, *Principles of International Politics: War, Peace and World Order* 5th ed. (Washington, DC: CQ Press, 2013), 211–220.

15. Frederick Kempe, *Berlin 1961* (New York: Penguin Group USA, 2011), 257.

16. John F. Kennedy, "Cuban Missile Crisis Address to the Nation"; see www.americanrhetoric.com/speeches/jfkcubanmissilecrisis.html.

17. Sergei N. Khrushchev, *Nikita Khrushchev and the Creation of a Superpower* (University Park: Penn State University Press, 2011), 532.

18. A video of the full speech as it was delivered can be seen on YouTube at https://www.youtube.com/watch?v=EgdUgzAWcrw.

19. Graham Allison and Philip Zelikov, *Essence of Decision: Explaining the Cuban Missile Crisis*, 2nd ed. (Reading, PA: Addison Wesley Longman, 1999), 339.

20. http://www.americanrhetoric.com/speeches/jfkcubanmissilecrisis.html.

21. See US Department of State, *Bulletin* 47, no. 1213 (September 24, 1962): 450 (read to news correspondents on September 4 by White House press secretary Pierre Salinger).

22. See http://nsarchive.gwu.edu/nsa/cuba_mis_cri/audio.htm.

23. Allison and Zelikov, *Essence of Decision*, 1.

24. Bruce Bueno de Mesquita and Alastair Smith, "Ukraine's Last Best Hope," *Foreign Affairs*, May 7, 2014, http://www.foreignaffairs.com/articles/141400 /bruce-bueno-de-mesquita-and-alastair-smith/ukraines-last-best-hope.

25. Ibid.

26. http://www.state.gov/e/eb/tfs/spi/ukrainerussia/.

27. Jonathan Weisman and David S. Joachim, "Congress Approves Aid of $1 Billion for Ukraine," *New York Times*, March 27, 2014, http://www.nytimes .com/2014/03/28/world/europe/senate-approves-1-billion-in-aid-for-ukraine .html; Alessandra Prentice and Natalia Zinets, "Ukraine Passes Laws to Unlock $3.2 Billion in Foreign Aid," Reuters, July 16, 2015, http://www.reuters.com /article/2015/07/16/us-ukraine-crisis-parliament-idUSKCN0PQ14E20150716.

CONCLUSION: FIXING FLAWS

1. John Jay, "The Federalist Number 4" [1787] in *The Federalist Papers by Alexander Hamilton, James Madison and John Jay*, ed. Gary Wills (New York: Bantam Books, 1982), 14.

2. James Madison, *The Pacificus-Helvidius Debates of 1793–1794* by Alexander Hamilton and James Madison, Liberty Fund, 2007.

3. Kenneth J. Arrow, "A Difficulty in the Concept of Social Welfare," *Journal of Political Economy* 58, no. 4 (1950): 328–345.

4. For a demonstration of this seemingly counterintuitive claim, see Bruce Bueno de Mesquita, *Principles of International Politics* (Los Angeles: CQ Press, 2014), 10–22.

5. Bruce Bueno de Mesquita and Alastair Smith, *The Dictator's Handbook* (New York: PublicAffairs, 2011).

6. https://www.cbo.gov/sites/default/files/107th-congress-2001–2002 /costestimate/hjres1140.pdf.

7. Stephen Daggett, "Costs of Major U.S. Wars," Congressional Research Service 7–5700, June 29, 2010, www.crs.gov RS22926.

8. D. Scott Bennett and Allan C. Stam III, "The Duration of Interstate Wars," *American Political Science Review* 90 (June 1996): 239–257.

9. Alexander L. George and William E. Simons, *The Limits of Coercive Diplomacy* (Boulder, CO: Westview Press, 1994); Kenneth E. Boulding, *Conflict and Defense: A General Theory* (New York: Harper, 1962); Bruce Bueno de Mesquita et al., "Testing Novel Implications from the Selectorate Theory of War," *World Politics* 56, no. 3 (2004): 363–388; D. Scott Bennett and Allan C. Stam III, "The Declining Advantages of Democracy: A Combined Model of War Outcomes and Duration," *Journal of Conflict Resolution* 42, no. 3 (1998): 344–366; D. Scott Bennett and Allan C. Stam III, "Revisiting Predictions of War Duration," *Conflict Management and Peace Science* 26, no. 3 (2009): 256–267; James D. Fearon, "Why Do Some Civil Wars Last So Much Longer Than Others?" *Journal of Peace Research* 41, no. 3 (2004): 275–301; Patrick M. Regan, "Third-Party Interventions and the Duration of Intrastate Conflicts," *Journal of Conflict Resolution* 46, no. 1 (2002): 55–73.

10. Mark Zuehlke, *For Honour's Sake: The War of 1812 and the Brokering of an Uneasy Peace* (Toronto: Knopf Canada, 2010), 54, 89.

11. Adam Smith, *The Wealth of Nations* [1776] (New York: Random House, 1937), book 5, chap. 3, 872.

12. Ibid.

13. CBO report, "The Distribution of Household Income and Federal Taxes, 2011" November 2014, www.cbo.gov/publication/49440.

14. Gustavo A. Flores-Macías and Sarah Kreps, "Borrowing Support for War: The Effect of War Finance on Public Attitudes toward Conflict," forthcoming in the *Journal of Conflict Resolution*.

Index

abolition. *See* slavery; Thirteenth Amendment

Adams, Henry, 86

Adams, John, 70, 77, 88, 177
    criticism of, 10
    on slavery, 99
    on Washington, G., 28

Adams, John Quincy, 87–88, 96, 123, 244, 255 (fig.)

Afghanistan, 12, 20, 193, 196
    cost of war in, 202, 204–205, 215, 235, 252
    public opinion and support of, 215

African Americans, 95
    in Declaration of Independence, 106, 107, 113
    Dred Scott decision on, 101–102
    FDR support from, 164–165
    LBJ on, 187
    Lincoln's varied support of, 136
    in military service, 166–168
    See also segregation; slavery

agriculture, 76

Algonquin (tribe), 49–50

ambition, 151
    FDR's reelection, 143, 153–155, 159, 163, 165, 169–170
    of Lincoln, 5, 20, 93–94, 95, 103, 107, 121, 138
    Madison on war and, 2, 4, 7–8, 10, 16, 53, 73, 89–90, 94, 138, 218, 239–240

national welfare and, 4–5
    war motives and political, 5, 6–8, 11, 188–189, 218, 242–243
    of Washington, G., 15, 28
    See also self-interest

American colonists. *See* colonists, American

American Indians
    Britain's collaboration with, 61–62, 68–71
    colonist treatment of, 24, 70, 90
    Declaration of Independence and, 47–52
    land rights battles with, 48–52, 61, 70–71, 189
    War of 1812 and, 61–62, 68–72, 73, 80, 90, 240
    wars with, 14, 24
    Washington, G., relations with, 23–24, 49–51, 52
    See also French and Indian War

American Revolution, 14, 17, 21–22, 28
    frontier security with, 69
    outcome alternative for, 52–55
    outcome overview of, 55–57
    slaves in, 98
    Stamp Act and origins of, 39

American revolutionaries, 21, 23, 28
    frontier land claims of, 47–48, 61, 68–69, 73
    grievances of, 42–43
    political theory of, 8–9

277

Bruce Bueno de Mesquita is the Julius Silver Professor of Politics and director of the Alexander Hamilton Center for Political Economy at New York University. He is the author of twenty books, including *The Predictioneer's Game* and, with Alastair Smith, *The Dictator's Handbook*.

Alastair Smith is a professor of politics at New York University. The recipient of three grants from the National Science Foundation and author of three books, he was chosen as the 2005 Karl Deutsch Award winner, given biennially to the best international relations scholar under the age of forty. He is the author, with Fiona McGillivray, of *Punishing the Prince* and, with Bruce Bueno de Mesquita, *The Dictator's Handbook*.